THE POWER OF ISRAEL IN THE UNITED STATES

THE POWER
OF ISRAEL
IN THE
UNITED STATES

JAMES PETRAS

 CLARITY PRESS, INC.
ATLANTA

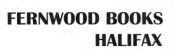 FERNWOOD BOOKS
HALIFAX

© 2006 James Petras
USA
ISBN: 0-932863-51-5
    978-0932863-51-8

Canada
ISBN: 1-55266-215-2
    978-155266-2151

Reprinted November 2006
    February 2007

In-house editor: Diana G. Collier
Cover: Mona Dovina Prodaniuk

Library of Congress Cataloging-in-Publication Data

Petras, James F., 1937-
  The Power of Israel in the United States / by James Petras.
    p. cm.
  ISBN 0-932863-51-5
1. Jews—United States—Politics and government. 2. United States—Politics and government. 3. Middle East—Foreign relations—United States. 4. United States—Foreign relations—Middle East. 5. Iraq War, 2003—Causes. 6. Iraq War, 2003—Influence. 7. United States—Foreign relations—Israel. 8. Israel—Foreign relations—United States. I. Title.

E184.36.P64P48 2006
327.730569409'0511—dc22

                  2006024379

Library and Archives Canada Cataloguing in Publication

Petras, James F., 1937-
The power of Israel in the United States / James Petras.
Includes bibliographical references and index.
ISBN 1-55266-215-2
1. Israel—Foreign relations—United States. 2. United States—Foreign relations—Israel. 3. Lobbying—United States. I. Title.

DS119.8.U6P47 2006 327.5694073 C2006-904222-5

Clarity Press, Inc.
Ste. 469, 3277 Roswell Rd. NE
Atlanta, GA. 30305
USA
http://www.claritypress.com

Fernwood Books
32 Oceanvista Lane, Site 2A, Box 5
Black Point, NS BOJ1BO
Canada
http://www.fernwoodbooks.ca

TO RACHEL CORRIE

US citizen and humanitarian
internationalist volunteer in Palestine
murdered by the Israeli military

ACKNOWLEDGMENTS

My wife, Robin Eastman-Abaya, for her substantial contributions, editing, comments and criticism; Jeff Blankfort for sharing his encyclopedic knowledge of the pro-Israel lobbies; Diana G. Collier for her outstanding and highly professional and supportive editing; and all the alternative websites that provided information not available in the mass media.

TABLE OF CONTENTS

INTRODUCTION

On January 25, 2006 the Palestinian people voted overwhelmingly in favor of Hamas in the cleanest election to take place in any Arab Middle Eastern country. The Israeli government immediately refused to recognize the democratic outcome. It refused to turn over Palestinian tax revenues, deliberately blocked all trading outlets to drastically reduce what was already Palestinian subsistence living, and began an intense and prolonged series of violent assaults on Palestinian cities and villages, killing and maiming hundreds.

In the two and a half weeks prior to the Palestinian suicide attack of April 17, 2006 that killed nine Israelis, Israeli forces had already killed 26 Palestinians, including five children, and injured 161 men, women and children. In fact, according to the internationally respected human rights group, the Palestinian Center for Human Rights, between April 6-12, 2006 alone, Israelis killed 19 Palestinians including three children. Ten of these were "extrajudicial executions," and 94 Palestinians, including 32 children, were wounded. The Israeli Occupation Forces conducted 27 incursions into Palestinian communities in the West Bank and 70 Palestinian civilians, including six children, were arrested. Israeli settlers attacked several farming communities, stealing livestock and destroying property. During that period overall, the Israeli military carried out 369 raids into the West Bank.

Similarly, according to UN reports, between March 30-April 12, Israeli forces launched 2300 artillery and tank shells and 34 missiles into Gaza. Defense for Children International reports that 4,000 Palestinian children have been arrested in the past five years (2001-2006) 400 of whom are currently still in prison. Then on April 19, 2006, after the Palestinian retaliation, Israelis seized the mothers and wives of men on their 'wanted' lists and held them hostage in detention centers to force the men to surrender. Mosques were broken into and scores of families were forced out of their houses while Israeli soldiers ransacked their homes.

Not a single US or EU leader stated a word of criticism of the preceding Israeli state terror.

None of these violent Israeli killing expeditions were reported in the electronic or print mass media, by National Public Radio or in any of the Jewish Lobby propaganda sheets like the *Daily Alert*. Not a single US or EU leader stated a word of criticism of the preceding Israeli state terror. Only when a Palestinian group took credit for the suicide bombing and Hamas defended the right to reprisal did the entire Washington political elite and mass media denounce terrorism. The Lobby's propaganda ploy of focusing exclusively on isolated and sporadic Palestinian attacks and ignoring Israel's daily systematic executions has become the daily fare offered by the US political elite and the mass media to the American public. This serves to legitimize and justify the Lobby's advocacy for starving the Palestinian people into submission and its proposal that the US Congress give an additional $10 billion dollar aid package to resettle Israelis in the West Bank.

Despite these genocidal policies, the Hamas government observed a ceasefire, even as it asserted that Palestinians had the internationally sanctioned right to resist colonial violence. Having ignored Israel's sustained 'storm trooper' assaults on Palestinians, the US propaganda media launched an all out campaign to overthrow the Hamas government following the Palestinian suicide bomber attack, while the Lobby linked Iran to the incident in an effort to provoke a US military attack upon that country.

In response to the triumph of Palestinian democracy and taking their cues from the Israeli state, the entire pro-Israeli lobby and its Congressional and Executive branch spokespeople launched a successful propaganda blitz binding US policy to the genocidal Israeli blockade. The result was Washington's total adherence to every tenet of Israeli policy toward Hamas. Aid, including humanitarian aid, was cut. US officials were prohibited from even meeting with any Hamas officials in any capacity, while US diplomats pressured every European, Asian, Arab, and Latin American country to join the total blockade of any humanitarian aid to the Palestinians. While several Arab states balked at cutting off all aid, as did France and Russia, long-time US client leaders in Jordan and Egypt, as well as China, refused to meet representatives of the Hamas government. The US repudiated its own ostensible policy of "democratizing" the Middle East. President Bush's initial welcome of the democratic elections in Palestine was quickly replaced by an embrace of Israel's policy of starving the Palestinians into submission. These shifting policies were largely the result of the power exercised by the *Jewish* Lobby— as practically all Israeli commentators fondly refer to it.

The US repudiated its own ostensible policy of "democratizing" the Middle East.

A review of the *Daily Alert* published for the Conference of Presidents of Major Jewish Organizations by the Jerusalem Center for Public Affairs (distributed daily to every member of the US Congress and Executive branch) between January to May, 2006 provides overwhelming evidence of the Jewish Lobby's intense efforts to strangle the Palestinian economy and promote a US military attack and embargo against Iran. The leading and most aggressive Senatorial proponent of a military attack on Iran is Senator Joseph Lieberman, an unfailing transmission belt of the Israeli Foreign Office. According to an interview in the *Jerusalem Post* (April 18, 2006) Lieberman, also a major leader and spokesman of the Jewish Lobby, stated, "I don't think anyone is thinking of this as a massive ground invasion, as in Iraq, to topple the government...[he envisioned] an attempt to hit some of the components of the nuclear program." Lieberman is not a loose cannon but the former Vice Presidential candidate for the Democratic Party and one of its most influential spokespersons on Middle East affairs. Lieberman's 'bombs over Teheran' position is a verbatim repetition of the current Israeli pro-war posture and in total accordance with the program of AIPAC, the Conference of Presidents of Major Jewish Organizations, the American Jewish Committee, the Anti-Defamation League and the Zionist Organization of America.

This book is about the power of the Jewish Lobby to influence US Middle Eastern policy. In addition to unconditional US backing of Israel, this includes launching an aggressive war against Iraq, inciting a military attack on Iran, and securing US backing for Israeli colonization of Palestine and the massive uprooting of Palestinians. The power of the Jewish Lobby in shaping US policy has long been recognized by Israeli leaders and certainly has allowed them to ignore the occasional Presidential pleas to cease and desist from massacres, assassinations, home demolitions, collective punishments, and other genocidal practices perpetrated against the Palestinians. As former President Ariel Sharon once boasted, regarding his influence over President Bush, "We have the US under our control". Yet despite their awareness of the massive, sustained, and unprecedented US funding to Israel, a great many otherwise progressive observers have been in denial or invented specious arguments for explaining away the link between the Israeli state/the Jewish Lobby and US Middle East policy. This book provides a chapter-by-chapter analysis and documentation of the power exerted by Israel via the Lobby on US Middle East policy.

Over 170 years ago, Alexis DeToqueville, an acute observer of US politics, expressed his fear of the "tyranny of the majority", of an unruly majority, which would override the rights of minorities in pursuit of their narrow interests.[1] Today the threat to democracy, at least as it involves US policy toward the Middle East and questions of war and peace, is not in an unruly majority of the *electorate*, but in the majority of *fundraisers* for the Democratic Party and the minority financiers of the Republican Party. J.J. Goldberg in his book, *Jewish Power: Inside the Jewish Establishment*[2] based on data in the early 1990's, noted that 45 percent of the fundraising for the Democratic Party and 25 percent of the funding for the Republicans came from Jewish-funded Political Action Committees (PACs). A more recent survey by Richard Cohen of the *Washington Post* shows higher figures: 60 percent of Democratic financing comes from Jewish pro-Israel PACs and 35 percent of the Republican fundraising. Almost all of the Lobby's party fundraising is tied to a single issue which cuts across the liberal-neocon divisions—unconditional and knee-jerk support for Israel, its policies, its institutions, its land grabs and its political-military definition of enemies. No single other lobby including Big Pharma, Big Oil and Agro-business plays such a dominant financial role in party funding. What would be interesting to study is the degree to which the $3 to $10 billion dollars in US aid to Israel is recycled back to the Lobby via money transfers, lucrative contracts between Lobby donors and Israeli enterprises and banks. In which case, US taxpayers would actually be subsidizing a network of local lobbyists working on behalf of a foreign power. The financial power of the Lobby over both parties allows it to influence and reward Israel loyalists and punish any doubters or dissidents, by funding alternative nominees and candidates or launching vituperative campaigns via the "friendly media".

The tyranny of the majority fundraisers is not exercised by the Jewish Lobby in order to secure private individual privileges but to secure the colonial expansionist goals of the Israeli State and its regional supremacy in the Middle East. As envisioned by the ZionCon ideologues and policymakers, the supreme goal is to convert the Middle East into a joint US-Israel 'Co-Prosperity Sphere', a project disguised as promoting democracy in the Middle East…by the barrel of a (US) gun.

The basis of the Lobby's PAC power is rooted in the high proportion of Jewish families among the wealthiest families in the United States. According to *Forbes*, 25 to 30 percent of US multi-millionaires and billionaires are Jewish. If we add the contributions to the Lobby by Jewish-Canadian billionaires with assets worth over 30 percent of the Canadian Stock Market, we can realize the scope and depth of the Lobby's power to dictate Middle East policy to Congress and the Executive.

The tyranny of Israel over the US has grave consequences for world peace and war, the stability and instability of the world economy, and for the future of democracy in the US. This study of the Lobby is not a discussion of 'another lobby' pressuring Congress for an increased budget subsidy, specific tax exemption or a piece of legislation benefiting a specific economic or regional interest. The demands of the Lobby led directly to US support of Israel's wars of aggression against Arab states in 1967, 1973, and 1982; the US wars against Iraq of 1991 and 2003; support of Israel's invasion of Lebanon and Gaza (2006); and ongoing military threats against Iran and Syria from 2001 to the present (2006). It is no surprise that a clear majority of Europeans perceived Israel as the greatest threat to world peace[3] and that the Lobby responded through its mass media acolytes with predictable shrill claims of "widespread anti-Semitism throughout Europe at all levels of society". This was subsequently echoed in Washington in response to the Lobby's campaign and manifested by the Bush Administration's bludgeoning Europe to support its belligerent posture toward the Middle East.

The issues raised by the tyranny of Israel and, by proxy, the Lobby, over the United States' Middle East policy are far too serious to be relegated to secondary consideration because of fear of verbal assaults, institutional blackmail, or ostracism by philo-Israeli colleagues. This is especially the case for US intellectuals, who are faced with the dilemma of how to respond to the fact that there are over 20,000 U.S.casualties (and climbing) in Iraq and over 250,000 Iraqis killed,[4] and 4 million Palestinians facing starvation thanks to a Lobby-backed US blockage of funding to the democratic Hamas government. We have a special responsibility to the American people to describe and expose the wealth, power, operations and influence of the Lobby, and its ties to the expansionist colonial and mass-supported apartheid state that is Israel. (A poll in Israel, published by the liberal newspaper *Haaretz* showed that 68 percent of Israeli Jews reject living near an Arab. Surveys show repeatedly that nearly half of Israeli Jews favor the forced emigration of Arabs from Palestine—a policy that both major Israeli parties practice through forced land grabs, geographical fragmentation and economic blockades.)

In confronting the tyranny of Israel and its Lobby, US intellectuals have the responsibility to affirm the freedom to debate, discuss and criticize the Israel-Lobby axis, and then to use that freedom to diagnose, criticize and organize for a democratic foreign policy free from imperial and surrogate wars. It is not enough to have 'private reservations' about our colleagues' submission to the tyranny of the Israel Lobby. It is unacceptable to voice our cowardice by refusing to contest the deceptions and apologies for Israeli terror in the Occupied Territories by our academic colleagues for fear of provoking hysterical verbal ejaculations and their predictable labeling of us as creeping or crypto-anti-Semites. US intellectuals must rediscover their freedom to debate publicly and forcefully the disastrous consequences of following the Israel/Lobby line promoting sequential Middle Eastern wars. We must call the system of power by its name, organization, and international alignment—without euphemisms. The task of US intellectuals is no more and no less than a democratic revolution: to overthrow the tyranny of the pro-Israel PAC over our Middle East foreign policy, over our academic marketplace of ideas, as well as the tyranny of the Lobby over our mass media leading to its blatant pro-Israel and pro-Lobby bias. Intellectuals must challenge the Lobby's tyranny over our foreign aid budget. More specifically, activist intellectuals must challenge peace movements that refuse to criticize the Lobby or Israel's militarist policies.

The Lobby and its ideologues have gained intellectual hegemony via coercion and persuasion in spheres of public life that are central to our Republic—the assessment of and response to threats to our freedoms and self-determination. It is time to launch a counter-hegemonic movement here in the US, not for a different kind of empire, free of Israeli entanglements, but simply for the reconstruction of a democratic republic offering true freedom of expression and debate in matters crucial to American well-being.

This book is a modest effort in pursuit of that goal. The first part, "Zionist Power in America", focuses on the role of pro-Israel officials in the government and the Lobby in leading the US into the Iraq War (Chapters 1 and 2). It also highlights the intra-elite conflict within the government between the 'Israel Firsters' and the traditional state apparatchiks (Chapter 3). Zionist power, however, is not confined to the Lobby but also is reflected in the reports by investigative journalists who systematically avoid the obvious role of the 'Israel Firsters' (Chapter 4). While investigative reporter Hersh failed to uncover the Israel-Zionist-war connection, the FBI discovered a triangular spy case involving leading AIPAC operatives linked to a strategically placed official and their Mossad spymaster in the Israeli embassy (Chapter 5).

In Part Two, we discuss the role of torture, assassinations and genocide as integral parts of US-Israeli empire buiding (Chapter 6). In particular we focus on Israel's savage invasion of Gaza as a clear example of ethnic cleansing via terror bombing and destruction of civilian infrastructure (Chapter 7).The Jewish state's ethnocide with impunity in Gaza was a dry run for its full-scale genocidal attack on Lebanon, demonstrating the relationship between impunity and genocidal recidivism. In both Gaza and Lebanon, the Jewish lobbies played a major role in securing Washington's unconditional backing for Israel's Lebanon holocaust (Chapter 8). The role of Israel and its US proxies in preparing the US for war against Iran and its potentially catastrophic consequences are outlined in Chapter 9. Israeli power is as much ideological as military. In Chapter 10, "The Caricature in Middle East Politics", we discuss the Israeli use of ideological warfare as a means of creating an advantageous polarization between Christians and Muslims.

In Part Three, we extend our analysis to the arena of psychological warfare and the moral basis of resistance. In Chapter 11 we analyze the role of Israeli and Lobby 'terror experts' who project the violence of the executioners onto the victims: the victims of course are Palestinians and Muslims, the Arab people and the Resistance. Through claims of 'expertise' and the use of prestigious institutional affiliations, the terror experts provide de-humanized descriptions of anti-Israeli and anti-imperialist adversaries that serve to justify the torture and abusive treatment, arbitrary mass arrests and collective punishment of entire peoples and communities. Contrary to the terrorist experts' opinionated judgments, we present (Chapter 12) an alternative perspective on the 'suicide bombers' which focuses on the negative impact of extreme material, spiritual and existential damage inflicted by colonial imperial powers as the detonator for suicide attacks in the face of overwhelming military imbalances.

In Part Four, we engage in ongoing political debate about the importance of the Lobby in shaping US imperial policy, relative to other interest groups (Chapter 13). Specifically we present a point-by-point refutation of Noam Chomsky's attempt to minimize the role of the Lobby and then proceed to critically examine the supposed role of the economic interests of Big Oil and Finance Capital in promoting the Iraq War and the impending Iranian confrontation. In Chapter 14, we discuss the possibilities of confronting Zionism and reclaiming freedom of discussion on American Middle East policy.

ENDNOTES

[1]   Alexis de Tocqueville, *Democracy in America*, Harper and Row, 1996.

[2]   J.J. Goldberg, *Jewish Power: Inside the Jewish Establishment,* New York, Basic Books, 1997.

[3]   The Poll was commissioned by the European Commission, and conducted by Taylor Nelson Sofres/ EOS Gallup Europe, between 8 and 16 of October. 2003. The poll found 59 percent of Europeans believe Israel represents the biggest obstacle to Mideast and world peace.

[4]   According to Les Roberts (Center for International Emergency Disaster and Refugee Studies at Johns Hopkins' Bloomberg School of Public Health, one of the world's top epidemiologists and lead author of *The Lancet* report) there might be as many as 300,000 Iraqi civilian deaths. (See Les Roberts, "Do Iraq Civilian Casualties Matter?" AlterNet, February 8, 2006.

PART I

ZIONIST POWER IN AMERICA

CHAPTER 1

WHO FABRICATED THE IRAQ WAR THREAT?

The debate and criticism in the US Congress and media of the Bush Administration's fabricated evidence of Iraq's possession of weapons of mass destruction and a host of other misconduct (lying to Congress, military tribunals in Guantanamo, torture in Abu Ghraib, CIA renditions, spying on Americans, and corruption in general) has finally reached the point of a Congressional attempt to generate an impeachment inquiry.[1] The initial investigation and testimony of top US military and civilian officials in the Pentagon and State Department, which revealed profound differences and divisions between themselves and the "political appointees", has now been embellished by public statements against the Bush administration from retired generals, who claimed to reflect the views of the active military, and called for the resignation of Donald Rumsfeld.[2] The testimony and evidence of the professionals' revelations have been crucial to understanding the structure of real power in the Bush Administration, since it is in times of crisis and divisions in the governing class that we, the public, are given insights into who governs, and for whom. The ongoing debate, criticism, and division in Washington today provide just such instances.

After years of UN inspections, and a comprehensive 15-month search by the Iraq Survey Group, following thousands of searches and interviews by close to ten thousand US military, intelligence and scientific inspectors, it has been definitively demonstrated, and at last admitted by President George W. Bush, that Iraq did not possess weapons of mass destruction (or even of useful national defense). This raised the key question: who in the Bush regime provided the fabricated evidence and for what purpose?

The initial response of the Bush apologists was to attribute the fabrications to "bureaucratic errors" and "communication failures" or as then Deputy Secretary of Defense Paul Wolfowitz cynically claimed, to the need to "secure a consensus for the war policy". CIA Director Tenant became the self-confessed scapegoat for the "mistakes". As the investigations progressed, however, testimony from a multiplicity of high level sources in the regime revealed that there were two channels of policy making and advisers, 1) the formal structure made up of career professional military and civilians in the

Pentagon and State Department, and 2) a parallel structure within the Pentagon made up of political appointees. From all available evidence it was the "unofficial" political advisers organized by Wolfowitz, Feith, and Rumsfeld in the Office of Special Plans (OSP) who were the source of the fabricated evidence, which was used to "justify" the invasion and occupation of Iraq. The OSP, which only existed briefly from September 2002 to June 2003, was headed by Abram Shulsky and included other neo-conservatives, who had virtually no professional knowledge or qualification in intelligence and military affairs. Douglas Feith, then Undersecretary of Defense, and Paul Wolfowitz set up the OSP. Shulsky was an avid follower and protégé of Richard Perle, the well-known militarist and long time supporter of military attacks on Arab regimes in the Middle East.

According to the testimony of a Pentagon insider, Lieutenant Colonel Karen Kwiatkowski, who worked in the office of the Undersecretary of Defense for Policy, Near East and South Asia Division and Special Plans in the Pentagon, the "civil service and active duty military professionals were noticeably uninvolved in key areas" of interest to Feith, Wolfowitz and Rumsfeld, namely Israel, Iraq and Saudi Arabia. Lieutenant Colonel Kwiatkowski went on to specify that "in terms of Israel and Iraq all primary staff work was conducted by political appointees, in the case of Israel a desk officer appointee from the Washington Institute for Near East Policy and in the case of Iraq, Abe Shulsky." Equally important, the ex-Pentagon official addressed the existence of "cross-agency cliques". She described how the members of a variety of neo-conservative and pro-Israel organizations (Project for a New American Century, the Center for Security Policy, and the American Enterprise Institute), also held office in the Bush regime and only interacted among themselves across the various agencies. She pointed out that major decisions resulted from "groupthink"—the uncritical acceptance of prevailing points of view and the uncritical acceptance of extremely narrow and isolated views. Kwiatkowski was forced to resign by her chief after she told him that "some folks (the cliques and networks) in the Pentagon may be sitting beside Hussein in the war crimes tribunal" for their destructive war and occupation policies.

What became very clear was that the OSP and its directors, Feith and Wolfowitz, were specifically responsible for the fabricated evidence of the "Weapons of Mass Destruction" that justified the war on Iraq. The OSP and the other members of the networks that operated throughout key US agencies shared a rightwing pro-militarist ideology and were fanatically pro-Israel. Feith and Perle authored an infamous policy paper in 1996 for Likud Party extremist, Benjamin Netanyahu, entitled "A Clean Break: A New Strategy for Securing the Realm", which called for the destruction of Saddam Hussein and his replacement by a Hashemite monarch. The governments of Syria, Lebanon, Saudi Arabia and Iran would then have to be overthrown or destabilized, the paper asserted, in order for Israel to be secure in a kind of 'Greater US-

Israel Co-Prosperity Sphere.' The finger clearly pointed to Zionist zealots who directed the OSP, like Abram Shulsky and Feith, as the source for the "phony intelligence" which led to the war that Wolfowitz and Rumsfeld were seeking. The manner in which the Zionist zealots organized and acted—as a clique of arrogant like-minded fanatics hostile to any contrary viewpoints from the professional intelligence, civilian, and military officials—indicated that their loyalties and links were elsewhere, most evidently with the Sharon regime in Israel. As the *Guardian's* Julian Borger wrote on July 17, 2003, the OSP "forged close ties to a parallel, ad hoc intelligence operation inside Ariel Sharon's office in Israel specifically to bypass Mossad and provide the Bush administration with more alarmist reports on Saddam's Iraq than Mossad was prepared to authorize." It is interesting to note that the influential rightwing Zionists in the Bush Administration actually provided "reports" on Iraq which were at variance with reports from the Israeli Mossad, which did not believe that Iraq represented any "threat" to the US or Israel. Mossad's skepticism was shared by the CIA, now known to have advised the Bush administration on the non-existence of WMD.[3] With the primary intelligence agencies of Israel and the US advising otherwise, is it credible to presume that their negative findings on Iraqi WMD were overruled due to better information, and not to better clout?

With the primary intelligence agencies of Israel and the US advising otherwise, is it credible to presume that their negative findings on Iraqi WMD were overruled due to better information, and not to better clout?

The Jewish Lobby, Not Big Oil

Contrary to the view of most American progressives that oil, and specifically the interests of Big Oil, is the primary mover, there is no evidence that the major US oil corporations pressured Congress or promoted the war in Iraq or the current confrontation with Iran. To the contrary: there is plenty of evidence that they are very uneasy about the losses that may result from an Israeli attack on Iran. Furthermore, it seems reasonable to suppose that Big Oil is far from happy about taking the rap for all that is happening in the Middle East, particularly when it combines with public anger at high gas prices, and leads to Senate inquiries.

There is an abundance of evidence for the past 15 years that:

1. The oil companies did not promote a war policy.

2. The wars have prejudiced their interests, operations and agreements with prominent Arab and Islamic regimes in the region.

3. The interests of the oil companies have been sacrificed to the state interests of Israel.

4. The power of the pro-Israel lobbies exceeds that of the oil compa-

nies in shaping US Middle East policy.

A thorough search through the publications and lobbying activities of the oil industry and the pro-Israel lobbies over the past decade reveals an overwhelming amount of documentation demonstrating that the Jewish lobbies were far more pro-war than the oil industry. Moreover the public records of the oil industry demonstrate a high level of economic co-operation with all the Arab states and increasing market integration. In contrast the public pronouncements, publications, and activities of the most economically powerful and influential pro-Israel Jewish lobbies were directed toward increasing US government hostility to the Arab countries, including exerting maximum pressure in favor of the war in Iraq, a boycott or military attack on Iran, and US backing for Israeli assassination and ethnic cleansing of Palestinians.

The most striking illustration of Jewish power in shaping US policy in the Middle East against the interest of Big Oil is demonstrated in US-Iran policy. As the *Financial Times* notes: "International oil companies are putting multi-billion dollar projects in Iran on hold, concerned about the diplomatic standoff [*sic*] [US economic-military threats] over the country's nuclear programme".[4] In fact, as Michael Klare pointed out:

> No doubt the major U.S. energy companies would love to be working with Iran today in developing these vast oil and gas supplies. At present, however, they are prohibited from doing so by Executive Order (EO) 12959, signed by President Clinton in 1995 and renewed by President Bush in March 2004.[5]

Despite the fact that billions of dollars in oil, gas and petro-chemical contracts are in play, the pro-Israel lobby has influenced Congress to bar all major US oil companies from investing in Iran. Through its all-out campaign in the US Congress and Administration, the US-Jewish-Israeli lobby has created a warlike climate which now goes counter to the interests of all the world's major oil companies including BP, the UK-based gas company, SASOL (South Africa), Royal Dutch Shell, Total of France, and others.

A question to ponder is whether "war for oil" is the same *as* "war *in the interests of Big Oil.*" Writing in the prestigious French monthly, *Le Monde Diplomatique,* in April 2003, Yahya Sadowski argued:

A question to ponder is whether "war for oil" is the same as "war in the interests of Big Oil".

> As part of their grand plan for using a "liberated" Iraq as a base from which to promote democracy and capitalism across the Middle East, [the Neocons] want Baghdad to explore for new reserves, rapidly increase production capacity

and quickly flood the world market with Iraqi oil. They know that this would lead to an oil price crash, driving it to $15 a barrel or less. They hope that this collapse will stimulate economic growth in the US and the West, finally destroy Opec (the Organisation of Petroleum Exporting Countries), wreck the economies of "rogue states" (Iran, Syria, Libya), and create more opportunities for "regime change" and democratisation…

Multinational companies—giants such as Exxon-Mobil, British Petroleum, Shell, Total and Chevron-Texaco—have diversified sources of production and have less to fear from a price collapse. But the US administration does not listen to them (most are not even American). When Bush Junior was elected, they lobbied hard for a repeal of the Iran-Libya sanctions act and other embargos that curbed their expansion of holdings in the Middle East. The Bush team rebuffed their pleas and Vice-President Dick Cheney produced his 2001 national energy policy that focused on opening new areas within the US for energy exploration.[6]

… Multinational oil companies, US and other, have plenty to be ashamed of, from their despoliation of the Niger Delta to their support for state terrorism in Indonesia. But they have not been pushing for a war against Iraq. The Bush administration planned its campaign against Baghdad without input from these companies, and apparently without a clue about the basics of oil economics.[7]

The neo-con objective of bringing down OPEC (while achieving access to oil for Israel) was foiled by the dismal state of the Iraqi oil infrastructure, after the impact of a decade of international sanctions (as Sadowski argued), and by the Iraqi resistance, [8] which has rendered the prospect of any bonanza from Iraqi oil revenues moot.

To understand the central role of the Zionist ideologues in shaping US foreign policy in the Middle East and elsewhere, it is important to frame it in the context of US-Israel relations and the powerful influence of the pro-Israel lobby inside of the US. As Patrick Seal described them in the liberal US weekly, *The Nation,* "The Friends of Ariel Sharon (among the Jewish pro-Israel zealots) loath Arabs and Muslims… What they wished for was an improvement in Israel's military and strategic environment".

The US invasion of Iraq and its aggressive military posture toward most Arab regimes in the Middle East made the names of these Zionist policymakers known to the world. Wolfowitz and Feith were second and third in command of the Pentagon. Their protégés in the OPS included

Abram Shulsky, Richard Perle, then chairman of the Defense Policy Board, and Elliot Abrams (a defender of the Guatemalan genocide of the 1980's), then Senior Director for Near East and North African Affairs for the National Security Council. Washington's most influential pro-Israel zealots include William Kristol and Robert Kagan of *The Weekly Standard*, the Pipes family and a large number of pro-Israel institutes which work closely with and share the outlook of the rightwing Zionists in the Pentagon. The consensus among US critics of the Bush Administration is that "9/11 provided the rightwing Zionist zealots with a unique chance to harness US Middle East policy and military power in Israel's interest and succeeded in getting the United States to apply the doctrine of pre-emptive war to Israel's enemies".[9] The evidence implicating the US Zionists in the war policy was so overwhelming that even the mainstream Zionist organizations refrained from crying 'anti-Semitism'.

Concerned more with Israeli supremacy than US military losses, the zealous Zionists ignored the emerging quagmire of the US military in Iraq, and went on to plan new wars targeting Iran, Syria, Lebanon, and even Saudi Arabia, raising a whole new series of "intelligence reports" accusing the Arab countries of funding, protecting and promoting terrorism. Their prefabricated intelligence continued to flow while they were in government office, and does so even today.

Concerned more with Israeli supremacy than US military losses, the Zionists ignored the emerging quagmire of the US military in Iraq, and went on to plan new wars targeting Iran.

As US military casualties mount daily in Iraq, with an unofficial estimate of 2579 US deaths by August 1st, 2006,[10] as the military costs of the war near 300 billion[11] and further undermine the US economy, the American public has become disenchanted with the Bush Administration. As the public investigations proceeded, the operations of the OSP, and the identity of its architects and propagandists who promoted the US war against Iraq and for Israel's supremacy were made public.

Yet what might have been anticipated as a harsh and righteous backlash by the American public against the neo-conservative Zionist ideologues and their networks in and out of the government in general is only slowly mounting—and may not rise sufficiently swiftly to deflect their plans for a forthcoming war against Iran. True, the OSP has been shut down, Paul Wolfowitz has been forced out of the Pentagon and moved to the World Bank,[12] Douglas Feith seems set to find a niche in academia,[13] and Richard Perle has resigned his chairmanship of the Defense Policy Board. But Elliot Abrams' star is on the ascendant,[14] Donald Rumsfeld, however attacked by his own generals, remains under presidential protection in the Department of Defense, Dick Cheney remains in the saddle, and the Bush Administration has moved on to target Iran in terms and processes startlingly similar to those which preceded the war against Iraq.

Though the understanding of the general public appears to have moved beyond the original official reasons for war (WMDs, the presence of Al Qaeda, and "bringing democracy"), and even beyond its supplemental pretexts (regime change, human rights), the present focus of both public and progressive criticism is directed largely towards the interests of Big Oil or "empire" as the source of the conflict. The notion that the US went to war against Iraq for the greater good of Israel remains largely absent from commentary in the major media.

A very small number of progressive Jews raised serious questions about the uncritical support of Israel by mainstream Jewish organizations and were sharply critical of the Zionist zealots in the Pentagon. However, in the wake of the firestorm ignited by the publication of the Mearsheimer and Walt article, "The Israel Lobby" in the *London Review* in March 2006, it seems clear that the extent of Israeli influence not only on US Middle East policy, but on America's democratic political institutions and processes as a whole poses a much greater problem for progressive Americans, especially since most progressive Jews went into denial—denying the relevance of the essay, and denying the power of the Jewish Lobby to impact American foreign policy, a point that will be more fully elaborated in a later chapter.

ENDNOTES

[1] Thirty US House Representatives signed on as sponsors or cosponsors of H. Res 635, which would create a Select Committee to "investigate the Administration's intent to go to war before congressional authorization, manipulation of pre-war intelligence, encouraging and countenancing torture, retaliating against critics, and to make recommendations regarding grounds for possible impeachment. " The bill was referred to the House Committee on Rules on December 18th, 2005.

[2] David S. Cloud and Eric Schmitt, "More Retired Generals Call for Rumsfeld's Resignation", *New York Times*, April 16, 2006. The generals are: Major General Paul D. Eaton, General Anthony C. Zinni, Lieutenant General Gregory Newbold, Major General John Batiste, Major General John Riggs, and Major General Charles H. Swannack Jr.

[3] Recent revelations by retired CIA officers, such as Paul Pillar and Ty Drumheller, indicate that the CIA advised the Bush administration on the nonexistence of WMD, but was ignored. See Larry Johnson, "Why Did Goss Resign?" Truthout, May 6th, 2006.

[4] *Financial Times*, March 18/19, 2006 p.1.

[5] Michael Klare "Oil, Geopolitics and the Coming War with Iran," TomDispatch.com, April 11, 2005. Klare totally ignores the role of the Zionist lobby, resorting to the oil interest ploy, even after demonstrating their inability to shape US policy!

[6] See Michael Klare, "United States: energy and strategy", *Le Monde diplomatique*, English language edition, November 2002.

[7] Yahya Sadowski, "No War for Whose Oil?" *Le Monde Diplomatique*, April 2003.

[8] The Iraqi resistance may have been a major factor in blocking the privatization of Iraqi oil. As Greg Palast noted: "Mr Aljibury, once Ronald Reagan's "back-channel" to Saddam, claims that plans to sell off Iraq's oil, pushed by the US-installed Governing Council in 2003, helped instigate the insurgency and attacks on US and British occupying forces...'We saw an increase in the bombing of oil facilities,

pipelines, built on the premise that privatization is coming.'" Greg Palast, "Secret U.S. Plans for Iraq's Oil", BBC News, March 17, 2006.

[9] Patrick Seale, "A Costly Friendship", *Nation*, July 21, 2003.

[10] For a running casualty count, see the Iraq Coalition Casualty Count website at <http://icasualties.org/oif/>

[11] For a running total of the costs of war to the US taxpayer, see National Priorities Project website at <http://nationalpriorities.org/index.php?option=com_wrapper &Itemid=182>

[12] See Chapter 5, concerning, inter alia, FBI investigations of Wolfowitz, Feith et al.

[13] Douglas Feith has just been appointed Visiting Professor and Distinguished Practitioner in National Security Policy at Georgetown University, commencing Fall 2006. Since leaving government, he served as a Distinguished Visiting Fellow of the conservative Hoover Institution of Stanford University and co-chaired a task force on strategies for combating terrorism at Harvard University's Kennedy School of Government.

[14] Elliot Abrams is making headway within the Bush regime, serving now as Deputy National Security Adviser and head of President George W. Bush's Global Democracy Strategy.

CHAPTER 2

US-IRAQ-ISRAEL-ZIONIST CONNECTION

Why did the US go to war against Iraq in March 2003 with further plans to attack Syria, Iran, and probably Lebanon? The reasons given thus far have all been discredited. No weapons of mass destruction have been discovered. No ties between Iraq and Al Qaeda have been established. No threats to US security existed. Many of the past and present allies of the US have equal or worse human rights records than did Iraq. The war, conquest, occupation, killing, and vile systematic torture and imprisonment of thousands of Iraqis have aroused the hostility and indignation of hundreds of millions of Christians, Muslims and free thinkers throughout the world, justly discrediting the entire political establishment in Washington and overseas.

Who Benefited from the Iraq War?

Who benefited, then, from the US war? By examining the beneficiaries we can get an idea who had a motive for promoting this crime against humanity.

America itself has reaped the opprobrium of the world, which continues to impact American individuals and businesses. Terrorism is on the rise, while US security might be presumed to have worsened.[1] The mounting costs of the war, which some forecast could surpass two trillion dollars,[2] are slowly eating through the American infrastructure. The prospect of extending an American empire faced by potential challenges to its hegemony is a growing concern for empire builders, given the growing ideological, human, and material costs in Iraq. While the OPEC countries for a time rejected US and EU pressures to pump more oil to lower sky-high prices—partly a hostile response to the US invasion of Iraq—today the price of oil seems resistant to efforts to lower it, with the attendant dismal impact upon the American and world economy.

US oil companies have been faced with a growing anti-colonial resistance, and their investments throughout the Middle East and South Central Asia are under siege. Big Oil may have enjoyed windfall profits, but these were unanticipated, and its operations in Iraq are in a shambles.[3]

The only major beneficiary of the war has been the State of Israel, which has succeeded in having the US destroy its most consistent Arab adversary in the Middle East—the regime that extended the greatest political support to the Palestinian resistance. The decades-long US assault on Iraq has achieved the forced demodernization[4] of Iraqi military and civilian technological infrastructure, the dissolution of its military, the disarray of its governing processes, and possibly incited the outbreak of civil war, which carries the potential for the dismemberment and actual disappearance of the country altogether. Iraq, together with Iran and Syria, had formed the core resistance to Israeli expansionist plans to expel the Palestinians and conquer and occupy all of Palestine.

The only major beneficiary of the war has been the State of Israel, which has succeeded in having the US destroy its most consistent Arab adversary.

What were the obstacles to Greater Israel?

1) The two Intifadas, the uprisings of Palestinians who refused to be driven out of their country, which were able to inflict losses on the self-styled Chosen People of God (Israel is by law an exclusively Jewish state, inhabited by immigrants mainly from Europe and their children, and governed by exclusionary religious dogma).

2) Hezbollah, an organization founded due to and for the purpose of counteracting the Israeli incursion into Lebanon, had inflicted a strategic military-political defeat on Israel, forcing them and their client Lebanese Maronite Christian mercenary allies to evacuate from Southern Lebanon.

3) Iraq, Iran and Syria, the three countries which were most consequential in their opposition to Israeli annexation and regional domination, were developing economic and political ties with a multitude of countries and especially in the case of oil contracts, signing trade and exploitation agreements with Japan, China, Russia as well as Western European corporations. Israel's hopes for sharing a co-prosperity economic sphere of domination with Washington based on servile, client Arab regimes were becoming increasingly doubtful.

4) The Iraqi regime was slowly recovering, despite the decade-long US-European boycott and constant US-UK military aggression. With time running out, the Israelis and their Zionist agents in the Bush administration realized that an agreement to end the boycott and normalize relations with Iraq was on the horizon following the UN inspection teams' certification of the absence of WMD, which would lead to Iraq forming joint ventures with French and Russian oil companies, a possible shift of the Iraqi oil trade into Euros, and diminishing influence of Israel's protector state in the region.

5) There was a deepening internal crisis in Israel over the economic costs and personal insecurity accompanying the policy of the colonial settlements and savage repression in the Occupied Territories. Israel's out-migration

was now exceeding its in-migration, its Jewish-based welfare policies were eroding, and hundreds of active reservists were refusing military duty in the dirty colonial war. The plan to "democratize" the Middle East proposed by US Zionists in the government in essence intended joint control by the US and Israel over the entire Middle East via a series of wars.[5] A series of US wars against independent Arab regimes, beginning with Iraq, was clearly in the interests of the Israeli state and so it was perceived by the Sharon regime, its secret police (Mossad), the Israeli military, and rightwing Zionists in positions of influence in Washington.

How was the Israeli state able to influence the US imperial state into pursuing a series of wars, which would imperil its own imperial economic and security interests and further those of Israel? The most direct answer is to be found in the role played by key pro-Zionist officials in and around the most important policy making positions in the Bush administration. These US officials had long-standing ideological and political ties to the Israeli state, including policy advisory positions. Throughout most of their political lives they had dedicated themselves to furthering Israel's state interests in the US.

While the design and execution of the US war strategy was in the hands of Zionist civilian militarists in the Pentagon, they were only able to succeed because of the powerful support exercised by Sharon's acolytes in the major Jewish organizations in the US. The Conference of Presidents of Major Jewish Organizations, the Anti-Defamation League, AIPAC, and thousands of their activists—doctors, dentists, philanthropists, real estate magnates, financiers, journalists, media moguls, and academics—acted in concert with key Jewish politicians and ideologues to press the case for a war because, they would argue, it was in the interest of the State of Israel to destroy Saddam Hussein and the secular Baath Party state apparatus.

But who can say that doing so was in the interests of imperial US, which in Saddam already had a strongman in place, prepared to act in the service of America? How did Saddam, another of those known as "our" son-of-a-bitch,[6] manage to get himself in the crosshairs of America? By invading Kuwait (which received the "go ahead" from US Ambassador April Glaspie, and was widely viewed in the Arab world as his entrapment)? Or by his noncooperation concerning the multiple interests of Israel (oil, water, and Palestine).

The issue of access to oil has long been problematic for Israel, due to its inability to purchase oil from neighboring countries. In typical fashion, this problem was resolved through the September 1st, 1975 Israel-US Memorandum of Agreement Concerning Oil, whereby the US agreed to guarantee Israel's access to oil—an agreement which has been regularly renewed over the subsequent period, at some cost to US taxpayers (see below). By 2003, however, with pro-Zionist forces calling the shots in the US government and Operation Iraqi Freedom afoot, the prospect of Israeli access to Iraqi oil neared fruition. Israeli National Infrastructures Minister Joseph Paritzky requested an assessment of the condition of the old oil pipeline from Mosul to Haifa, with an eye toward renewing the flow of oil "in the event of a friendly postwar regime in Iraq". [7] Paritzky noted that the pipeline would cut Israel's energy bill drastically, probably by more than 25 per cent, since the country was currently largely dependent on expensive imports from Russia. On June 21, 2003, Reuters reported: "Netanyahu says Iraq-Israel oil line will open in near future." By August 2003, *Haaretz* was to report that: "The United States has asked Israel to check the possibility of pumping oil from Iraq to the oil refineries in Haifa. The request came in a telegram last week from a senior Pentagon official to a top Foreign Ministry official in Jerusalem." [8] (Now who might that have been…?) By 2006, three US bases were under construction in the north of Iraq falling along the potential construction line of an oil pipeline from Kirkuk oil fields to the Israeli shipping seaport and petroleum-refining city of Haifa (see diagrams below), with a view to turning that city into a "New Rotterdam". [9]

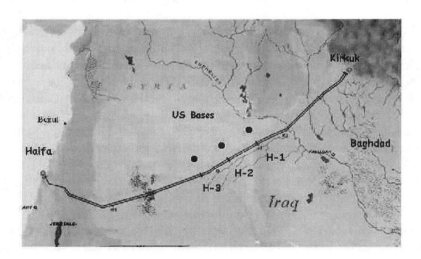

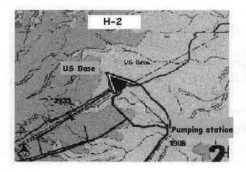

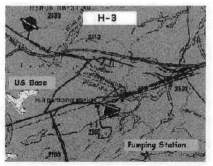

US-Israel relations have been described in a variety of ways. Politicians refer to Israel as the US 's most reliable ally in the Middle East, if not the world. Others speak of Israel as a strategic ally. Some speak of Israel and the US as sharing common democratic values in the war against terrorism. On the Left, critics speak of Israel as a tool of US imperialism for undermining Arab nationalism, and a bulwark against fundamentalist Islamic terrorism. Very few writers point to the "excess influence" which the Israeli governments exercise on US government policy via powerful Jewish lobbies and individuals in media, financial and governmental circles, or their exercise of that influence for the primary benefit of Israel, irrespective of how that impacts the well-being of the United States.

While there is a grain of truth in much of the above, there are numerous unique aspects in this relationship between the US, an imperial power, and Israel, a regional power. Unlike Washington's relation with the EU, Japan and Oceania, it is Israel which pressures and secures a vast transfer of financial resources (by 2004, $2.8 billion per year, $84 billion over 30 years).[10] Israel secures the latest arms and technology transfers, unrestrictive entry into US markets, free entry of immigrants, unconditional commitment of US support in case of war and repression of colonized people, and guaranteed US vetoes against any critical UN resolutions.

From the angle of inter-state relations, it is the lesser regional power which exacts a tribute from the Empire, a seemingly unique or paradoxical outcome. The explanation for this paradox is found in the powerful and influential role of pro-Israel Jews in strategic sectors of the US economy, political parties, Congress and Executive Branch. The closest equivalent to past empires is that of influential white settlers in the colonies, who through their overseas linkages were able to secure subsidies and special trading relations.

The Israeli "colons" in the US have invested and donated billions of dollars to Israel, in some cases diverting funds from union dues of low paid workers to purchase Israel Bonds, which in turn were used to finance new colonial settlements in the Occupied Territories. In other cases Jewish fugitives from the US justice system have been protected by the Israeli state, especially super rich financial swindlers like Mark Rich, and even gangsters and murderers. Occasional official demands of extradition from the Justice Department have been pointedly ignored.

In turn, the colonized Empire has gone out of its way to cover up its subservience to its supposed ally, but in fact hegemonic power. In 1967, the *USS Liberty*, a communications and reconnaissance ship sent to monitor belligerents in the third Israeli-Arab war, was bombed and strafed by Israeli fighter planes in international waters for nearly an hour, killing 34 seamen and wounding 173 of a crew of 297. Intercepted Israeli messages as well as the clearly displayed US flag demonstrate that this was a deliberate act of aggression. Washington acted as any Third World country would when faced with an embarrassing attack by its hegemon: it silenced its own naval officers who witnessed the attack, and quietly received compensation and a pro-forma apology.[11]

Not only was this an unprecedented action in US military and diplomatic relations with an ally, there is no case on record of an imperial country covering up an assault upon itself by a regional ally.[12] On the contrary, similar circumstances have been followed by diplomatic and bellicose responses. This apparent anomaly cannot in any way be explained by military weakness or diplomatic failures: the US is a military superpower, and its diplomats are capable of forceful, even bullying, representation to allies or adversaries, when the political will is present. But the Jewish-American Lobby, Congress people, media and Wall Street moguls strategically located in the US politico-economic system ensured that President Johnson would behave like a docile subject. No direct pressures were necessary, for a hegemonized political leadership acts seemingly on its own beliefs, having learned the rules of the political game. The bottom line is this: the Israel-US relationship is so entrenched that not even an unprovoked military attack could call it into question. Like all hegemonized powers, Washington threatened the US Naval witnesses with a court marital if they spoke out, while they coddled their attackers in Tel Aviv.[13]

Washington reacted to the attack on the *Liberty* as any Third World country would when faced with an embarrassing attack by its hegemon.

Another illustration of the asymmetrical relation is found in one of the most important espionage cases during the Cold War involving an Israeli agent, Jonathan Pollard, and the Pentagon. Over several years Pollard stole and duplicated bagfuls of top-secret documents about US intelligence, counter-intelligence, strategic plans, and military weaponry, and turned them over to his Israeli handlers. This was the biggest case of espionage carried out against the US by any ally in recent history. Pollard and his wife were convicted in 1986. The US Government privately protested to the Israeli government. The Israelis, on the other hand, through their Jewish-American allies, organized a lobby to propagandize in his favor. Eventually all top Israeli leaders and Jewish-American lobbyists campaigned for his pardon, and almost succeeded with President Clinton.

The unequal relation is clearly evident in the case of a major fugitive from justice, Marc Rich. A financier and trader, he was indicted in the US federal court on several counts of swindling and defrauding clients. He fled to Switzerland and subsequently obtained an Israeli passport and citizenship, investing hefty sums of his ill-gotten wealth into Israeli industries and charities. Despite the seriousness of his offense, Rich hobnobbed with top political leaders in Israel and its economic elite. In the year 2000, the Prime Minister of Israel and numerous pro-Israeli Jewish personalities, including Rich's ex-wife, convinced Clinton to pardon him. While an outcry was raised about a linkup between the Rich pardon and his wife's $100,000-plus contribution to the Democratic Party, the underlying relationship of subordination to Israeli influence and the power of the Israeli Lobby in the US was clearly more important. It is worth noting that it is extraordinarily unusual for a US President to consult with a foreign ruler (as Clinton consulted with Barak) in dealing with an accused swindler. It is unprecedented to pardon an indicted fugitive who fled his trial and never served any sentence. But then, the US faces great difficulty in securing any extraditions whatsoever from Israel—even private citizens wanted for committing murder in the US are not returned for trial,[14] despite the purported closeness of the two states. What are the implications for the American criminal justice system of a "home free" territory for Jewish-American criminals?

The power of Israel is manifested in the numerous annual pilgrimages that influential US politicians make to Israel to declare their loyalty to the Israeli state, even during periods of intensive Israeli repression of a rebellious subject people.[15] Rather than reprimanding Israel for an aggressive act of war against another state and for internationally-condemned human rights violations in the Occupied Territories, US satraps of the Israeli mini-empire applauded its bloody repression of Intifadas I and II, and the Jewish state's invasion of Lebanon in 1982—as they do in 2006— and opposed any international mediation to prevent further Israeli massacres, thereby sacrificing US credibility in the United Nations and in world public opinion.

In votes in the United Nations, even in the Security Council—despite overwhelming evidence of human rights violations presented by EU allies— Washington has toiled in the service of its hegemon. Sacrificing international credibility and deliberately alienating 150 other nations, Washington labeled criticisms of Israeli racism as "anti-Semitic". But this does not mark the high point of Washington's servility to Israel.

The most recent and perhaps the key indicator of US servility occurred in the months preceding and following the September 11 attacks on the World Trade Center and the Pentagon. On December 12, 2001 Fox News learned from US intelligence sources and federal investigators that 60 Israelis engaged in a long-running effort to spy on US government officials had been detained since 9/11. Many of those arrested were active Israeli military or intelligence operatives. They had been arrested under the anti-terrorist USA Patriot Act. Many failed polygraph questions dealing with surveillance activities in and against the United States.

More seriously, federal investigators had reason to believe that the Israeli operatives gathered intelligence about the September 11 attacks in advance and did not share it with its Washington ally. The degree of Israeli involvement in September 11 is a tightly guarded secret. A highly placed federal investigator told Fox News there are "tie-ins". When asked to provide details, the federal investigator refused. "Evidence linking these Israelis to 9/11 is classified. I cannot tell you about evidence that has been gathered. It is classified information."[16]

Nothing so exemplifies the power of Israel over Washington as this case of Israeli espionage. Even in the case of the worst attack on the American mainland in US history, Washington suppressed federally collected evidence linking known Israeli spies to possible evidence about prior knowledge. Clearly this evidence might raise questions about the links and ties between political and economic elites, as well as undermine strategic relations in the Middle East. More important, it would pit the Bush Administration against the Jewish-American Lobby and its powerful informal and formal networks in the media, finance, and in government.[17]

Fox News obtained numerous classified documents from federal investigators probably frustrated by the cover-ups of Israeli espionage by political leaders in Washington. These documents brought to light by Carl Cameron revealed that even before September 11, as many as 140 other Israelis had been detained or arrested in a secret investigation of large-scale, long-term Israeli espionage in the United States. Not one of the other major print or electronic media reported on these arrests. Neither the President nor any Congressional leaders spoke out on Israeli's pervasive and sustained effort to obtain key US military and intelligence information.

Even before September 11, 140 Israelis had been detained or arrested in a secret investigation of large-scale, long-term Israeli espionage in the US.

The classified documents detailed "hundreds of incidents in cities and towns across the country" that investigators claimed could be Israeli-organized intelligence gathering activities. Israeli agents targeted and penetrated military bases, the Drug Enforcement Administration, the Federal Bureau of Investigation, the IRS, the INS, the EPA, the US Marshalls' Service, dozens of government facilities, and even secret office and unlisted private homes of law enforcement and intelligence personnel, according to the Federal documents cited by Fox News. A document issued by the Government Accountability Office (an investigatory arm of the US Congress), also cited, referred to Israel as "Country A", saying "the government of Country A conducts the most aggressive espionage operation against the US of any US ally." A Defense Intelligence report said Israel has a "voracious appetite for information… It aggressively collects military and industrial technology and the US is a high priority."

Carl Cameron's Fox News Report appeared on the Fox News internet site briefly in December, 2001 (Dec. 12, 2001) and then disappeared—there was no follow up—or, as might be expected in cases of error, no disclaimer or official correction and/or apology. None of the other mass media picked up on this major espionage report. No doubt the powerful pro-Israeli influentials in the mass media played a role. More significantly than direct "pressure", Israeli hegemony "persuades" or "intimidates" the media establishment and political leaders to operate with maximum discretion in limiting reporting about Israel's appropriation of strategic information.

While the web of Israeli agents are sometimes subject to arrest, interrogation and expulsion, the Israeli state and the ministers in charge are never publicly condemned, nor are there any official diplomatic ripostes such as the symbolic temporary withdrawal of the US Ambassador. The closest parallel to US behavior toward Israeli spies is the response of poor, dependant Third World countries to US espionage. In that context docile rulers quietly ask the Ambassador to rein in some of the more aggressive agents.

Unanswered Questions: September 11 and the Israelis

Following September 11, rumors circulated throughout the Arab East that the bombing was an Israeli plot to incite Washington to attack Muslim-Arab adversaries. These stories and their authors provided nothing more than circumstantial evidence and motive, namely that Bush's anti-terrorism campaign would legitimate Sharon's "anti-terrorist" repression of Palestinians. The stories implicating Israel were completely dismissed by all the media and political leaders across the spectrum.

Now, however, that US federal investigators have revealed that the Israelis may have known about the attack before it occurred and did not share the information, this raises further questions concerning the relationship between the Arab terrorists and the Israeli secret police. Did the Israelis penetrate the group or pick up information about them?[18] Federal investigators' confidential information could probably clarify these vital questions. But will the confidential information ever become public? Most likely not—for the very reason that it would expose the extent of Israeli influence in the US via its secret agents and more importantly via its powerful overseas lobby and allies in the US government and finance. The lack of any public statement concerning Israel's possible knowledge of 9/11 is indicative of the vast, ubiquitous and aggressive nature of its powerful Diaspora supporters.[19] Given the enormous political and economic importance which the mass media have given to 9/11, and the sweeping powers, funding, and institutions created around the issue of national security, it is astonishing that no further mention has been made about Israel's spy networks operating in the US's most delicate spheres of counter-terrorism.

But then, it is not astonishing at all if we understand properly the "unique relationship" between the US Empire and Israel, a regional power.

Theoretical Issues

The relationship between the US—a global imperial power—and Israel, a regional power, provides us with a unique model of inter-state relations. In this case the regional power exacts tribute ($2.8 billion annually in direct contributions from the US Congress), free access to US markets, protection of overseas felonious Jews from prosecution or extradition to the US, while engaging in pervasive espionage and money laundering.[20] On Friday, June 23, 2000 *Haaretz* reported Israel as one of the world's leading havens for illegal international money laundering.

Moreover Israel establishes limits on US-Middle Eastern policy in the international forums. Israel's hegemonic position has endured under both Democratic and Republican presidencies for almost half a century. In other words it is a structural historical relation, not one based on personalities, or particular transitory policy making configurations.

> **Israel's hegemonic position has endured under both Democratic and Republican presidencies for almost half a century. In other words it is a structural historical relation.**

Several hypotheses emerge from an examination of this unique relationship.

The first stems from the fact that the territorial Israeli state has little power of persuasion, economic reach, or military clout in comparison to the major powers (Europe and the US). The power of Israel is based on that of the Diaspora, the highly structured and politically and economically powerful Jewish networks which have direct and indirect access to the centers of power and propaganda in the most powerful imperial country in the world. Tribute is exacted via the influence of these "internal colonialists" who operate at the level of mass media opinion makers and via Congress and the Presidency. Close to 60 percent of Democratic Party funding and 35 percent of Republican Party funding comes from pro-Israeli Jews. For every dollar spent by the Jewish networks in influencing voting outcomes, the Israeli state receives $50 in aid to finance the building and arming of colonial settlements in the Occupied Territories complete with swimming pools, Rumanian gardeners and Filipino maids.

> **Close to 60% of Democratic Party funding and 35% of Republican Party funding comes from pro-Israeli Jews.**

Through overseas networks the Israeli state can directly intervene and set the parameters to US foreign aid in the Middle East. The overseas networks play a major role in shaping the internal debate on US policy toward Israel. Propaganda associating Israeli repression of Palestinians as the righteous response of the victims of the Holocaust has been repeated and circulated throughout the mass media. Iranian President Ahmadinejad's suggestion that Holocaust victims might more properly be compensated by land located in Europe or in the countries that victimized them was misreported, then highly circulated to fuel, instead, the notion of a rabid anti-Semitic Iran. From the height of the network to the lawyers' boardrooms, and the doctors' lounges, the pro-Israel supporters of the network aggressively attack as "anti-Semites" any critical voices. Through local intimidation and malicious intervention in the professions, the zealots defend Israeli policy and leaders, contribute money, organize voters, and run for office. Once in office they tune in to Israeli policy needs.

The phenomenon of overseas expatriates attempting to influence an imperial power is not an exclusively Jewish phenomenon. The Cuban exiles in Miami exercise significant influence in both major parties. But in no other case has linkage led to the establishment of an enduring hegemonic relationship: an empire colonized by a regional power, with the US paying tribute to Israel, subject to the ideological blinders of its overseas colons, and launching aggressive wars on its behalf.

Many questions remain to be answered as the Empire aggressively pursues its military expansion and the internal voices of repression narrow the terms of public debate.

As the colons extend their influence throughout the political and intellectual spheres of the US, they feel more confident in asserting Israel's superiority to it, particularly in the areas of political coercion and war. They brazenly boast of Israel's superior security system, its methods of interrogation including its techniques of torture, and demand that the US follow Israel's war agenda in the Middle East. In Israel, there is acknowledged state-sanctioned physical and mental abuse of prisoners in interrogation, which has broad public support.[21]

Seymour Hersh even urged the US FBI and intelligence agencies to follow the Israeli secret police's tactics and use or threaten to use torture of family members of terror suspects.[22] (See more on Hersh's pro-Israel bias in Chapter 4.) The US followed suit by imprisoning the wives and daughters of wanted Iraqi Baathists. Richard Perle, then highly influential in Rumsfeld's Defense Department, advocated the Israeli tactics of offensive bombing of adversaries. "In 1981 the Israelis faced an urgent choice: should they allow Saddam Hussein to fuel a French built nuclear reactor near Baghdad or destroy it? The Israelis decided to strike preemptively. Everything we know [*sic*] about Saddam Hussein forces [*sic*] President Bush to make a similar choice: to take a pre-emptive action or wait, possibly until it is too late."[23]

Another prominent colon, Senator Joseph Lieberman, called on the US to bomb Syria, Iraq and Iran immediately after 9/11, echoing Prime Minister Sharon's policy advice to President Bush. Alan Dershowitz, Harvard Law professor, publicly endorsed both torture and repressive legislation in the US—modeled on the Israeli system of unlimited detention of Palestinians.[24]

The colons subordinate US policy to Israel's foreign policy needs, independent of the US's own circumstances and in reflection of the extremities to which Israel's colonial policies push it. Moreover as representatives of Israeli hegemonic power in the US, they even try to micro manage security measures—torture in interrogation—as well as becoming vociferous advocates of a generalized Middle East war. The colons have successfully influenced the US government to block any EU initiatives toward international mediation, as well as the US-sponsored Mitchell Plan, advocating peace observers in the occupied territories. In a word, the US, despite its occasional inconsequential criticism of Israel's excesses, has not only been an unconditional supporter of Israel, but it has done so in the context of a prolonged bloody repression and occupation of Palestinian territories, which Washington is a party to securing. Israeli hegemony over the US via its colons affords it a formidable weapon for neutralizing the US's NATO allies, Arab petroleum clients, the vast majority of the General Assembly in the United Nations, and even its own public on certain Middle Eastern issues.

Even more dangerous is the irrational paranoia that the colons transfer from Israeli politics to the US. All Arabs are suspect as was evident in the Zionist-instigated congressional outcry about the purchase of US ports by a Dubai firm. Middle Eastern adversaries should be threatened if not bombed. Secret military tribunals and summary justice should be meted out to suspected terrorists. The mass media is especially tuned to pick up the Israeli paranoid syndrome: magnifying every threat, celebrating Israeli resolution and efficiency against Arab "terrorists". The paranoid style of politics had led to Israel's attacks on Arab countries in the Middle East, espionage on the US, illegal purchase of nuclear devices in the US, and unremitting violence against the Palestinians and Lebanese. The assimilation of the Israeli hyper-paranoid style by the US has vast and dangerous consequences not only for the Mideast but also for the rest of the world, and for democratic freedom in the US.

What the intellectual colons and other Israeli publicists forget to mention is that Israeli security policy in the Occupied Territories is a total disaster: bus stations, public malls, five star hotels, and pizzerias in Israel and all Israeli frontiers have been attacked. Hundreds of Israeli citizens have been killed and injured. Tens of thousands of educated Israelis have fled the country precisely because of insecurity and the proximity of violence, which neither the

What the intellectual colons and other Israeli publicists forget to mention is that Israeli security policy in the Occupied Territories is a total disaster.

Shin Ben, the Army nor the settlers are capable of preventing. A few Israeli intellectuals are especially embittered by the enormous costs of the settlement movement.[25]

Blind to Israel's security failures, the colons insist on creating conditions for internal repression and external war. Given their influential role in the mass media, their prominence in the editorial and opinion pages of the most prestigious newspapers, the colons' message reaches far beyond their limited numbers and the mediocrity of their intellect. Location and money can make up for their psychological and political pathologies as well as override any qualms about dual loyalties.

Who Finances the State of Israel?

The question of who is financing the Israeli state is basic because Israel as we know it today is not a viable state without massive external support. As the July 2004 updated Congressional Research Service Issue Brief for Congress titled "Israel: U.S. Foreign Assistance" points out in its opening statement: "Israel is not economically self-sufficient, and relies on foreign assistance and borrowing to maintain its economy."[26] Despite what might seem an insurmountable obstacle not just to Israel's prosperity, but to its sustainability, the country has nonetheless done rather well. Billions of dollars are raised from a variety of Jewish and non-Jewish institutions to sustain the Israeli war machine, its policy of generous subsidies for Jews enticed to settle in colonies in the Occupied Territories and in Israel—sufficient to place the country as the world's 28th highest in living standards for Israel's Jewish citizens.[27]

Israel is not economically self-sufficient, and relies on foreign assistance and borrowing to maintain its economy.

Without external aid Israel's economy would require severe cutbacks in living standards and working conditions, leading to the likely flight of most Israeli professionals, businessmen, and recent overseas immigrants. The Israeli military budget would be reduced and Israel would be obligated to reduce its military interventions in the Arab East and the Occupied Territories. Israel would cease being a rentier state living on overseas subsidies and would be obligated to engage in productive activity—a return to farming, manufacture and services minus the exploitation of low paid Asian maids, imported Eastern European farm workers, and Palestinian construction laborers.

Europe continues to privilege the importation of Israeli exports[28] and financial services, despite overt and malicious attacks by leaders of both Israeli parties. Prominent Jewish organizations linked to major parties in France and England have muted any efforts to use the "trade card" to pressure Israel to accept European Union or United Nations mediation. European trade and financial ties to Israel however are not the basic prop for the Israeli war machine. The principle basis for long-term, large-scale financial support is found in the US, among public and private institutions.

In the United States there are essentially four basic sources of financial, ideological and political support for the Israeli rentier economy:

1. Wealthy Jewish contributors and powerful disciplined fund-raising organizations.
2. The US government—both Congress and the Presidency.
3. The mass media, particularly the *New York Times*, Hollywood, and the major television networks.
4. The trade union bosses and the heads of pension funds.

There is substantial overlap in these four institutional configurations. For example, Jewish supporters in the Israeli lobby work closely with Congressional leaders to secure long-term, large-scale US military and economic aid for Israel. Most of the mass media and a few trade unions are influenced by unconditional supporters of the Israeli war machine. Pro-Israel Jews are disproportionately represented in the financial, political, professional, academic, real estate, insurance and mass media sectors of the American economy. While Jews are a minority in each and every one of these categories, their disproportionate power and influence stems from the fact that they function collectively: they are organized, active, and concentrate on a single issue—US policy in the Middle East, and specifically in securing Washington's massive, unconditional, and continuing military, political and financial support for Israel. Operating from their strategic positions in the power structure, they are able to influence policy and censor any dissident commentators or views from circulating freely in the communications and political system.

Jewish influence stems from the fact that they function collectively: they are organized, active, and concentrate on a single issue— US policy in the Middle East.

In the political sphere, pro-Israeli politicians and powerful Jewish organizations have joined forces with (and even animate)[29] pro-Israel ultra rightwing mass-based Christian fundamentalist powerful political leaders tied to the military-industrial complex, such as Secretary of Defense Rumsfeld and Vice President Cheney. Israel's unconditional support of Washington's Cold War and subsequent anti-terrorist military offensive has further strengthened ideological and military ties between US rightwing political leaders, pro-Israeli politicians and the leaders of the leading Jewish organizations. The politics of Washington's new imperialism coincides splendidly with the Sharon-Olmert conquest and destruction of the Occupied Territories.

Wealthy and organized Jewish organizations, compliant Congressional representatives and rightwing fundamentalist organizations are not the only financial supporters of Israel. US taxpayers have been funding the Israeli war machine with over $3 billion a year of direct assistance for over 35 years (now totaling over $100 billion and continuing to mount).

Support for Israel from the US Government

Jewish support for Israel exercised in the above-mentioned sectors of American society leads in turn to an exacerbated support for Israel by the US government that is demonstrable in the lavish dispensation of US aid to Israel. As the CRS Issue Brief notes, "Israel receives favorable treatment and special benefits under U.S. assistance programs that may not be available to other countries." The CRS Issue Brief elaborates these benefits under the following topics: cash flow financing, ESF cash transfer, FMF offsets, early transfers, FMF drawdown, unique FMF funding arrangements, FMF for R&D, FMF for in-country purchase.

The data below, compiled by the CRS Issue Brief in 2004,[30] provide some notion of the extent of U.S. aid and its special features:

• Israel has received more than $90 billion in US aid up to 2003, of which $75 billion has been in grants (i.e. non-repayable), and $15 billion in loans.

• Since 1985, the United States has provided $3 billion in grants annually to Israel.

• Resettlement assistance for Soviet and Ethiopian immigrants peaked in 1992 at $80 million, but continues to be subsidized at $60 million for 2003, $50 million in 2004 and again in 2005.

• In 1990, Israel requested $10 billion in loan guarantees, which would enable Israel to borrow from US commercial establishments, with their loans guaranteed against default by the US government. In 2004, a further $9 billion in loan guarantees was included in P.L. 1088-11. (NOTE: Loan guarantees is the area of financial support to Israel that the US government attacks to indicate its displeasure with Israeli settlement activities. The $10 billion authorized in loan guarantees for 1993-1996 was reduced by $774 million in penalties for settlement expansion.[31] No matter: Israel only drew loans on the $10 billion worth about 6.6 billion—annulling any effect from the purported penalty.)

• Economic aid became all grant cash transfer in 1981, and military aid similarly in 1985.

What might be called optimization techniques are employed to further increase (and disguise?) the actual extent of financing, such as:

• Loans with repayment waived (or a pledge to provide Israel with economic assistance equal to the amount Israel owes the United States for previous loans). Since 1974 through 2003, Israel received more than $45 billion in waived loans.

• Since 1982, the US pays Israel ESF funds in one lump sum early in the fiscal year, rather than in four quarterly installments, as is the usual practice with other countries. "The United States pays more in interest for the money it borrows to make lump sum payments. AID officials estimate that it cost the United States between $50 million and $60 million per year to borrow funds for the early, lump-sum payment. In addition, the U.S. government pays Israel interest on the ESF funds invested in U.S. Treasury notes, according to AID officials. It has been reported that Israel earned about $86 million in U.S. Treasury note interest in 1991."[32] The practice has continued in subsequent years.

In addition, the US has supported the development of the Israeli military-defense industry, inter alia through:

• $625 million to develop and deploy the Arrow anti-missile missle.

• $1.8 billion to develop the Lavi aircraft. "On August 20, 1987, the Israeli cabinet voted to cancel the Lavi project, but asked the United States for $450 million to pay for canceled contracts. The State Department agreed to raise the FMF earmark for procurement in Israel from $300 million to $400 million to defray Lavi cancellation costs."[33]

• US military assistance for military purchases in Israel (26.3%). This meant that in 2004, $568 million in military aid could be spent in Israel. (Most US military aid is for purchases of US arms.)

Further support comes through the US government's guarantee of Israel's access to oil, via the Israel-United States Memorandum of Agreement, 1 September 1975. According to Ed Vuillamy, writing in the London *Observer*:

The memorandum has been quietly renewed every five years, with special legislation attached whereby the US stocks a strategic oil reserve for Israel even if it entailed domestic shortages—at a cost of $3 billion (£1.9bn) in 2002 to US taxpayers.[34]

Any major development in or initiated by Israel seems to give rise to its own "special costs" which in turn are placed at the door of the United States, whether it concerns support for the migration of Soviet or Ethiopian Jews, or withdrawal from occupied territories. In 2005, Israel moved to request American aid to cover some of the $2 billion to $3 billion cost of its "disengagement" from Gaza, but withdrew that request once hurricanes hit America's Gulf coast.[35] With the ascendancy of Olmert, however, the putative costs of the disengagement plan as a whole (which was unilateral despite the US government's demand that it be negotiated) far superceded that, witness his "future intention to seek international financial assistance to defray the cost of the plan, estimated by Israeli economists at $10 billion to $25 billion."[36]

Israel Bonds

Over its fifty years of existence, the sale of Israel Bonds raised some $22 billion for the State of Israel. Gideon Pratt, CEO of Israel Bonds, claims the bonds have financed over 50% of Israel's development,[37] though this is clearly disputable, in view of its proportion to grants, etc. from the US government as outlined above.

According to the Development Corporation for Israel prospectus, the bonds are used for eight categories of infrastructure development projects, such as building ports, power grids, transportation, communications, etc. But as Russell Mokhiber points out:

> What the prospectus does not mention, however, is that such 'development' projects also include Israeli settlements in the West Bank and Gaza. Other bond revenues are transferred from the Israeli government's development account to its ordinary budget, to be spent on the military, the Israeli intelligence services, and other agencies, according to the statistical abstract published each year by the Israeli government.[38]

Rank and file trade union members might have been surprised to learn that their pension funds had been invested in Israel Bonds with below normal rates of return and higher risk. Despite the poor investment quality of

Israel Bonds, some of the largest US trade unions, employee pension funds, and major multi-national corporations have collectively loaned billions of dollars to the Israeli regime. In all cases, the decisions to purchase a foreign government's bonds were made by the trade union bosses and corporate fund managers without consulting the membership or stockholders.[39] Nathan Zirkin, a financial director of the Retail, Wholesale and Department Store Union, when asked if his union would continue to purchase Israel Bonds despite Israel's repression and arrest of Palestinian trade unionists and activists, replied "Absolutely. The Palestinians didn't have a damn thing until Israel came in."[40]

Many of the trade unions, which are purchasers of Israeli bonds, are controlled or influenced by the Mafia. The Teamsters Union is the biggest purchaser of Israel Bonds; it is also the union which has seen more senior officials indicted for Mafia ties, illicit use of union funds, and massive robbery of membership pension funds. In this case the trade union Mafioso were buying favorable propaganda from the mass media and support from the "respectable" Jewish organizations via the purchase of Israel Bonds.

Union pension funds have also been used by trade union bureaucrats to purchase Israel Bonds. The most notorious case is the former International Ladies Garment Workers Unions (ILGWU), now called UNITE, a union whose workers are 95% Black, Hispanic, and Chinese, most earning at or below the minimum wage. UNITE's leadership and staff is overwhelming Jewish and earning between $100,000 to $350,000 a year plus expenses.[41] By channeling over $25 million in pension funds to Israel, the US workers are deprived of access to loans for housing, social services, legal defense, etc. Clearly the Jewish trade union bosses have a greater affinity for the State of Israel and its oppression of Palestinian workers than they have with their own poorly organized workers, employed under some of the worst working conditions in the US.

Israel Bond promoters, with support from Mafia-influenced corrupt trade union bosses, have sold vast holdings of Israel bonds to 1500 labor organizations at interest rates below **The American labor community holds $5 billion in Israel Bonds.** those of other available securities and well below what most investors would expect from loans to an economically troubled foreign government like Israel. On March 22, 2002, the Jewish weekly *Forward* actually put a figure on that amount, quoting the director of the National Committee for Labor Israel as estimating that "the American labor community holds $5 billion in Israel Bonds."

Many factors accounted for the US trade union bosses channeling their members pension funds and union dues into Israel Bonds: political protection and respectability in being associated with Israel and its lobbyists—this was especially important to Mafia-linked and corrupt officials.

Ideological and ethnic ties between Jewish trade union leaders and Israel has been a second factor.

While Israel bonds may represent a diminishing factor in the contemporary Israeli economy—perhaps because the $US 10 billion loan guarantee terminated in 1998?[42]—they are nonetheless still purchased and held, inter alia, by state and city governments, teachers, universities, and police in the United States, as well as 100,000 individuals.

Accomplices to Genocide

In April 2002, over 100,000 people, mostly Jews and Christian fundamentalists, marched in support of the Sharon regime in the midst of the siege of Jenin, and were addressed, inter alia, by Paul Wolfowitz, William Bennett, Hillary Clinton, Dick Armey, Rudy Giuliani, Dick Gephardt, and AFL-CIO president John Sweeney. In Israel two out of three Israelis (65 percent) polled in late April 2002 supported Sharon and almost 90 percent believed the regime's propaganda that the UN commission to investigate Israeli devastation of the Occupied Territories "will not be fair to Israel." The Israeli public, the US trade union bosses, and the American political and financial elites who financed Sharon thereby became accomplices to the crimes against the Palestinian people. Obviously the shrinking minority of Jews in Israel who oppose the military machine have little or no influence in policy, in the media, or in securing overseas financial support.

Interestingly, the US did vote in favor of the resolution creating a UN investigatory commission of Israel's near total destruction of Jenin in the spring of 2003. But the UN investigation got no further than its creation. It evoked the hostility of the entire Israeli political class. Shimon Perez (then the self-styled labor moderate in Sharon's government) accused the 170-plus member United Nations Organization of "blood libel". The Israeli security cabinet decided that Kofi Annan, the UN Secretary General, had not met its demands for amending the mission's mandate, "so there is no possibility of beginning the inquiry…." As Alan Philips of the *Daily Telegraph* put it:

> Apparently having lost his trial of strength with Ariel Sharon, the Israeli prime minister, Mr Annan recommended to the UN Security Council that the team—which has been waiting in Geneva for three days for permission to go to Israel—should be sent home.[43]

Wealthy and powerful reactionary Jews in the Diaspora also gravitated toward Sharon. Seven of the eight billionaire Russian Mafia Oligarchs have donated generously to the Israeli state, were on excellent terms with Sharon and Shimon Peres, and have no use for dissident military reservists.

In fact, two of these, Israeli-Russian partners of the Russian oil company, Yukos, have taken up residence in Israel to avoid Interpol interdiction, while a third, Boris Berezovsky, though resident in London, is an Israeli citizen.[44] Six out of the seven are Jews.[45]

Because of powerful unconditional external financial and military support primarily from influential Jews in the US, Christian Fundamentalists, the military industrial complex, Pentagon extremists, and corrupt US trade unionists, Israel is able to defy world public opinion, slander humanitarian organizations and human rights leaders, and brazenly continue its genocidal policies. Israeli leaders know "their people": they know they have uncondi-tional supporters who have already been tested. They know that their bankers, professionals and fundamentalists will back them up to the last murdered Palestinian: the march of the 100,000 pro-Zionists in Washington in the midst of the Jenin massacre proved it. The huge turnout of politicians at the annual AIPAC conference during the massacres in the Rafah refugee camp in the Gaza strip confirms that they in turn supported the butchers of Rafah.

The Zionist Power Configuration in the United States

C. Wright Mills once wrote that the US "power elite" ruled by deny-ing it held power. The Zionist elite follows this formula, but defends itself by accusing its adversaries of being "anti-Semites" and pursuing retributive mea-sures that would please former Senator Joseph McCarthy. The Zionist power configuration (ZPC) cannot be un-derstood merely as the "Jewish Lobby" or even the AIPAC, as for-midable as it is, with 150 full-time functionaries. The ZPC can best be understood as a complex net-work of interrelated formal and informal groupings, operating at the international, national, regional and local levels, and directly and systematically subordinated to the State of Israel, its power holders and key decision makers.

The ZPC can best be understood as a complex network of interrelated formal and informal groupings, operating at the international, national, regional and local levels, and directly and systematically subordinated to the State of Israel.

Influence is wielded via *direct influence* by Zionist representatives in the Government (most notably in the Pentagon under Bush) both in the Ex-ecutive branch as well as in the Congress, and indirectly via its use of campaign funds 1) to influence the selection of candidates within the two major political parties and 2) to defeat critics of Israel and reward elected officials who will toe the Israel line.

The parameters of political debate on Israel-related issues—which have broadened over time—are shaped by pervasive Zionist and Jewish orga-nizational influence in the mass media, censoring and virulently attacking critics, and pushing pro-Israel "news" and commentaries. The mass media in the US, particularly the "respectable" *New York Times,* has been in the forefront of propagandizing Israeli conquest and destruction as a "defensive", "anti-terrorist war". Not a single voice or editorial in the *New York Times* has spoken of the mass killing of Palestinian civilians and Israel's destruction of priceless Christian historical and religious sites that go back over 2000 years.[46] While Israel's war machine destroys ancient monasteries and the heritage of world culture, the pro-Israeli mass media in the US focus their critical lenses on the scandals of the Catholic clergy. The Church's protests at the Israeli shelling of the Church of the Nativity and the murder of those seeking sanctuary are thus silenced.

The fourth circle of influence is through local and sectoral organizations, local and state Jewish federations, and through them in local professional bodies, trade unions, pension funds. Activists may be affiliated with the national apparatus and/or embedded in local "civil society". This is probably the most serious threat as it inhibits average US citizens from voicing their doubts and criticisms of Israeli policy, and mutes the effectiveness of the advocacy sector of American society, which in other arenas has assumed a critical progressive role in relation to US policy. All over the US, local editors, critical intellectuals and activists, and even doctors have been branded as "neo-Nazis" and have suffered threatening phone calls and visits by local pro-Israel zealots—including 'respectable' members of the Jewish community. The threatened consequences usually stop discussions and/or intimidate local citizens advocating an independent and democratic foreign policy.

Moreover the ZPC's formal and informal *structure* has a crucial dynamic element to it: each power center *interacts* with the rest, creating a constant "movement" and activity, which converges and energizes both leaders and followers. Secondly those non-Jewish or even non-Zionist political, media and civic leaders influenced by the ZPC in turn influence their constituency, multiplying several fold the initial influence of their "hegemons". The relative absence of an informal, organized and active grassroots democratic foreign policy movement, particularly in relation to Mideast policy, had for some time given the ZPC a clear field with virtually no competitors. Only recently has it been challenged by a growing campaign for divestment from Israel which has won varying degrees of support from Christian denominations (Presbyterians, Methodists, Episcopalians) and on university campuses—though this movement proceeds only tentatively and with much organized opposition. As an instance, the City of Somerville, MA intended to divest from Israel, then backed off after Jewish representations to city council.

Over time the same pattern of Zionist influence has manifested itself in US executive agencies. The State Department's "Arabists" are being replaced by pro-Zionists as is the case with senior civilian militarists in the

Pentagon, in the Mideast think tanks and the Council of Foreign Relations, among others. It should be noted that the so-called "single issue" (US-Middle East Policy) focus of the ZPC of the past has been replaced by the new Zionist strategies in the Pentagon and rightwing think tanks who link the expansion of Israeli power beyond Palestine to US-European relations (especially French bashing), US nuclear policy, and US military and energy strategy. This analytical framework is useful in understanding the US-Iraq war, and macro-imperial policy as well as micro-colonial practices.

The ZPC in Action: The Iraq War

The major theoretical strategist of US World Empire is Paul Wolfowitz who first presented a detailed outline of action in 1992.[47] The argument for permanent wars, unilateral action, pre-emptive warfare and colonial conquest was spelled out for the first Bush Administration, and later supported implicitly during the Clinton Administration's continued military attacks against Iraq, its unconditional backing of Israel's war against the Palestinians, the Balkan wars, and the de facto takeover of the ex-Communist states of Eastern Europe, the Baltic states and the South-Central Republics of the ex-USSR.

The Clinton Administration's vigorous intervention in favor of Yeltsin's seizure of power and backing of the Russian (Jewish) Oligarchs played a major role in dismembering and weakening its former adversary to world domination. Clinton's unconditional support for Israel and more importantly, for the formulation of a Mideast strategy convergent with Israeli foreign policy was tied to three sets of policies:

1) destroying the military and economic power of one of Israel's main critics in the Mideast (Iraq) via economic boycotts, arms inspections and unilateral disarmament of Iraq, while Israel stockpiled nuclear and other weapons of mass destruction;

2) financing and arming Israeli expansion and colonization of Arab Palestine;

3) maintaining an economic boycott of Libya and Iran (supporters of the Palestinians) while subsidizing Arab client states friendly to Israel (Egypt and Jordan), whose recognition of and relations with Israel required increasing repression of opinion and resistance within those states (and further expenditures by the US in order to be accomplished).

Direct Zionist influence over US Mideast policy was shaped by Secretary of State Madeleine Albright who, while a convert from Catholicism to the more elite Episcopalian Church, benefited from her newly-discovered Jewish ancestry. Albright infamously justified the US-induced deaths of 500,000 Iraqi children during her tenure in office, declaring "It was worth it." Secretary of Defense Cohen was instrumental in promoting Israeli military dominance in the Middle East and Richard Holbrooke, a closet Zionist, was one of the most influential Clinton advisers on the Middle East "peace negotiations". President Clinton and the Democrats laid the basis for the eventual capture of US foreign policy making by the Zionists in the subsequent Bush administration by accepting Zionists in strategic foreign policy positions influencing Mideast policy and shaping US policy to fit Israeli expansionist aims.

To be sure, Clinton and his "moderate" Zionists did not threaten Israel's critics such as Saudi Arabia or the rest of the Arab countries with military attacks—as did the Bush regime dominated by the ultra-Zionist militarists. Nor did his regime follow the Israeli line of accusing all of Europe, especially France, of being anti-Semites for criticizing Israel's slaughter of Palestinians. The Clinton regime and its moderate Zionist influentials believed it was possible to establish US dominance by consulting with Europe and conservative Arab regimes and sharing the economic benefits of imperial spoils in the Mideast while supporting Israeli expansionism.

The Bush regime represented a qualitative advance in Zionist power in US policies, both foreign and domestic. The key economic policymaker was Alan Greenspan, head of the US Central Bank (Federal Reserve Bank), a long time crony of Wall Street financial interests and promoter of the major pro-Israeli investment houses—responsible for the speculative boom and bust economy of the 1990's.

The influence on US Middle East policy of this neo-conservative cabal far exceeded their formal positions because they were backed by an array of influential Zionist academic ideologues (Kagan, Cohen, Pipes), political pundits (Kristols, Krauthamer, Peretz etc) and directors of war think-tanks (Pipes, Rubin) who continue to be given constant access to the opinion pages of the major US newspapers, or interviewed as Middle East "experts" on pro-Israeli television and radio shows—advancing their war propaganda designed to promote US defense of Israel's Middle East agenda, despite the evident quagmire in Iraq, and growing public rejection of that war. These policy and opinion makers, backed by the mass media, worked in close consultation and in tandem with the major Jewish organizations in the US and in close "consultations" with top officials in the Sharon regime—and will continue to do so with Olmert. Mossad agents, Israeli diplomats and key officials in the Sharon regime had free access to the offices of the Zionist officials in Washington and interchanged information on how to optimize Israeli interests.

Prior to the US invasion of Iraq, all the Zionists in key policy positions and their counterparts in Congress backed a US war with Iraq. After 9/

11, Wolfowitz and Senator Lieberman immediately proposed a war against Iraq—demanding that the intelligence agencies "find" the connection and accusing the military of being cowards for not engaging in war to "protect" Israel. Despite Herculean efforts by Feith et al. to twist CIA and MI reports to serve their pro-war Israeli line, their bellicose rhetoric lacked substance. They then invented the—now callously admitted—BIG LIE (by Wolfowitz) of the Iraqi weapons of mass destruction threat to US security. It was a classic case, as became evident when the secret Downing Street Memo was made public, of fitting the facts to suit the policy.[48]

To pursue this line, the Zionists in the Pentagon bypassed the traditional military/intelligence agencies and created their own propaganda–"intelligence" agency or "Office of Special Plans". The Committee for the Liberation of Iraq (CLI) was set up by Bruce Jackson, a former director of the neo-conservative Project for a New American Century, to press for regime change in Iraq. Other members of the CLI included Bush advisor Richard Perle, former Republican House Speaker Newt Gingrich, former CIA Director James Woolsey, and the editor of the of the *Weekly Standard*, William Kristol, as well as Senators John McCain and Bob Kerry.

Zionist power manifested itself first in the making of the war and then in imposing impunity on the crimes of the war makers in the government. The Zionists had knowingly painted a totally unrealistic and false picture of the war, its consequences and the likely response of the Iraqi resistance to an Israeli-style conquest and colonization—knowingly, indeed, since it was they who put the figures in place whose purported special knowledge supported their arguments. The Zionists were initially able to marginalize high military officials like General Anthony Zinni who questioned the war and opposed the way the war was launched, and the length and breadth of the engagement. They shut out all debate on who would benefit and who would lose from the war: US soldiers killed, rising oil and energy costs, huge budget deficits, and, of course, massive loss of life and property among the Iraqis.

Wolfowitz claimed that the invading army would be welcomed as liberators (evoking the liberation of Paris). Perle claimed "the Arabs" would offer little or no resistance (being a "tribal" society). Kagan claimed that "one big bomb" would silence the Arab street and public opinion.

While the US military had conducted a campaign of forced demodernization in the first Iraq War, attacking even civilian technological infrastructure related to water and sewage, in the second attack on Iraq by the Bush, Jr. administration, Feith and Wolfowitz concentrated on the destruction of Iraqi society, as such. They promoted the massive purge of the entire Iraqi civil service, professions, universities, schools and hospitals of Baathists, as well as the dismantling of the Iraqi army and dismissal of 400,000 Iraqi military and police personnel—over the shocked objections of experienced senior US military officers who had expected to work with the surrendered military and administrative structure of Iraq to control the colony. This opened the way for the pillage of Iraq's complex infrastructure and historic treasures and libraries, as well as the growth of criminal gangs involved in theft, kidnap for ransom, murder and rape—activities virtually unknown under the tight Baathist regime. Rumsfeld dismissed the massive destruction of Iraqi society as the "messiness of freedom".

Many top US military officials objected, as did the first US proconsul, former general Jay Garner, who stated that he "fell out with the Bush circle because he wanted free elections and rejected an imposed programme of privatization."[49] But the Zionists in the Pentagon and their partners in crime, Rumsfeld and Cheney, were determined to dismantle the secular Iraqi state in order to institute a policy to turn Iraq into a desert kingdom—a loose collection of at least three "tribal" client mini-states based on ethnicities, religious-tribal loyalties, and forever incapable of opposing Israeli expansionism, particularly in Northern Iraq.[50]

However, instead of easy conquest, the 'Israel First' Pentagonistas provoked a massive popular opposition, which unified the religious and secular groups in opposition to the US occupation, and swelled the ranks of the armed resistance with thousands of discharged armed professionals. In the course of pursuing a policy of strengthening Israel's regional position, the Zionists weakened the US colonial occupation and any medium term plans to convert Iraq into a US oil colony. The result has been thousands of US military and client collaborators dead, maimed and wounded, and a burgeoning worldwide opposition, particularly in the Arab East, and among several hundred million Muslims.

The Israel First Pentagonistas successfully promoted the idea that the Israeli military and intelligence experts had a lot to teach their ignorant American counterparts on "urban warfare" and "information gathering" drawing on Israel's wealth of experience of over 50 years of expelling and destroying Palestinian communities and developing interrogation and torture techniques on Palestinian and Lebanese captives.[51] The purpose of the Pentagon Zionists was to deepen the ties with Israel's security apparatus as part of a middle term goal of making "the cause of Israel as the cause of America" (as prostrate Presidential candidate Kerry pledged).[52] The long-term goal

The Grand Scheme of a Greater Middle East US-Israel Co-Prosperity Sphere would provide Imperial Israel with access to water, oil, capital and markets, which the heavily subsidized rentier militarist state presently lacks.

was to leverage military security and the co-manufacture of military weaponry between the US and Israel into the Grand Scheme of a Greater Middle East US-Israel Co-Prosperity Sphere.[53] Imperial Israel would then have access to water, oil, capital and markets, which the heavily subsidized rentier militarist state lacks at the present.

The torture-interrogation techniques taught by the Israeli instructors converged nicely, updating and refining the older CIA torture manuals, more specifically introducing specificities pertaining to torturing Muslims and especially Arabs.[54] But once again the Zionist-Israeli priorities undermined US imperialist policies: the photo revelations of US soldiers torturing, raping and humiliating Iraqi prisoners discredited the US occupation worldwide, heightened Arab and Muslim resistance throughout the Middle East and discredited the Bush regime. Congressional hearings and mass media reportages even provoked a burst of public disapproval of the invasion of Iraq and Bush's handling of the occupation. Throughout the country there were calls, including from members of Congress, for Rumsfeld's resignation.

Curiously enough, there were virtually no calls for the resignation of the Israel First Pentagonistas—who were equally implicated and responsible for the mass torture of Muslim detainees. According to *Newsweek*, it was Douglas Feith who was actually in charge of setting policy on Iraqi detainees.[55] Even in the face of this horrible crime against humanity, even in the general national outcry to investigate, impeach and hold responsible those involved, Paul Wolfowitz, the top Zionist architect of the war and responsible head (number 2) of Pentagon intelligence in the Iraq war involved in ordering the torture, has escaped official public censure, protected as he has been up to now by the pro-Israel pundits, political fundraisers, presidential campaign fundraisers and influentials, (see Chapter Four on the exposé of Seymour Hersh's exposé). As for number 3, despite the fact that he is still a key subject of a Phase II Senate Intelligence Committee investigation on pre-war planning and post-invasion failures (Phase I focused primarily on intelligence failures), Douglas Feith was invited to teach a course on the Bush Administration's strategy behind the war on terrorism to students in the Edmund A. Walsh School of Foreign Service at Georgetown University in Fall 2006.

While the Zionists in the Pentagon may have been publicly criticized and even investigated, they have yet to be officially and publicly reprimanded for their collaboration *with the Mossad*.

While the Mossad was later chastised for "intelligence failures" by the Israeli Knesset after release of the Steinitz Report on March 29, 2004, their Zionist counterparts in the Pentagon—Shulsky, Wolfowitz, Feith, and Abrams—however they may have been publicly criticized and even investigated, have yet to be officially and publicly reprimanded for their collaboration *with the Mossad*. Much will depend on an ongoing investigation by the FBI—which holds more promise than the Congressional whitewashing. As Robert Dreyfuss put it in *The Nation*: "Did Ariel Sharon, the Prime Minister of Israel, run a covert program with operatives in high-level US government positions to influence the Bush Administration's decision to go to war in Iraq? The FBI wants to know."[56] In fact, the FBI appears to be one American institution which is willing to address the issue of Zionist power in America, as its efforts related to the AIPAC-spying scandal (see Chapter 5) seem to indicate.

Amid the widespread condemnation of these war crimes and the media exposure of the systematic lies of the Pentagonistas, the fear that the highly influential and visible role of the Israel Firsters might lead to an anti-Israel backlash raised alarm bells among some of the most astute Congressional Zionists.[57] Senator Frank Lautenberg (Democrat-New Jersey) a committed Zionist, called for the "replacement" of Wolfowitz and Feith in order to get them out of view and further, louder, anti-Zionist-related condemnation. "The men in charge have let down the soldiers in uniform. Simply replacing Secretary Rumsfeld will change little at the Pentagon if his discredited team of advisers remains in high-level positions. It is time for us to bring in new civilian leadership at the Defense Department".[58] Lautenberg made it abundantly clear whom he thought was central to the whole US war effort, from beating the war drums, to cooking the data, designing the war strategy, to micromanaging the business of interrogation-torture.

Several former top US military professionals objected to the Zionist control over US policy and their close network of collaborators. Colonel Karen Kwiatkowski has given us an inside picture of the Feith/Shulsky operation whose links to the Mossad seemed closer than to the US military. The Rumsfeld-Zionist group's monopolization of military policy, war strategy, military calculations and military promotions all alienated the military high command. Some who clearly foresaw the disastrous consequences of the policies of the Israel First crowd on US global ambitions were silenced and marginalized.

It is likely that the release of the torture photos to the media was deliberately encouraged or promoted by highly placed military officials or former officials as a way of discrediting Rumsfeld and the Pentagon Zionists.[59] This move severely undercut the war effort, which more and more of the military high command sees as destined to fail, but they were determined not to become the neo-cons' scapegoats. However to gain an "honorable" withdrawal they must know that they have to remove Rumsfeld and his Zionist colleagues, whose criteria for evaluating the war has less to do with the aims and standing of the US military and more to do with Israeli expansionist goals in the Middle East.

While the Pentagon Zionists and the powerful network of pro-Israel Jewish organizations have seen their Iraqi serial war strategy fall behind schedule, they have succeeded in securing Presidential economic sanctions against Syria and binding US political support for Sharon's (and now Olmert's) destruction and annexation of the remnant of Palestine. Moreover the leading Jewish organizations were able to secure a near unanimous vote in Congress

(407 to 9) in favor of Bush's declaration supporting Israel's "new borders" in Palestine.[60]   Once again the Zionist Lobby demonstrated its power—even turning Bush and Congress into self-effacing political idiots before Sharon. After Bush put all of his limited credibility in Mideast politics in his "Roadmap" for a Middle East peace accord, Sharon unilaterally declared a policy of "annexation and separation" and told Bush to swallow it. All the major Jewish organizations backed Sharon's plan. Bush submitted and endorsed this, alienating virtually every European country and all Arab countries, and clearly demonstrating the slavish complicity of US policymakers who once again renounced US Middle East imperial interests in order to accommodate Israel's expansion into the remnants of Palestine. Bush's policy reversal was backed by the vast majority of Congress who are forever fearful of Zionist-Jewish retaliation for the least deviation from unconditional and total support for Israel.

During the invasion and occupation of Iraq, some Congress members have been critical of the war. Hundreds of thousands of people have demonstrated their disapproval. Many Jewish Americans have participated in the protests and in some cases have led the protests. Mass media outlets have on occasion (especially after the torture exposé) publicized adverse news on the war (tortures, civilian victims, wedding parties bombed, and homes and orchards bulldozed). While the US pursues the war in Iraq, the Israeli government has been equally brutal: engaging in premeditated assassination of Palestinian leaders, systematically destroying thousands of homes, farms, orchards, stores, schools, mosques and factories, and killing and maiming thousands of Palestinians activists, civilians, women and children. They have also resorted to the routine hooding, manacling and torture of detainees.

All the major pro-Israel Jewish groups in the US, high and low, have defended all these crimes against humanity, successfully pressuring both major parties, the Congress and President, to say nothing—no protest, no investigation, no punishment. This, while the US, smarting from the exposure of torture at Abu Ghraib and pursued by the UN Committee on Torture, Amnesty International and other human rights groups, has been forced to put on trial more than 100 armed forces' staff accused of prisoner abuse in Afghanistan and Iraq, the scope of which in and of itself points to a practice rooted in policy.[61] More perversely in the face of the Israeli mayhem, pro-Israel Jewish groups have secured $10 billion dollars more in aid and lucrative joint-venture military contracts (no outcry here about Halliburton-type contracting).

Israel and the Right of Free Speech

There is presently an inability in America even to formulate or sustain a discourse related to the subject of Israeli influence on the United States. Such an opportunity seemed to open with the courageous publication of a well-documented essay written by Professor Walt of Harvard University and Professor Mearsheimer of University of Chicago critical of the Lobby's influence on US Middle East policy. However, a virulent campaign against Mearsheimer and Walt was then waged by all the major Jewish publications and pro-Israel organizations. From the ultra-rightwing Orthodox *Jewish Press* (which claims to be the largest "independent" Jewish newspaper in the US), to the formerly social democratic *Forward*, to the *Jewish Weekly*, all have launched, together with all the major Jewish organizations, a propaganda campaign of defamation ("the new Protocols of Zion", "anti-Semitic", "sources from Neo-Nazi websites...") and pressure for their purge from academia.

There is presently an inability in America even to formulate or sustain a discourse related to the subject of Israeli influence on the United States.

The Jewish authoritarians have already partially succeeded. Their press releases have been published by the mass media without allowing for rebuttal by the academics under attack. Harvard University has demanded that the identification of the Harvard Kennedy School be removed from the paper. The financier of the professorial chair (in his name) which Professor Walt, as academic dean, occupies at the Harvard Kennedy School, is no longer mentioned in his publication. Ultra-Zionist and torture advocate Professor Dershowitz and his fellow Harvard zealots called into question their moral and academic qualification to teach—this concerning professors of the highest standing, with an established record at America's top universities.

In both the United States and France, legislation is being prepared to equate anti-Zionism with anti-Semitism and to criminalize as a 'hate crime' the free expression of outrage over Israeli atrocities and any criticism of the Lobby's control of US Middle East policy. [62] In the US, the proposed legislation[63] would take the form of withdrawing federal funding from any academic institution where the policies of Israel are criticized.

Other attacks on American academics include the effort by Daniel Pipes, director of Middle East Forum, to establish a campus blacklist through his neo-McCarthyite Campus-Watch website. Pipes is part of a "band of neo-conservative pundits with strong allegiances to Israel [who] took on the task of launching a more focused assault on Middle East Scholars."[64] This effort was but the latest in a long history of attempts to curtail academic discussion of issues that might relate to Israel.[65]

In New York City, a major theater production of the life of Rachael Corrie, an American humanitarian volunteer murdered in the Occupied Territories by an Israeli Defense Force soldier driving a bulldozer, was cancelled because of Jewish pressure and financial threats. The theater admitted that the cancellation had to do with the "sensitivities" (and pocket book) of the Israel-Firsters. Even the progressive magazine, *Mother Jones,* went to the trouble of running an article critical of Corrie, heading it:

> **NEWS:** Martyr, idiot, dedicated, deluded. Why did this American college student crushed by an Israeli bulldozer put her life on the line? And did it matter?[66]

The pro-Israel lobby's defense and support of a minority opinion in favor of Middle East aggression is now extending its authoritarian reach into undermining the basic right of Americans to free and open expression. There is no group of investors or financiers willing to fund a civil rights campaign in defense of free speech, academic and artistic freedom, to counter the minority Zionist financial and professional elite.

The leaders of the peace movement, both Jews and non-Jews, reject any effort to include Israel's genocidal war against Palestine for fear of alienating the "public" (read the major Jewish organizations) and the self-styled progressive Jews, who are ever protective of everything Jewish—even war crimes. Worse still, with a few rare exceptions, the "progressive" Jewish critics of the war and Israel are forever and adamantly determined to avoid criticizing the role of powerful Zionist policymakers in the government, their ties to Israel and the significant support they receive from the major Jewish organizations in all matters which pertain directly or remotely to Israeli interests.

With blind simplicity, they all see Israel as simply a "tool" of the US for weakening the Arabs in the service of US oil interests. Apparently they have never consulted US petrol CEOs, advisers or investment brokers, who all agree that US support for Israel is destabilizing the region, threatening oil supplies, boosting prices to US consumers and creating enemies out of Arab client rulers who invest in the US, buy US currency to keep it from collapsing, and raise OPEC quotas to help lower US prices. By its blind support for Israeli colonial brutality, the US has alienated several hundred million Muslims, millions of Arabs of all faiths, the great majority of Europeans, Africans and Asians, thereby heightening US global isolation. The American alliance with Israel has been one of the world's greatest energizers of anti-imperialist movements, crossing racial, religious and gender boundaries.

The American alliance with Israel has been one of the world's greatest energizers of anti-imperialist movements, crossing racial, religious and gender boundaries—everywhere but among the American Left.

Even the crude, virulent anti-European ideology propagated by Israeli ideologues and their transmission belt Jewish organizations in the US and Europe has influenced the US government. At a time when Muslims and Arabs are conquered and persecuted, with thousands jailed and many "disappeared" by the US, Israeli and European governments, Secretary of State Powell convened a meeting in Europe on the rising danger of ... "anti-Semitism"!! And the UN, under Kofi Annan, followed suit with its own meeting on 'anti-Semitism' during the ongoing devastation in the Rafah refugee camps in the Gaza Strip! The major Jewish organizations repeat the Sharon and now Olmert line that "anti-Zionists" are "anti-Semites"—and it becomes established policy in the US and in some countries of Europe... to the point that individuals critical of Zionism are fired, cultural institutions are pressured into censoring anti-Zionist events and creating a general culture of fear of offending the hegemonic Jewish organizations. Even Webster's recent dictionary equates anti-Zionism with anti-Semitism. Surprisingly, in the midst of this, the major Jewish organizations in France openly condemned the manufactured hysteria as an Israeli mechanism to encourage the migration of French Jews to Israel.[67]

Jews in North America, South America and Europe are disproportionately in the highest paid positions, with the highest proportion in the exclusive, prestigious private universities, with disproportionate influence in finance and the media. It is clear that "anti-Semitism" is a very marginal global issue and, in point of fact, that Jews are the most influential ethnic group.

The tragic myopia or perverse refusal of leftist Jews to face up to the prejudicial role of the major Zionist and Jewish groups promoting the Israel First policy and imposing it on the electoral agendas substantially undermines their and our efforts to secure peace and justice in the Middle East and to forge a democratic US foreign policy.

ENDNOTES

[1]   The U.S Country Reports on Terrorism 2005 indicates that terrorism is on the rise, with the bulk of the increase in Iraq.

[2]   Tom Regan, "Report: US war costs could top $2 trillion", *Christian Science Monitor*, January 10, 2006.

[3]   As Bernhard Zand points out, "On the eve of the war, Iraq was pumping about 2.5 million barrels of crude oil per day. In the first three months of this year, the rate of export was just over 1.7 billion barrels." See Bernard Zand, "On the Verge of Collapse," *Der Speigel*, May 1, 2006.

[4]   Steven Graham, "Switching Cities Off", Routledge, 2005.

[5]   "A Clean Break: A New Strategy for Securing the Realm", Richard Perle, Douglas Feith, David Wurmser, et al, Institute of Advanced Strategic and Political Studies. 1996.

[6]   There are actually numerous contenders for this epithet. See Kevin Drum, "Political Animal", *Washington Monthly*, May 16, 2006, who lists Anastasio Somosa, Francisco Franco and Dominican dictator Trujillo. Geoffrey Kemp, head of the National Security Council, is cited as the source of the epithet in relation to Saddam. See Judith Miller and Laurie Mylroie, *Saddam Hussein and the Crisis in the Gulf*, New York, Times Books, 1990, p. 85.

[7]   See Akiva Eldar, "Infrastructures Minister Paritzky dreams of Iraqi Oil Flowing to Haifa", *Haaretz*, March 31, 2003.

8   Amiram Cohen, "US checking the possibility of pumping oil from northern Iraq to Haifa via Jordan", *Haaretz*, August 23, 2003.

9   This pipeline, once the Mosul-Haifa pipeline, closed in 1948 with the advent of the Zionist state, is now resurrected as the Kirkuk-Mosul-Haifa pipeline. Our source for the maps is http://judicial-inc.biz/pipeline_blown_mossad.htm, though they appear elsewhere on the internet.

10   US Financial Aid to Israel: Facts, Figures and Impacts, *Washington Report on Middle East Affairs*. 2004

11   Forty years later, on June 8, 2005, the *USS Liberty* Veterans Association filed a formal report with the US Department of Defense of War Crimes Committed Against U.S. Military Personnel on June 8, 1967 by elements of the Israeli military forces.

12   James Bamford, *Body of Secrets: Anatomy of the Ultra-Secret National Security Agency*, Doubleday, New York, 2001.

13   James Ennes, *Assault on the Liberty*, Random House, 1980. See also Statements by Ward Boston, Jr., Captain, JAGG USN (Ret), January 9, 2004 and Admiral Thomas Moorer, USN (Ret) January 11, 2003.

14   Alison Wier, "Russia, Israel and Media Omissions", Counterpunch.org, February 7, 2005.

15   *Washington Report on Middle East Affairs*, Pro-Israel PAC Contributions to 2002 Congressional Candidates, June 2003.

16   See Carl Cameron Investigates (Parts 1-4) Fox News Network, Dec. 17, 2001, available at <http://www.informationclearinghouse.info/article5133.htm>.

17   Compare this to the Bush Administration's prosecution and heated call for the death penalty for Zacarias Moussaoui, for just such a pre-knowledge of 9/11 and failure to forewarn.

18   Richard Reid, the ex-con and would-be shoe bomber, convicted for trying to blow up an American Airlines passenger jet over the Atlantic in December 2001, managed to enter Israel on an El Al flight despite his unusual background, BBC News, Dec. 28, 2001.

19   See Gordon Thomas and Martin Dillon, *Robert Maxwell, Israel's Superspy: The Life and Murder of a Media Mogul*, (Caroll and Graf, New York, 2002) for in depth discussion of the powerful media links with Israel.

21   Frankel, Glenn, "Prison Tactics a Longtime Dilemma for Israel", *Washington Post*, June 16, 2004, p. A01.

22   National Public Radio Interview, October 2004.

23   *New York Times*, December 28, 2001, p. 19.

24   CBS News September 20, 2002.

25   Gideon Levy, "Compensate settlers for what?", *Haaretz*, June 15, 2004.

26   Congressional Research Service Issue Brief for Congress titled "Israel: U.S. Foreign Assistance" by Clyde R. Mark, updated July 12, 2004. Order code IB86055.

27   See Global Income Per Capita 2005, compiled from World Bank Development Indicators, at <http://www.finfacts.com/biz10/globalworldincomepercapita.htm>

28   The EU's effort to curtail duty-free imports by Israel of goods produced in the Occupied Territories was resolved by its decision to charge duty on products labeled, say, "made in Ariel, Israel" but not on those marked "made in Tel Aviv, Israel". "It appears to save Israeli face by using the word 'Israel' to describe the location of the settlements, but allows the EU to make its point by charging a tariff on goods produced beyond the pre-1967 Green Line", noted the August 5, 2004 Reuters article "EU, Israel resolve trade dispute over settlements". However, Reuters might more significantly have pointed out that this decision resulted in the EU officially referring to contested territories as being in Israel.

29   Eli Kintisch, "Group Raising Millions to Launch a Christian AIPAC", *Forward*, June 21, 2002. Kintisch writes:

          While a handful of pro-Israel Christian groups exist around the country, Reed and Eckstein believe their connections and the International Fellowship's $30 million annual budget will bring heighten advocacy for the Jewish state.

"It's always been an informal relationship," Reed said of the Christian right's ties with Israel. Reed added that organizations such as the Christian Coalition had always taken pro-Israel positions, but "it was always one of 25 issues."

What Stand for Israel would add to the pro-Israel mix, Eckstein said, is the ability to mobilize the groups' 100,000 affiliated churches and 250,000 donors to call into Washington at crucial times.

30 Supra, endnote 26.
31 The CRS Issue Brief for Congress by Clyde R. Mark pointed out that "no US aid can be used by Israel in the occupied territories because the United States does not want to foster the appearance [*sic*] of endorsing Israel's annexation of the territories *without negotiations* [italics added]."
32 CRS Issue Brief, supra, endnote 26.
33 CRS Issue Brief, supra, endnote 26, p. 9.
34 Ed Vuillamy, "Israel Seeks Pipeline for Iraqi Oil", *The Observer*, April 23, 2003. Also see endnote 7, supra.
35 Ori Nir, "Olmert Begins to Lay Out Unilateral Plan", *Forward*, May 19, 2006.
36 Ibid.
37 Avi Machlis, "As Israel Bonds turn 50, Is once critical role waning?", *Jewish News Weekly*, June 16, 2000.
38 Ibid.
39 "Israel Bonds Raise $130 million from US Labor", *Jerusalem Post*, July 25, 2001. See also "El Al Moves to Avoid Tiff with Big Labor—Sharon Steps in", *Forward*, Feb. 21, 2003.
40 Russel Mokkiber, "Bonds of Affection", Multinational Monitor1988. See <http://multinationalmonitor.org>
41 Rachel Donadio, "Talking the Talk at Jewish Labor Dinner", *Forward*, March 22, 2004; see also Robert Fitch, "The Question of Corruption", *Metro Labor Press Association*, October 21, 1999, and Robert Fitch, Testimony, House of Representatives, Hearing on Workplace Competitiveness, March 31, 1998.
42 "Since 1995, the Israeli government has secured a foothold on international markets in order to create alternative stable financing frameworks following the end of a $10 billion U.S. loan-guarantee program in 1998." Machlis, supra
43 Alan Philips, "UN Team to disband as Jenin inquiry is derailed", *Daily Telegraph*, May 1, 2002.
44 Weir, supra, endnote 14.
45 Uri Avnery, cited in Weir, Ibid.
46 William Dalrymple, *From the Holy Mountain*, Harper Collins,1997. Chapter 5 chronicles the systematic devastation of the ancient Orthodox Christian communities in Israel and the Occupied Territories, including the Armenians.
47 Defense Planning Guidance for the 1994-1999 fiscal years, February 18, 1992.
48 "Bush wanted to remove Saddam, through military action, justified by the conjunction of terrorism and WMD. But the intelligence and facts were being fixed around the policy." See the secret Downing Street Memo, posted on Information Clearing House website at <http://www.informationclearinghouse.info/article8709.htm>
49 David Leigh, "General Sacked by Bush Says He Wanted Early Elections", *Guardian*, March 18, 2004. However, as Robert Dreyfuss noted, "For more than a decade, both during his military service and then in retirement, Garner established a pattern of close ties to the Israeli military and its U.S. supporters. *Forward*, the English-language version of the venerable Yiddish weekly newspaper, recently carried a headline referring to Garner that read, 'Pro-Israeli general will oversee reconstruction of postwar Iraq.'" Robert Dreyfuss, "Humpty Dumpty in Baghdad", *American Prospect*, May 1, 2003. Since Garner was also a member of the Jewish Institute for National Security Affairs (JINSA), and must have been fully aware of the true program he had been chosen to implement, the actual reasons for his removal may lie elsewhere.

50 "A Clean Break: A New Strategy for Securing the Realm", Richard Perle, Douglas Feith, David Wurmser, et al, Institute of Advanced Strategic and Political Studies. 1996. See also Leslie Gelb, "The Three-State Solution", *New York Times*, November 25, 2003 and Seymour Hersh,"Plan B", *The New Yorker*, June 28, 2004 on Israeli activity in Kurdish Northern Iraq.

51 Glenn Frankel, "Prison Tactics A Longtime Dilemma for Israel", *Washington Post*, June 16, 2004.

52 John Kerry, *Perspectives: An Israel Review*, Brown University Publication, November 19, 2003.

53 How this might shape up is foreshadowed in the new Free Trade Agreement (FTA) with Jordan, which has already been described as having descended into "human trafficking and involuntary servitude" by the National Labor Committee for Worker and Human Rights.

54 Matthew Clark, "Concrete, razor wire, ID cards", *Christian Science Monitor*, December 8, 2003.

55 *Newsweek Magazine*, June 7, 2004, p. 35.

56 Robert Dreyfuss, "Agents of Influence", *The Nation*, October 4, 2004.

57 See *Haaretz*, April 24, 2004 where Israeli deputy ambassador to UN, Arye Mekel, complained that criticisms "only enhance suspicions ... linking us with Iraq where we have no business", and Nathan Guttman, "Prominent US Jews and Israel Blamed for Start of Iraq War", *Haaretz*, May 31, 2004.

58 *Newsday* May 13, 2004.

59 Martin Sieff, "Army, CIA want torture truths exposed", United Press International, May 18, 2004.

60 "Sharon praises US on West Bank Refugees", *Haaretz*, June 25, 2004.

61 "US Gives New Details on Iraq, Afghan Abuse Probes", Reuters, May 8, 2006.

62 Canada and some other European countries that claim to honor free speech have already passed laws making "Holocaust denial" a criminal offense. United Nations Secretary-General Kofi Annan (whose Jewish wife is related to the prominent Swedish Raoul Wallenburg family) stated that the world must challenge those who deny the Holocaust happened.

63 The International Studies in Higher Education Act (HR 3077) passed the House in 2003 and is presently with a Senate Committee.

64 Joel Beinin "The new American McCarthyism: policing thought about the Middle East", *Race and Class*, Vol. 46(1), p. 104.

65 Beinin's article includes a valuable history of the intimidation of American academics in relation to issues pertinent to Israel. Ibid.

66 Joshua Hammer, "The Death of Rachel Corrie", *Mother Jones*, September-October 2003.

67 Xavier Ternisien, "Des responsables communautaires protestant contre un "plan" israelien incitant les juif francais a emigrer," *Le Monde*, June 17, 2004.

CHAPTER 3

THE LIBBY AFFAIRE AND THE INTERNAL WAR

The national debate that the indictment of Irving Lewis Libby for perjury and obstruction of justice has aroused in the mass media has failed to address the most basic questions concerning the deep structural context, which influenced his felonious behavior. The most superficial explanation was that Libby, by exposing Valerie Plame (an undercover CIA agent), acted out of "revenge" to punish her husband Joseph Wilson for exposing the lies put forth by Bush about Iraq's purported importation of uranium from Niger. Other journalists claim that Libby acted to "cover up" the fabrications to go to war. The assertion however raised a deeper question: who were the fabricators of war propaganda, who was Libby protecting? And not only the "fabricators of war", but the strategic planners, speech-makers and architects of war who acted hand in hand with the propagandists and the journalists who disseminated the propaganda? What was the link between all these high-level functionaries, propagandists and journalists?

Equally important, given the positions of power which this 'cabal' occupied and the influence they exercised in the mass media as well as in designing strategic policy, what forces were engaged in bringing criminal charges against a key operative of the cabal?

To best understand the rise and apparent fall of Irving Lewis "Scooter" Libby, it is essential to recognize that he was a member of an ideologically cohesive group with a long history of a shared ideology, common purpose, and organizational collaboration. Libby's rise to power was part and parcel of the ascendancy of the Zionist neo-conservatives to the summits of US policymaking. Libby was a student, protégé, and collaborator with Paul Wolfowitz for over 25 years. Libby along with Wolfowitz, Elliot Abrams, Douglas Feith, Kagan, Cohen, Rubin, Pollack, Chertoff, Fleisher, Kristol, Shulsky and a host of other political influentials are long term believers and aggressive proponents of a virulently militaristic tendency of Zionism organically linked with the rightwing Likud Party of Israel. Early in the 1980s,

Libby and a host of other political influentials are long term believers and aggressive proponents of a virulently militaristic tendency of Zionism organically linked with the rightwing Likud Party of Israel.

Wolfowitz and Feith were charged with passing confidential documents to Israel, the latter temporarily losing his security clearance. This posed no blockage to their subsequent advancement. It's hard to conceive of such a charge being raised in relation to any other country that would leave the parties concerned with a still-ascendant career path within American government.

The ZionCon ideologues began their "Long March" through the institutions of the state—in some cases as advisers to rightwing pro-Israel congressmen, and others in the lower levels of the Pentagon and State Department; in other cases as academics or leaders of conservative think tanks in Washington during the Reagan and Bush senior regimes. With the election of Bush in 2001, they moved into major strategic positions in the government, and served as the principal ideologues and propagandists for a sequence of wars against Arab adversaries of the Israeli State. Leading ZionCons, like Libby, drew up a war strategy for the Likud government in 1996, and then recycled the document for the US war against Iraq *before* and *immediately after* 9/11/01.

Along with their rise to the most influential positions of power in the Bush administration, the ZionCons attracted new recruits, like *New York Times* reporter, Judith Miller. What is striking about the operations of the ZionCon 'cabal' is the very open and direct way in which they operated. Lt. General William Oden (former Director of the National Security Agency under Reagan), General Anthony Zinni (retired Marine Commandant), Colonel K. Wilkerson (former chief of staff of Colin Powell), Brent Scowcroft (National Security Adviser to President George Bush the First), and numerous disenchanted officials, including veterans of the intelligence agencies, high level observers, and former diplomats, openly criticized the ZionCon takeover of the US policy and their promiscuous relationship with Israeli generals and Israel's secret international police, the Mossad, who had total access to their offices.

In the run-up to the invasion of Iraq, ZionCons Wolfowitz and Libby were the architects of the military strategy for Rumsfeld and Cheney, their putative bosses. Douglas Feith established the Office of Special Plans to fabricate the lies to justify the war. Judith Miller, David Frum and Ari Fleisher served to disseminate the lies and war propaganda through articles, interviews, press conferences, and speechwriting for President Bush. A review of the leading newspapers and government documents reveals that at every point in time and policy, the ZionCons echoed—to the letter—the policy demands emanating from the Sharon regime: that the US should invade and destroy the Iraq regime and state apparatus. Not a single ZionCon in the government, or outside in the prestigious private universities or think tanks, voiced the minimum deviation from the war policy of the Sharon regime. In what is probably one of the most cynical ploys in recent history, the ZionCons

Anti-Arab, Anti-Islam crusade on behalf of Greater Israel was portrayed as a policy of democratizing the Middle East… by those who bombed Jenin into rubble to those who would napalm Fallujah into ruin.

The War Within

In their overweening drive for total control of government policy, motivated by their fanatical loyalty to Greater Israel, the ZionCons pushed to manipulate and marginalize many of the key institutions in the US imperial state. To circumvent intelligence from the CIA that didn't promote the Israeli agenda of war with Iraq, ZionCon Douglas Feith's Office of Special Planning, fabricated propaganda and channeled it directly to the President's Office bypassing and marginalizing any critical review from the CIA. Wolfowitz and Rumsfeld totally marginalized the leading generals, promoting nondescript "loyalists" and outsiders to the top positions, and discarding any advice which opposed or conflicted with their plans for war with Iraq. Colin Powell, the Secretary of State, referred to a speech prepared for him by Irving Libby as "bullshit" because of its blatant falsehoods. His chief aide, Colonel Wilkerson, has written disparagingly of the ZionCon cabal, which marginalized the State Department including his boss, Powell. Nonetheless, Powell went on to front a further range of lies to the world at large at the UN.

Finally the FBI has been engaged in permanent warfare with the Israeli Mossad regarding the massive and conspicuous entry of Israeli spies into the US—hundreds have been deported since September 2001.

Libby's crime (perjury over revealing a CIA agent) is a minor crime, compared to the large-scale, long-term crimes against humanity, international law and the US Constitution committed by the ZionCons embedded in the US State. The prosecution of Libby, however, reveals the intense internal struggle over the control of the US imperial state between the ZionCons and the traditional leaders of its major institutions. Along with the arrest of Libby by the Federal Prosecutor, the FBI has arrested the two leading policymakers of the most influential pro-Israeli lobby (AIPAC) for spying for the State of Israel. These are not simply isolated actions by individual officials or investigators. To have proceeded against powerful ZionCon leader Irving Libby and AIPAC leaders (Rosen and Weissman), they had to have powerful institutional backing—otherwise the investigations would have been terminated even before they began.

The prosecution of Libby reveals the intense internal struggle over the control of the US imperial state between the ZionCons and the traditional leaders of its major institutions.

The CIA has been deeply offended by the ZionCon usurpation of their intelligence role, their direct channels to the President, their prime loyalty to the State of Israel and their 'ignorance' of reliable sources. The military is extremely angry at their exclusion from the councils of government over questions of war; the disastrous war policy which has depleted the armed forces of recruits, and devastated troop morale; and at the ZionCons' grotesque ignorance of the costs of a colonial occupation. It is no wonder that General Tommy Franks referred to ZionCon Douglas Feith as "the stupidest bastard I have ever met."

The current institutional war recalls an earlier conflict between the rightwing Senator Joseph McCarthy and the Defense Department. At the time of the mid 1950's, Senator McCarthy was accumulating power first by purging trade unions, Hollywood, and the universities, and by promoting likeminded conservative officials. He successfully extended his investigations and purges to the State Department and finally to the military. It was here that Senator McCarthy met his 'Waterloo'. His attack backfired, the Army stood its ground, refuted his accusations, and discredited his fabrications and grab for power.

Are we witnessing a similar process unfolding today? Will the ZionCon power grab be thwarted by its 'overreach' into the core of the US State? Or does the appointment of General Michael Hayden to head the CIA reflect the subservience of the CIA to the Pentagon, and in turn, to the ZionCons? In any open hearings between the ZionCons and the constituted bodies of the State, the public would be exposed to the real nature of the conflict and what is at stake: namely the choice between 'Israel First' or US political interests.

In the meantime, the ZionCons are not at all daunted by the trials of their colleagues in AIPAC and the Vice President's office: they are pressing straight ahead for the US to attack Syria and Iran via economic sanctions and military bombing. On October 30, 2005 the former head of the Israel Secret Police (Shin Bet) told AIPAC to escalate their campaign to pressure the US to attack Iran (Israel National News.com). Despite Syrian post-9/11 assistance to the US, AIPAC secured a near unanimous vote in the US Congress in favor of economic sanctions against it. Despite mass demonstrations, and because of a 'captured' Congress, it appears, paradoxically, that the only force capable of defeating the ZionCon juggernaut, like the earlier Joe McCarthy, are powerful voices in the State threatened by new disastrous wars not of their making.

CHAPTER 4

EXPOSING THE EXPOSÉ

SEYMOUR HERSH AND THE MISSING ZIONIST-ISRAELI CONNECTION

As I read Hersh's highly publicized and influential reports in *The New Yorker* on torture in US-occupied Iraq,[1] it became increasingly apparent that this was not a thoroughly researched exposé of the higher-ups responsible for the policy of torture. Hersh's reportage was a selective account guided by selected questions about selected officials. As one reads through Hersh's version of events with increasing incredulity, one comes to realize that Hersh hangs his whole argument and exposé of US officials involved in the use of torture on one person—Defense Secretary Donald Rumsfeld (important to be sure)—but not on the other top Defense officials who were extremely influential and responsible for war policy, establishing intelligence agencies and co-coordinating strategy and tactics during the occupation. Rumsfeld was *part* of an elite, which sanctioned and promoted torture. Throughout his exposé, Hersh deliberately omits the role of the Zionists (Wolfowitz, Feith—numbers 2 and 3 in the Pentagon) who supported and promoted the war and torture-interrogation, and particularly the Israeli experts who led seminars teaching the US Military Intelligence their torture-interrogation techniques of Arab prisoners based on their half-century of practice.

Hersh omits the role of the Zionists and particularly the Israeli experts who led seminars teaching the US Military Intelligence their torture-interrogation techniques of Arab prisoners based on their half-century of practice.

In looking for documentary sources of torture interrogation Hersh relies on academic texts and 20-year-old CIA manuals, not Israeli practice widely disseminated by the Mossad and Shin Bet advisers presently involved in torture in neighboring Palestine and Iraq today.

Hersh is presented in the mass media as an iconoclastic investigative journalist, a role which gives his reportages and exposés a great deal of credibility. Yet it was Seymour Hersh who publicly defended torture of suspects and their family members as a method of interrogation, citing the Israeli examples in the wake of September 11, justifying torture in the same way as the Pentagon now justifies the torture of Iraqi suspects. Instead of citing an obscure professor at the University of Chicago, Hersh should have cited the influential tract defending torture by Harvard Law Professor Alan Dershowitz (a fellow Zionist) widely read by the 'civilian militarists' who run the Pentagon today and direct the chain of command leading to interrogation through torture.

Seymour Hersh publicly defended torture of suspects and their family members as a method of interrogation, citing the Israeli examples in the wake of September 11.

Hersh's account fails to provide a political context in the Pentagon and in the Middle East for the systematic use of torture. To understand the issue of the US practice of torture and violent abuse of Iraqi prisoners and civilians requires an examination of the ideological demonization of the Iraqi population—"the Arabs"—and the US unconditional political and military support for the state of Israel, the principal long-term, large-scale practitioner of torture against Arabs. The most vitriolic systematic denigration of Arabs and Muslims in the Middle East is found in the writings and speeches of influential US-based Zionist ideologues, like the Pipes (father and son), the Kristols (senior and junior), the Kagans, Cohens, Goldhagens and others.

The first step toward justifying torture is to "dehumanize' the victim, to label them as 'untermensch' (congenitally violent savages). The Zionists in the US were merely following the pronouncements of their ideological mentors in Israel who not infrequently proclaimed that "the only thing the Arab understands is force" (Sharon, Golda Meir, Dayan, Rabin, etc.). The Zionist ideologues in the Pentagon were influential in arousing hatred of "Arabs" in several ways. In their defense of Israel they deliberately distorted the nature of Israel's colonial war, blaming the Palestinian victims for the systematic violence that Israel inflicted on them. The ideologues defended every Israeli violent action: the massacre in Jenin, new Jewish settlements in the West Bank, the murderous assault on Rafah, the killing of UN aid workers and peace activists, the monstrous Wall ghettoizing a whole people, the mass murder of hundreds of Palestinians and the destruction of thousands of homes in Gaza. Israeli violence against Palestinians made a deep impression on US Zionists who generalized and deepened their animus to Arab Muslims throughout the Middle East, but particularly in Iraq where they were in a position to implement their policies.

The Zionists and Torture in Iraq

The Pentagon's main source of "intelligence" and propaganda for the invasion and occupation of Iraq was in part provided by the Office of Special Plans . The Special Group bypassed normal CIA and military intelligence agencies and secured its own intelligence prior to the war, and was involved in *securing intelligence* during the first stages of the occupation (before it was dismantled). As the Iraqi resistance increased its effectiveness and the US justification for the war (weapons of mass destruction) was proved to be a total fabrication of the Special Group, the top echelon of the Pentagon, Rumsfeld and the Zionists grew desperate—they collectively passed the orders to intensify and extend torture to all Iraqi suspects in all the prisons. It is a gross simplification—even disinformation?—to say that the line of command was limited to Rumsfeld, when Wolfowitz, Feith and Abrams were so intimately involved in everyday policies prosecuting the war, defending the occupation and controlling intelligence.

Even more than Rumsfeld, the Zionist zealots in the Pentagon were the most ardent promoters of introducing Israeli methods of torturing and humiliating Arab suspects, and lauding Israeli "successes" in dealing with the "Arabs". They, not military intelligence, promoted the use of Israeli 'experts' in interrogation; they encouraged Israeli-led seminars in urban warfare and interrogation techniques for the US military intelligence officers and private contractors.

Nothing about the responsibility of the Pentagon Zionists in the torture of Iraqis appears in Hersh's "exposé". The glaring omissions are deliberate—as they are obvious. They form a systematic pattern and serve the purpose of exonerating the Pentagon Zionists and Israel, and hanging the entire responsibility for war crimes on Rumsfeld.

A Close Look at Hersh's Method

A close reading of Hersh's series of articles in *The New Yorker* reveals his premises and political perspectives, none of which have anything to do with democratic values or concern with human rights. Hersh's principal concern is that Rumsfeld's blanket order to use torture disrupted the operations of an elite group made up of professional commandos involved in a secret "special access program" designed to murder, kidnap, torture "terror suspects" throughout the world. In other words by involving thousands of everyday US soldiers (referred to by one of Hersh's sources as "hillbillies") as torturers in Iraq, Rumsfeld was endangering the operation of professional killers throughout the world. Hersh's second major concern was that the discovery of the torture would "hurt America's prospects [*sic*] in the war on terror"—in other words, a tactic he attributed (solely and wrongfully) to Rumsfeld was endangering the US empire-building capacity. Hersh's empire-centric view refuses to recognize the elementary rights of self-determination and international law's nonderogable prohibition against torture and extrajudicial executions.

Hersh's third apparent concern is with Rumsfeld's *bypassing* the CIA and other intelligence agencies and his attempt to monopolize intelligence. This is a bit disingenuous. Wolfowitz and Feith set up the special intelligence agency that fed Rumsfeld the fabricated intelligence, they promoted Chalabi (known throughout Washington intelligence circles as totally unreliable) as an impeccable source of "inside information" on Saddam's non-existent weapons of mass destruction, *knowing in advance that they were passing phony "data"*. As Wolfowitz later cynically admitted, the decision was made to launch the US invasion over banned weapons because it was the only issue they could agree upon.

Hersh is not stupid, he knew what everyone else in Washington and out of government knows: the Zionists in the Pentagon were pushing for war with Iraq before 9/11 (even before they took office in Washington and were working with the Israeli state) and were intent on having the US destroy Iraq *at any price,* including the loss of American lives, budget busting deficits, imperiling oil interests and jeopardizing US global imperial interests. They launched the invasion bypassing the military central command by deliberately falsifying the anticipated response of the conquered Iraqi people ("they will welcome us as liberators"—Wolfowitz and Perle) and were intent on destroying Iraqi civil and state structures (under the guise of de-Baathification purges) in order to forever undermine Iraq's capacity to challenge Israel's domination of the Middle East.

None of Hersh's questions explore these well-known facts about who is responsible for the atrocities against Iraqis. He didn't have to cite unnamed intelligence or Pentagon sources—General Anthony Zinni and many non-Zionists insiders, as well as the CIA and Central Command, knew about the Zionist promoters' plans and moreover, knew the role Feith played in pushing for harsher interrogation techniques. But Hersh ignored these questions, these Zionists and their ideological supporters and advisers who have, post-invasion, done everything possible to undermine any Iraqi economic recovery and capacity to run their own education, health and electoral systems. De-Baathification was meant to turn Iraq into a backward tribal, divided desert country run by their protégé Chalabi, the only "candidate" who would recognize Israel, supply it with oil and water, and support Mideast "integration" under Israeli hegemony.

The Zionist Pentagonistas succeeded in securing the war, they succeeded in destroying basic Iraqi social services, and they destroyed the Iraqi state (courts, military, civil services). However in their blind subservience to Israel, they overlooked the fact that the disbanded professional soldiers and purged civil leaders and professionals would become part of an experienced armed resistance, that Iraq would become ungovernable, that US rule would crumble, that the US would become bogged down in a politically lost war, and that its puppet regime would have neither legitimacy nor popular support. The Zionists did what they thought was best for Israel, even if it provoked greater opposition worldwide, including in the US, where a majority had turned against the occupation by May 2004. Only the Israeli transmission belt, AIPAC, would cheer Bush and his continuation of the occupation and pledge allegiance to the Israeli war against Palestinians. When their self-serving "prediction" of an Iraqi welcoming committee turned into a valiant popular anti-colonial war, Feith and his underlings called for greater use of more forceful interrogation methods—Rumsfeld and Feith encouraged Israeli-type torture to "humiliate the Arabs". Meanwhile Kagan's call to "bomb the Arab street" was tried and failed to intimidate the Iraqi resistance.

Hersh's exposé of Rumsfeld as the *only* top culprit turned up at a convenient moment: when US policy had failed and most knowledgeable officials were moving closer to identifying the role of the Pentagon Zionists. It was clever by half: Rumsfeld was universally despised in Congress, among the professional military and a host of others for his policies and arrogant public face. Even in "exposing" Rumsfeld, however, Hersh was careful to do so in a fashion that allowed his Zionist colleagues to continue in office unscathed. Furthermore, Hersh justified some of Rumsfeld's acts of illegal terror by describing "legalistic obstacles" to eliminating terrorists. Hersh's support for Rumsfeld's resort to unaccountable commandos engaging in assassination, kidnapping, and torture of suspects around the world serves in effect to condone those tactics after Rumsfeld leaves office.

Requiring a "perp", Hersh dragged in a fifth level functionary working under Feith, Stephan Cambone, whom he tells us "was deeply involved" in the torture of prisoners—more involved than his Zionist superiors? We might ask the peerless investigatory journalist: how is it that Hersh blames those above (Rumsfeld) and those below (Cambone) but never focuses on Feith and Wolfowitz, who designed and directed the policy?

How is it that Hersh blames those above (Rumsfeld) and those below (Cambone) but never focuses on Feith and Wolfowitz, who designed and directed the policy?

In setting up Cambone for the exposé, Hersh profiles Cambone in terms that fit the Zionists with greater pertinence: he advocated war with Iraq (following Wolfowitz, Feith, Perle, and Abrams); he disdained the CIA whom the Pentagon Zionists viewed as "too cautious", attacking it for not finding WMD. Since Cambone functioned under Wolfowitz and Feith, he was simply repeating what his bosses wanted to hear and perhaps that's why they entrusted him with the relevant dirty tasks of extracting 'intelligence' via torture.

Hersh tries to link Cambone with the extension of the torture practiced "selectively" by the Special Agency Program. But SAP was already operative before Cambone took office and its operations were under the direction of Rumsfeld, Wolfowitz, Feith and Abrams. Hersh's dating of the torture as commencing in August 2003 with Cambone and Major General Miller's assignment (from Guantanamo) is false. It started earlier under the SAP, and with Israeli-trained interrogators. Moreover it was the Pentagon, headed by the same three (Rumsfeld, Wolfowitz and Feith), that ordered Miller's use of torture on "suspects" at Guantanamo in the first place—then moved him to Iraq as a reward for exemplary work. Hersh does not explore Miller's links with Rumsfeld, Wolfowitz and Feith before going to Iraq. He simply aborts the analysis—looks at the middle and lower levels of power: Cambone, Miller, interrogators, and enlisted soldiers. Out of this framework Hersh comes up with a detailed piece of selective investigatory journalism. He exposes some but covers up for those most actively involved in invoking the war and directing it in a way that served Israeli interests. The cost in US lives and the degradation of young US servicemen forced to assume the role of torturers is of little concern to the Pentagon Zionists.

The Pentagon's Zionists are under attack. Marine General Anthony Zinni, Senator Fritz Hollings and other prominent political, diplomatic and military leaders have openly identified the role of the Pentagon Zionists in launching and directing the war to favor Israel. What seemed a visible move toward the marginalization of the pro-Israel Chalabi—the protégé of Wolfowitz, Feith and Abrams—by raiding his house and carting off his records, ostensibly to investigate financial irregularities, seemed a symbolic setback.[2] So was the US abstention in the Security Council on Israel's rape of Rafah—much to the chagrin of the Israel First crowd at the AIPAC convention.

In response all the major Jewish organizations and publications from *Forward* to the Anti-Defamation League, AJC and others denounced the critics of the Pentagon Zionists. Despite all the exposés of torture, killings and rapes, major Zionist ideologues like Kristol, Krauthammer, Rubin, Perle, Kagan, and Frum launched attacks on Bush for "backing off" from the war.

Hersh's attempts to head off the anti-Zionist headhunting coalition by focusing on the two Goyim—Rumsfeld and Cambone—have been to no avail. The knives were drawn. Because of Zionist power in and out of the government, the anti-Zionist coalition and their supporters used code words, the most common of which is "neo-conservative", which everyone now knows means Wolfowitz, Feith, Abrams, and other Zionists in and out of the government. AIPAC, the Anti-Defamation League and other Israel Firsters, sensing the danger to their co-thinkers, turned to labeling critics of the neo-conservative militarists "anti-Semites" and arousing Congress, the media, and their propaganda machine into cowing the coalition into submission.

But the photos of torture, which have discredited the war policy, threaten to isolate the Zionist zealots. Faced with the indignation of the whole civilized world at the war crimes, the 'progressive' Zionist apologists, like Hersh, take to isolating blame on Cambone and Rumsfeld and minimizing the responsibility to "a few soldiers in a cell block" as did Senator Lieberman— though the US military say there have now been over 100 persons indicted, itself an indicator of the scope of the problem, and its origins in policy—while the AIPAC elite cheer Bush, ignoring the muck and blood of torture.

Rumsfeld shrewdly tied his future to his Zionist partners in the Pentagon and outside, counting on riding on their coat tails and reaping the support of the powerful Jewish lobby and their leaders in the Israeli state, who stand behind them. He has few other influential allies.

Conclusion

In the final analysis the removal from office of key members of the then-current crop of Zionist Pentagonistas—Wolfowitz, Feith, Abrams, Rubin, Libby—was only a temporary setback. The Zionist political organizations remain intact, their influence over Congress remains overwhelming and they have pledges from both major parties that "Israel's cause is America's cause" (Bush and Kerry). The Zionist juggernaut grinds on, securing sanctions against Syria, calling for the bombing of Iran's supposed nuclear facilities, and trying to instill an atmosphere of crisis. During his visit to Washington in May 2006, Prime Minister Olmert got Bush's backing for Israel's unilateral setting of "final boundaries", thus forcing Washington to repudiate its own "road map" and its closest EU allies.

In the meantime, for those who still deny Zionist power in US foreign policy, one only has to read the accounts of the AIPAC conference in Washington in May 2004. At a time when Israel was killing children in the streets of Rafah and destroying hundreds of homes under the horrified eyes of the entire civilized world, when an indignant UN Security Council finally rose to its feet and unanimously condemned Israel, US Congressional leaders and the two major Presidential candidates pledged unconditional support to Israel, evoking the bloodthirsty cheers of investment brokers, dentists, doctors, lawyers—the cream of the cream of American Jewish society.

"The cause of Israel is the cause of America" rang out from the mouth of every candidate as the Israelis bulldozed homes and snipers shot small girls on their way to buy candy. It was almost as if Sharon had wanted to demonstrate the power of the Zionists in the US, timing the vile destruction of

Rafah to coincide with the AIPAC convention and the disgusting appearance of the spineless American politicians supporting ongoing crimes against humanity. Not one voice was raised in even meek protest. To those who claim that the Zionists are just one of a number of "influential lobbies"—try explaining the unconditional support for Israel's genocide of the Palestinian people by the most powerful politicians in the US.

It was almost a perverse pleasure to watch Sharon smear the muck and gore of Rafah on the groveling faces of US politicians—they deserve each other. But for those of us who support a democratic anti-imperialist foreign policy, this was one of the most humiliating moments in US history. Something we won't read in the exposés by Hersh or the erudite Zionist treatises in defense of endless wars.

ENDNOTES

[1]   Seymour Hersh, "Torture at Abu Ghraib: American soldiers brutalized Iraqis. How far does responsibility go?", *The New Yorker,* May 10, 2004; "The Gray Zone: How a secret Pentagon program came to Abu Ghraib", *The New Yorker*, May 25, 2004, and "Mixed Messages: Why the government didn't know what it knew", *The New Yorker,* June 3, 2004.

[2]   Chalabi's career continues to take extreme bounces. After his abysmal showing in the Iraqi election of December 15th, 2005, he was then chosen to replace then-Oil Minister Ibrahim Bahr Uloom, who had previously threatened to resign over the government's decision to raise gas prices for Iraqis. He was then replaced by Hussain al-Shahristani. Recently he appeared at the 2006 Bilderberg Conference meeting outside of Ottawa, Canada.

CHAPTER 5

THE SPY TRIAL

A POLITICAL BOMBSHELL

What country has had hundreds of spies, moles, and collaborators working for a foreign government in the US for over 30 years with impunity? According to former and present knowledgeable news reporters, some recently interviewed by the FBI, federal agents point to the Israeli secret police Mossad as the organizer and promoter of the espionage network within the US.

In one of its biggest spy investigations ever, over 100 FBI agents from city offices throughout the country interviewed thousands of potential witnesses, informants, and suspects in connection with Israeli espionage in the United States.

One former news reporter for an influential British weekly told me that he was interviewed twice, over twelve hours, about mass media collaboration with the Mossad in transmitting 'disinformation' and pro-Israel propaganda as "news". From conversations with journalists interviewed by the FBI, a picture emerges of large-scale, deep penetration of American society and its government by Israeli spies and their collaborators. According to my sources, the FBI has been investigating Israeli espionage networks for over 30 years; the spy investigation has been hampered by politicians of both parties in the pay of Israeli lobbies and wealthy pro-Israel campaign funders. Even the FBI has been infiltrated, according to a writer for the British *Economist*: testimony filed by the writer in the early 1980's implicating Richard Perle and Paul Wolfowitz in handing over documents to Mossad agents, "was removed from FBI files and disappeared."

Over the years the Israeli secret services have become ever more brazen and crude in their operations in the US. The scope includes hundreds of Israelis, Israeli-Americans (dual citizens) and their local collaborators (*'sayanim'* or volunteer Jewish supporters of Israeli agents outside Israel). In the aftermath of 9/11, hundreds of Israeli agents who were canvassing Government offices were rounded up and *quietly* deported. Quietly, not because they were not committing serious crimes, but in order to avoid arousing politi-

> **Over the years the Israeli secret services have become ever more brazen and crude in their operations in the US.**

cal attacks from the major pro-Israel organizations and their Congressional clients.

The mass expulsion of Israeli spies was a response to Israel's failure to cooperate in preventing the massacre of thousands of people in New York on September 11, 2001. The FBI appear to have proof that Israeli Intelligence had detailed evidence of the 9/11 terror attack and failed to provide the information to US authorities. My sources go on to state that Israelis relayed information just prior to the attack that threw the FBI off the track. While the Mossad has the biggest spy-network and the most powerful support system of any country operating in the US, what is of special interest is that these operations penetrate the highest spheres of the US government, including the office of Vice President Cheney, according to FBI investigators. The prolonged investigation and the recent massive allocation of resources and agents to the Israeli connection was precisely due to the spiny issue of dealing with suspects in the highest spheres of government. According to one Philadelphia-based Fed, one wrong step could lead to the higher-ups quashing the investigation. So the investigators extended interviews, covering all possible sources, accumulating thousands of pages of transcripts, affidavits, wiretaps, videos of anyone and everyone knowledgeable or potentially implicated in Israel's longstanding espionage operations. Despite the intensified investigations, scores of Israeli agents and recent recruits continued their operations, many receiving "protective cover" from the Philo-Zionist Christian evangelicals as well as the *'sayanim'*. A key target of the FBI investigation, but one very difficult to crack, was the AL—a secret unit of experienced *'katsas'* (Mossad case officers who recruit enemy agents as described by former Mossad agent, Victor Ostrovsky, in *By Way of Deception*).

According to my newspaper sources, passing Israeli disinformation, as instanced by the case of Judith Miller, was common practice throughout the 1980's and 1990's. Many of the top journalists and editorial writers knowingly accepted and published or broadcast Israeli disinformation disseminated by Mossad agents acting as political officers in the Israeli Embassy. A recent example: in May 2006, AIPAC—and the Senator for Tel Aviv, Charles Schumer—spread the malicious rumor that the Iranian parliament had passed a law that would require Jews, Christians and Zoroastrians to wear colored badges to identify themselves as non-muslims. This brazen falsehood was parroted predictably by the State Department, which said it instanced "clear echoes ... of Germany under Hitler." No such law was passed; in fact, Iranian lawmakers, including a Jewish member of parliament, said there had been no such discussion.[1]

The FBI investigation of Israel's extensive espionage operations in the US stemmed from several factors. After years of close collaboration between Israeli intelligence and the FBI, the latter (along with the CIA) took the blame for the "9/11 intelligence failure", without any mention of the lack of

Israel's cooperation and in the face of its disinformation. Secondly the brazen large-scale invasion of Israeli operatives on FBI turf (in the US), undermined the agency's own activities, eroded its position as a security agency, and particularly challenged its counter-espionage operations. Thirdly the ascendancy of Wolfowitz, Feith, and Perle to the top echelons of the Pentagon and Elliot Abrams, Rubin and Libby to the National Security Council, State Department and the Office of the Vice President, led to the massive and ready transfer of confidential documents and sensitive decisions to the army of Mossad operatives and Israeli high military intelligence officers both here and in Israel.

The flow of information from the US to Israel became an unchecked torrent, and worst of all, as far as it was concerned, the FBI was rendered organizationally marginal if not scorned. What was particularly galling to the FBI was that they had at least 5 witnesses willing to testify against Wolfowitz and Feith in an earlier spying incident who, because of their high positions and presidential backing (especially after 9/11), could not be touched. The FBI was certainly aware of the deep penetration of the US state and the key role which Israel played in advising, directing and passing propaganda and directives to their agents, collaborators, and the major Zionist organizations in the run-up to the US invasion of Iraq. Given the war hysteria and the "anti-terrorist" propaganda pumped out by the entire pro-Israel ideological apparatus, the Israeli supporters in the government operated openly and with impunity, defying both the FBI and the CIA by setting up their own Office of Special Plans as the key "intelligence operation" to transmit Israeli disinformation directly to the White House.

The onset and immediate aftermath of the Iraqi war and the subsequent occupation marked a high point of Israeli tyranny over Washington. Pro-Israel 'advisers', cabinet members, ideologues, spokesmen or women, AIPACers and their allies in the Conference of Presidents of Major Jewish Organizations (CPMJO) celebrated their success in pushing the US to utterly destroy Israel's principle adversary (Iraq), its army, economy, administrative and educational systems, and infrastructure.

The celebration and victory of Israel over US good sense and national interest was short-lived. As the Iraqi resistance gained force, as US casualties mounted and war costs ballooned, the American public turned against the war and support for the Bush Administration fell precipitously. With these political changes, the Israeli agents and collaborators in the government, authors and architects of the war, lost some of their immunity from investigation. The FBI, sensing the favorable change in the political climate, vastly expanded their investigation; interrogations followed including Feith, Wolfowitz, Perle, and other ZionCons closely identified with Israeli intelligence.

Fearful of attacks from unconditional supporters of Israel in the US Congress and Executive (Senators Clinton and Lieberman, Secretary of State

Condi Rice and Vice President Cheney), the ever-cautious agency focused on the offenses of several notorious pro-Israel targets: Irving "Scooter" Libby of the Vice President's office for revealing the identity of an undercover CIA agent; Larry Franklin, a second-level Pentagon official linked to Feith and Wolfowitz, for spying for Israel; and two leaders of the major pro-Israel lobby, AIPAC (American Israel Political Action Committee), Rosen and Weissman, for passing confidential documents to Mossad agents in the Israeli embassy and to "knowing" journalists in the Washington press corp. As the FBI investigation of the Israeli connection proceeded to reach higher in the state hierarchy, Wolfowitz, whose life-long ambition was to be number one in the Defense Department, suddenly resigned and was appointed to head the World Bank; Feith also resigned and rejoined his US-Israeli law firm, as the investigation touched on one of his major conduits for supplying Israeli intelligence (Franklin).

AIPAC On Trial

In August 2004, the FBI and the US Justice Department counter-intelligence bureau announced that they were investigating a top Pentagon analyst suspected of spying for Israel and handing over highly confidential documents on US policy toward Iran to AIPAC which in turn handed them over to the Israeli Embassy. The FBI had been covertly investigating senior Pentagon analyst, Larry Franklin, and AIPAC leaders, Steven Rosen and Keith Weissman, for several years prior to their indictment for spying. On August 29, 2005 the Israeli Embassy predictably hotly denied the spy allegation. On the same day Larry Franklin was publicly named as a spy suspect. Franklin had worked closely with Michael Ledeen and Douglas Feith in fabricating the case for war with Iraq. He was also the senior analyst on Iran, which is at the top of AIPAC's list of targets for war.

As the investigation proceeded toward formal charges of espionage, the pro-Israeli think tanks and 'ZionCon' ideologues joined in a two-prong response. On the one hand, some questioned whether "handing over documents" was a crime at all, claiming it involved "routine exchanges of ideas" and lobbying. On the other hand, Israeli officials and media denied any Israeli connection with Franklin, minimizing his importance in policy-making circles, while others vouched for his integrity.

The FBI investigation of the Washington spy network deepened and included the interrogation of two senior members of Feith's Office of Special Plans, William Luti and Harold Rhode. The OSP was responsible for feeding bogus intelligence leading to the US attack on Iraq. The leading FBI investigator, Dave Szady, stated that the FBI investigation involved wiretaps, undercover surveillance, and photography that documented the passing of classified information from Franklin to the men at AIPAC and on to the Israelis.

The Franklin-AIPAC-Israeli investigation was more than a spy case, it involved the future of US-Middle East relations and, more specifically, whether the 'ZionCons' would be able to push the US into a military confrontation with Iran. As a top Pentagon analyst on Iran, Franklin had access to all the executive branch deliberations on Iran. AIPAC lobbying and information gathering was aggressively directed toward pushing the Israeli agenda to a US-Iranian confrontation against strong opposition in the State Department, CIA, military intelligence and field commanders.

Franklin's arrest on May 4, 2005 and the subsequent arrest of AIPAC foreign policy research director, Steve Rosen, and Iran specialist and deputy director for foreign policy, Keith Weissman, on August 4, 2005 was a direct blow to the Israeli-AIPAC war agenda for the US. The FBI investigation proceeded with caution, accumulating detailed intelligence over several years. Prudence was dictated by the tremendous political influence that AIPAC and its allies among the Conference of Presidents of Major Jewish Organizations wield in Congress, the media and among Fundamentalist Christians, which could be brought to bear when the accused spies were brought to trial.

The first blow was struck on August 29, 2004, when CBS publicized the FBI investigation just when Franklin confessed to have passed highly confidential documents to a member of the Israeli government and began cooperating with federal agents. He was prepared to lead authorities to his contacts inside the Israeli government. Subsequently Franklin stopped cooperating. Abe Foxman of the Anti-Defamation League (a leading Jewish pro-Israeli lobby) called for a special prosecutor to investigate "leaks" of the FBI investigation, because they were "tarnishing" Israel's image (called "magna chutzpah"). Then Attorney General Ashcroft intervened to try to apply the brakes to the investigation, which spread into the 'ZionCon' nest in the Pentagon: Feith, Wolfowitz, Perle, and Rubin were "interviewed" by the FBI. ZionCon Michael Rubin, former Pentagon specialist on Iran and resident "scholar" at the American Enterprise Institute, blasted Bush for "inaction in the spy affair" and called the investigation an "anti-Semitic witch hunt".[2] AIPAC launched a massive campaign against the spy probe and in support of its activities and leaders. As a result scores of leading Congress members from both parties vouched for AIPAC's integrity and pledged their confidence and support of AIPAC.

Never in the history of the United States had so many leading Congress members from both parties pledged their support for an organization under suspicion of spying, a support based only on information supplied by the suspect, and in total ignorance of the federal prosecutor's case.

Never in the history of the United States had so many leading Congress members from both parties pledged their support for an organization under suspicion of spying, a support based only on information supplied by the suspect, and in total ignorance of the federal prosecutor's case. Contrary to the bipartisan Congressional support for AIPAC, a poll of likely voters found that 61 percent believed that AIPAC should be asked to register as an agent of a foreign power and lose its tax-exempt status. Only 12 percent disagreed. Among American Jews, 59 percent were not sure, while 15 percent strongly agreed and 15 percent strongly disagreed.[3] Clearly many Americans have serious doubts about the loyalty and nature of AIPAC activities, contrary to the views of their elected representatives. The federal spy investigation proceeded despite Executive and Congressional opposition, knowing that it had the backing of the great majority of US citizens.

In December 2004, the FBI subpoenaed four senior staffers at AIPAC to appear before a grand jury, and searched the Washington office of the pro-Israel lobby seeking additional files on Rosen and Weissman. AIPAC continued to deny any wrongdoing, stating: "Neither AIPAC nor any member of our staff has broken any law. We believe any court of law or grand jury will conclude that AIPAC employees have always acted legally, properly and appropriately."[4] Nevertheless a few months into the investigation and with the arrest of the two top leaders, AIPAC was to terminate their employment and, after a few months, cut off paying their legal defense bills. Likewise Israel's categorical denials of espionage evaporated, as video and transcripts of their intelligence operative receiving classified documents surfaced.

A Grand Jury was convoked in early 2005. As the FBI's spy investigation extended into AIPAC-Pentagon's inner recesses, self-confessed spy Franklin's superiors, Paul Wolfowitz and Douglas Feith, announced their sudden resignations from the number 2 and 3 positions in the Pentagon, most likely reflecting a deal with the Justice Department to free themselves from further investigations into their ties with Israeli intelligence and Franklin.

In February 2005, Bush announced that former convicted felon, defender of Central American death squads, and long-term Zionist fanatic, Elliott Abrams, would be in charge of Middle East policy in the National Security Council. Abrams would serve as a channel to the White House for directing Israeli policies, and as day-to-day source of the most essential policy decisions and discussions. Apparently Abrams was smart enough to keep his distance from the Franklin/Feith and AIPAC/Embassy operations, and deal directly with Ariel Sharon and his Chief of Staff, Dov Weinglass.

In April 2005, AIPAC dismissed Rosen and Weissman, saying their activities did not comport with the organization's standards. On May 4, Franklin was arrested on charges of illegally disclosing highly classified information to two employees of a pro-Israel lobbying group. On June 13, 2005 an expanded indictment explicitly named AIPAC and a "foreign country" (Israel) and its Mossad agent, Naor Gilon, who had, in the meantime, fled to Israel.

Despite AIPAC being named in a major espionage indictment involving Steve Rosen, head of its foreign policy department and Keith Weissman, head of its Iran desk, US Secretary of State Condoleezza Rice gave the keynote address at AIPAC's convention (May 22-24, 2005). Leaders from Congress and the Republican and Democratic parties also spoke, declaring their unconditional support for AIPAC, Israel, and Ariel Sharon. The list included Senator Hillary Clinton, Senate Majority Leader Bill Frist (Republican) and Senate Democratic leader Harry Reid. More than half of the US Senate and one-third of US Congress members were in attendance.

Clearly AIPAC, with 60,000 wealthy members and a $60 million annual budget, had more influence on the political behavior of the US executive, political parties and elected representatives than a federal indictment implicating its leaders for espionage on behalf of Israel. Could there be a basis for charging our political leaders as "accomplices after the fact"... of espionage, if the AIPAC leaders are convicted? Or is the very notion of hard-edge (as opposed to blurred) sovereignties separating the two countries moot?

On August 4, 2005 Paul McNulty of the Justice Department formally indicted AIPAC leaders Steven Rosen and Keith Weissman of receiving and passing highly confidential documents via the Israeli embassy to the State of Israel. Their trial was set for April 25, 2006. Franklin's trial was set to begin on January 2, 2006 but has been postponed. Franklin has been cooperating with the FBI and Justice Department in its investigations of AIPAC and the Pentagon's 'Israel Firsters' in the run-up to the invasion of Iraq and the further plans to attack Iran. The indictments are based on a prolonged investigation. AIPAC had been targeted for investigation as early as 2001, while the indictment of Rosen and Weissman cites illegal activities beginning in April 1999.

After Rosen and Weissman came under intensive federal investigation as co-conspirators in the Franklin spy case, AIPAC decided to cut its losses and cover its backside by throwing them overboard: it fired them on March 2005, arguing that their "conduct was not part of their job, and beneath the standards required of AIPAC employees".[5] In effect AIPAC was making Rosen and Weissman the "fall guys" in order to shake off a deeper federal probe of AIPAC's activities. Moreover AIPAC stopped payments to Rosen's and Weissman's lawyers, potentially sticking them with almost a half-million dollars in legal fees. AIPAC does not intend to pay the fees before the trial is over—not for lack of funds (they raised over $60 million in 2005 and are tax-exempt) but for *political* reasons. AIPAC wants to see how the trial goes: if they are acquitted, it will be safe to pay their lawyers. But if they are found guilty AIPAC will refuse to pay (citing the organization's by-law technicalities) in order to avoid being implicated with convicted spies. AIPAC leaders are putting their organizational interests and their capacity to promote Israeli interests in Congress and the media over loyalty to their former officials.

Facing up to 10 years in federal prison, up against detailed, well-documented federal charges based on wiretaps, videos, and the testimony of self-confessed spy and Pentagon contact Franklin, fired and denounced by their former colleagues and current leaders of AIPAC, Rosen and Weissman are striking back with unexpected vehemence. The defense attorneys are expected to argue that receiving information from administration officials was something the two *were paid and encouraged to do and something AIPAC routinely does.*[6] In other words, Rosen and Weissman will say that pumping top US government officials for confidential memos and handing them over to Israeli officials was a common practice among AIPAC operatives. To bolster their case of "just following AIPAC orders", Rosen and Weissman's defense lawyers will subpoena AIPAC officials to testify in court about *their* past access to confidential documents, their contacts with high-placed officials, and their collaboration with Israeli Embassy officials. Such testimony could likely bring national and international exposure to AIPAC's role as a two-way transmission belt to and from Israel. If Rosen and Weissman succeed in tying AIPAC to their activities and if they are convicted, that opens up a much larger Federal investigation of AIPAC's role in aiding and abetting felonious behavior on behalf of the State of Israel.

In the almost two years since Rosen and Weissman came into the public limelight as spy suspects, AIPAC has successfully fended off adverse publicity by mobilizing leading politicians, party leaders, and senior members of the Bush Administration to give public testimonials on its behalf. It successfully dumped Rosen and Weissman, and pushed ahead with lining up the US Congress with Israel's pro-war agenda against Iran. And then out of the blue, Rosen and Weissman threaten to blow their cover "as just another influential lobby" working to promote US and Israeli mutual security interests.

Rosen and Weissman's defense will certainly bring out the fact that AIPAC at no point informed their employees about what the law states regarding the obtaining and handing over of highly confidential information to a foreign power. Weissman and Rosen will argue that they did not know that receiving confidential information from administration officials and handing it over to Israel was illegal since everybody was doing it. They will further argue that their alleged spy activity was not a 'rogue operation' carried on by them independently of the organization, but was known and approved by their superiors—citing AIPAC's employee procedures for reporting to superiors. This action will promote AIPAC from the secondary role of aiding and abetting, to a primary role of soliciting and instigating illegal espionage against the government of the United States.

Rosen and Weissman are taking on biblical stature. According to one former AIPAC employee with connections to the organization's current leadership, Rosen and Weissman are perceived as acting "like Samson trying to bring the house down on everyone":[7] "everyone" that is involved in exploiting US wealth, power and military forces to serve Israel's expansionist interests. What started out as a small scale spy trial, no different from other recent cases, is growing into a major *cause célèbre*, involving the most powerful lobby influencing the entire direction of US Middle East policy.

If Rosen and Weissman are convicted and they effectively make the case that they were following orders and informing AIPAC of their felonious activities, it is possible that this will drive away many wealthy Jewish donors and activists, and perhaps put some shame into the politicians who kow-tow and feed at the AIPAC trough. With a weakened AIPAC and its neo-con/ 'ZionCon' allies in the government wary of continuing to "liaison" with Israeli intelligence on Middle East policy, it is possible that a free and open debate based on US interests can take place. With a public debate relatively free of the constraints imposed by the Israel First lobbies and ideologues, perhaps the US public's opposition to Middle East wars and occupations can become the dominant discourse in Congress if not the Executive. Perhaps the some $3 billion dollars plus of annual foreign aid to Israel can be reallocated toward rebuilding all the industrially ravaged cities and towns of Michigan, upstate New York, and elsewhere.

A move from Middle East militarism to a democratic foreign policy will not happen just because of a spy trial no matter how severe the sentence and no matter how deeply AIPAC is implicated, unless the American public is organized as a democratic majority capable of confronting party, congressional and executive leaders with the choice: *You are either for America or for AIPAC.*

ENDNOTES

1. *Financial Times*, May 23 2006.
2. *Forward*, Sept. 10, 2004.
3. Zogby International, Sept. 25, 2004.
4. AIPAC December 1, 2004.
5. *Forward*, December 23, 2005.
6. *Forward*, December 23,2005.
7. *Forward*, December 23, 2005.

CHAPTER 6

THE HOUSE OF HORRORS

TORTURE, ASSASSINATIONS AND GENOCIDE

When future historians write of the US empire, they will emphasize the process of empire building, its methods of rule, the principle ideologues, and how at a particular moment in time a small, dependent state—Israel—was able to shape US war policy to suit its needs.

Empire Building

Military violence, direct and through surrogates, was crucial to the expansion and consolidation of the empire in South and Central America and the Caribbean—from 1964 to 1990 US-backed surrogate military regimes and paramilitary forces took power in Argentina, Brazil, Peru, Chile, Uruguay, Bolivia, Dominican Republic—and later in Guatemala, El Salvador, Honduras, Nicaragua and Panama. Over 500,000 people were slaughtered in order to impose the imperial-centered system of accumulation (later called "neo-liberalism"). The imperial strategy of invasion and intervention established the parameters for long-term consolidation: an economic system 'open' to imperial penetration and control ("free market economies") and a state apparatus (judiciary, military, central bank, etc.) capable of deepening and consolidating the imperial-centered economy. Subsequently the domesticated electoral politicians accepted the imperial parameters and Washington encouraged political competition. In the case of Mexico, voter fraud ensured the election in 1988 of "President" Salinas who proceeded to "integrate" Mexico via NAFTA into the US Empire.

A similar process took place in Africa. From 1970 through to the 1990's, massive US military intervention and support of "surrogate" mercenaries aided by US strategic ally, South Africa, killed millions in Angola, Mozambique, Guinea Bissau, and Congo, destroying the economic and political basis for development and establishing client regimes. These mineral and oil rich countries were incorporated into the empire. In the case of South Africa, the leadership of the African National Congress was coerced and then co-opted and became an integral part of the Euro-US imperial system. Similar processes took place in Asia where imperial wars were followed by economic 'openings' extending imperial dominance throughout the region…at the cost of over 11 million dead Koreans, Indochinese, Filipinos, Indonesians, Timorese.

Between the 1990's and the present the US empire expanded into the Balkans, Eastern Europe, the Baltic countries, Central Asia and the Caucasus by aggressive ideological intervention aided by the corruption and deep rot in the dominant Communist parties ruling in those countries. The Middle East, Southwest Asia and the Balkans were next, in part because they are integral to exploiting oil resources, building pipelines and building military bases. Yugoslavia, Afghanistan and Iraq were invaded. Satellite regimes were established in Kosova, Macedonia and Serbia. A US puppet regime in Kabul rules in alliance with opium-subsidized mercenary warlords. Iraq was invaded, occupied and ruled initially by a US pro-consul. The US Empire has been built on wars, using its own military forces, surrogate mercenaries and paramilitary forces.

Imperial Consolidation

To sustain power in the face of mass anti-imperial resistance, the US state has repeatedly violated all international conventions and laws related to torture of prisoners, mass killings of civilians, destruction of infrastructure and historical sites, pillaging of natural resources, and establishment of client colonial states and imperial-centered economies.

The US conquest of Iraq is the latest example of empire building, but with its own particularities. The most salient feature of the imperialist conquest of Iraq is the widespread and public exposé of the brutal methods of imperialist rule. We have all read and seen photos of large-scale, systematic torture of thousands of Iraqi citizens suspected of being freedom fighters. Torture has been the principle source of "information" to buttress colonial rule, as well as a technique of repression. The model of rule via mass torture and sexual violence has been heavily influenced by the Israeli experience, where nearly half of the male adult Palestinian population has been incarcerated and subject to "legalized" Israeli torture. This is not a circumstantial coincidence. The main ideologues defending torture include the most prestigious Zionist academics and policymakers in the United States: Harvard Law Professor Alan Dershowitz, Princeton Professor Bernard Lewis, William Kristol, Yale Professor Robert Kagan, John Hopkins Professor Eliot Cohen, to name only a few of the Zionist totalitarian ideologues defending Israeli terror and US imperial force.

Mass systematic torture in Iraq was the first but not the most important revelation of imperial rule: that rulers of an empire acknowledge no legal restraint, whether domestic or international. Within the Pentagon the top leaders, Rumsfeld, Wolfowitz, and Feith specifically ordered the use of torture while the Justice and Defense Departments insisted that the President could override any laws—international or national as well as the US Constitution—in defending the empire. In other words, torture was seen as a special Presidential power beyond any legislative or legal restraint. De facto and de jure dictatorial powers of the President have been defended and assumed as requisite to establishing 'Imperial Security'.

Targeted Assassinations

A further revelation resulting from the exposé of torture was that the American empire was operating with a highly organized network of assassins throughout the world, killing, kidnapping and torturing "suspects" and sympathizers of resistance movements. This 'Murder Incorporated' operates under the name of the Special Agency Program (SAP) and is composed of highly trained Special Forces (Army), SEALS (Navy), and DELTA Force. The SAP violates the sovereignty of every country in the world, and engages in criminal behavior conducive to capital crimes including frequent arbitrary extra-judicial murder of suspected "terrorists" or sympathizers. Their model is the Mossad policy of "selective assassinations" of suspects. As the empire expands and the anti-imperialist resistance grows worldwide, the SAP acts as an international death squad of the US imperial terror network. Israeli patented assassinations occur throughout the world and are openly supported by the Jewish state: in that sense they differ from the US covert assassination program (Phoenix program) in Vietnam, and the Pentagon-backed paramilitary death squads in Latin America .

As the Israeli newspaper *Haaretz* has just revealed, the Israelis' assassinations policy accompanied the very birth of the Israeli state.

> On December 27, 1947, about a month after the decision by the UN General Assembly to establish two countries, one Jewish and one Arab, and before the bloody clashes between the two nations turned into a war—Israel's War of Independence—the Haganah (the pre-state army) issued an order for what was called Operation Zarzir (Starling). In this order one can see the first comprehensive, operational plan for what would several decades later be called "targeted assassinations."[1]

The assassinations undertaken by Operation Zarzir were part of a nationally orchestrated campaign of violence against the Palestinian people—a violence that was initiated by Israel, unprovoked by any Palestinian actions. As *Haaretz* put it:

> Although assassinations of Palestinian murderers have existed since the beginning of the Israeli-Palestinian conflict, Operation Zarzir was exceptional. For the first time, a nationwide program involving such assassinations was planned, with operational rules. Targeted assassinations are not, therefore, as we tend to believe, a result of the intifadas or of the suicide attacks...[2]

Targeted assassinations are not, as we tend to believe, a result of the intifadas or of the suicide attacks.

The violence was covert and duplicitous, seeking to shift the blame onto the Arabs.

> ... The orders emphasized the need to act cautiously so as not to arouse an extreme Arab reaction. In addition, there was a directive not to carry out the assassination near "weak Jewish settlements." ...There was also a piece of advice from headquarters, to the effect that "the operation should look like an Arab action"—in other words, as though it was an Arab who had murdered an Arab...

And it was directed against a broad swath of the Palestinian leadership:

> ...The original list of candidates for assassination included 23 Arab leaders and high-ranking officers from all over the country. The largest group was in the Jerusalem area; the second largest was in Jaffa. Several of them, like Emile Ghouri, were political leaders. Others were prominent military leaders...[3]

While initiated by the Haganah, Operation Zarzir carried on through what *Haaretz* calls the "Israeli War of Independence", to terminate after the Sinai campaign of 1956, where it had been employed against Egyptian intelligence deploying Palestinian commandos. But Operation Zarzir was nothing on the scale of the Israeli targeted assassination policy of today, Schiff muses.

The means for assassination were primitive. The commandos

did not even dream of firing missiles or using helicopters or unmanned aerial vehicles.[4]

Clearly, targeted assassinations has been an Israeli policy since its inception, which over time has not terminated, but only found better technology to implement its modus operandi. In so doing, Israel has become the instrument for the creation of one quarter of the world's refugees,[5] with that percentage likely to be augmented due to its current assault on the civilian populations and infrastructure of Lebanon.

Israel has become the instrument for the creation of one quarter of the world's refugees—or more.

Destruction of Civilian and Military Infrastructure

According to the UN's International Leadership Institute, "84% of Iraq's higher learning institutions have been burnt, looted or destroyed."[6] The destruction of Iraq's historical existence as a sovereign nation—the pillage of its archeological museums and historical sites, libraries and archives; the violent intrusions into sacred sanctuaries; the humiliation of its people via torture, collective punishment and sexual violence are all designed to destroy the country's historical identity as an Arab nation. The attacks on Iraq's physical and institutional infrastructure have since been supplemented by attacks which target its capacity to restructure what has been disassembled:

> The assassinations of Iraqi scientists started shortly after the US-led invasion of Iraq, [London-based Iraqi political analyst Haroun] Muhammed said. In the beginning it was thought that the target was scientists who worked in Iraq's former programme of weapons of mass destruction.
> But the assassinations have taken the lives of many experts in fields that have nothing to do with weapons and military sciences, such as Arabic and history…"As for scientists, it is clear that several foreign forces are interested in evicting Iraq of its qualified people," Muhammad said.
> The Ministry of Higher Education has announced that 146 university professors were assassinated in the past two years.[7]

Addressing an International Seminar held in Madrid on March 22-23, 2006 on the subject of assassinated Iraqi academics, Dirk Adriaensens of the Bertrand Russell Tribunal pointed out that targeted assassinations extended beyond academics: there were " 311 teachers killed the past 4 months, 182 pilots, 416 senior military officers killed in the first 3 months of 2006; 20.000 people kidnapped since the beginning of 2006."[8] Contrary to the claim that these kidnappings have been carried out by criminal gangs, Adriaensen noted:

> What we are witnessing is the result of a carefully planned US campaign to liquidate every Iraqi who opposes the occupation of his country, the so-called "Salvador option". In fact, since 1945 the U.S. developed counterinsurgency policies based on the model of Nazi suppression of partisan insurgents that emphasized placing the civilian population under strict control and using terror to make the population afraid to support or collaborate with insurgents.

John Pilger argued similarly concerning the Salvador Option, in a column appearing in *The New Statesman* on May 8, 2006.[9] As the World Socialist Web Site noted:

> This is a part of a program of cultural destruction, and it emanates from Washington.
> The appearance of death squads in Iraq stepped up after the installation of John Negroponte as ambassador to Iraq in June 2004. Negroponte was the ambassador to Honduras at the height of the American-sponsored counter-insurgencies in Central America in the 1980s. He is an experienced operative in creating and managing extra-judicial killings, the so-called Salvador option.
> Similarly, veterans of US "dirty wars" in Latin America—James Steele, who oversaw counterinsurgency operations in El Salvador during the height of the killing there 20 years ago, and Steve Casteels, who worked with US anti-guerilla and anti-drug operations in Colombia, Peru and elsewhere—were brought in to oversee the Iraqi Interior Ministry's operations.
> The goal, however, is not simply to silence critics of the puppet regime. The assassination policy is an attempt to create a tractable population… the killing of art historians, geologists, and writers must be explained as an attempt to destroy the intellectual health of Iraq.
> The loss of academics "is causing a drop in the quality of higher education," according to the UN's *IRINnews.org*. "The best professors are leaving the country and we are losing the

best professionals, the real losers are the next generation of students—the future of Iraq,' Abbas Muhammad, a student of Pharmacology at Baghdad University, said."

The country's intelligentsia was already depleted in the period from 1990 to 2003, when an estimated 30 percent had left the country for economic reasons.

The goal now, encouraged or allowed by the Bush administration, and implemented by its stooges in Iraq, is to destroy the historical consciousness of the Iraqi people, as a means of further subjugating them to US imperialism and its Iraqi supporters.[10]

The dissolution of the Iraqi military by Paul Bremer, widely viewed as a mistake when it occurred, was followed by ineffective, half-hearted efforts to reconstitute it, awarding only pittance salaries, and withholding medical treatment and proper gear. America's primary human rights agency interviewed Iraqi deserters, reporting on April 4, 2003 that:

All of the deserters interviewed by Human Rights Watch were men, regular soldiers between the ages of 20 and 38. They looked gaunt and several suffered from skin ailments as a result of the conditions on the battlefield. They spoke of low pay (approximately US$2 a month) or going for months without any pay.

"Some days we were so hungry we would eat grass which we mixed with a little water," said a 21-year-old soldier from Baghdad whose unit was part of the Fifth Corps. "We didn't wash ourselves for forty days. Often there was no drinking water and they would give us jerry cans and tell us to go and fill them from the pools of water that gathered on the ground when it rained."

Some of the Iraqi soldiers described inhumane punishments including being beaten, or being forced to crawl across stones on their bare knees or backs. One showed the scars on his back from this punishment. Their officers frequently warned them that they would be executed if they tried to escape. Several deserters said their officers forced them to remain in their positions during the air strikes, telling them "to die like men."[11]

The stories of scandal concerning the corrupt and ineffective reconstruction of Iraq are legion. Billions of dollars have been spent, US corporations, notably Halliburton, have won huge no-bid contracts, but they have ended up doing the job insufficiently—or not at all. While such failures are often passed off as due to the difficulties posed by the growing insurgency, or failing that, as extreme ineptitude, this does not address the question of how such ineptitude can proceed without investigation or reprimand, while on the other hand, miraculously, the construction of the massive Green Zone US embassy proceeds without a hitch.[12]

In early 2006, the administration indicated its intention to end aid for Iraqi reconstruction. This, when of the $18.4 billion it allocated to the rebuilding effort, "roughly half of the money was eaten away by the insurgency, a buildup of Iraq's criminal justice system and the investigation and trial of Saddam Hussein."[13]

Meanwhile, the *Los Angeles Times* reported that the latest emergency appropriation for the Iraq war includes $348 million to improve and expand the four military bases in Iraq which are central to US strategic purposes—Balad and Taji, north of Baghdad; Tallil, near Nasiriya in the south; and Al Asad in the western desert.

Clearly, the extent of destruction demands a broad prospect on its intended goals. The purpose is to divide and rule, to create mini-states based on tribes, religion and ethnicity, separating the oil resources from any substantial population base. The idea of breaking Iraq into statelets was originally proposed by staunch zionophile Leslie Gelb, former *New York Times* editor, now a director in the Council of Foreign Relations. This follows the UK precedent in establishing the Gulf states and the EU-US strategy in destroying Yugoslavia in the early 1990s.

The model for treatment of the local population imitates the Israeli policy toward the Palestinians. Israel's practice of sexual humiliation of Palestinians (and Lebanese) has been routine (rapes, stripping and hooding of prisoners). Collective punishment and taking family members hostage are legally condoned and extensively practiced in Israel despite their prohibition in international law. The recent Rafah/Jenin refugee camp invasions demonstrate the extremities of colonial savagery and inhumanity against entrapped and helpless populations.

The Israelis deny the Palestinians their past as a nation, their land as a place to live, and their right to govern themselves. So do the US imperial rulers in Iraq. They constantly work to ethnicize the conflict, deny the existence of the Iraqi nation, the people and their history. The US, like Israel, has taken land and resources, and built fortresses and walls of segregation. A group of extremist Zionist scholars have contributed to the totalitarian denial of Arab culture led by the virulent Bernard Lewis.[14] Recently Martin Wolf of the *Financial Times* justified imperial wars throughout the world, rejecting national sovereignty and defending US-European and Israeli conquest of "failed states".[15]

Conclusion

We in the United States appear to have accepted to live in a House of Horrors—where empire building via torture and assassination is executive policy, where White House-approved torture is exposed in the media but continues to be state practice. The mass media promoters and publicists of the House of Horrors count on our short memory: they praise Ronald Reagan, whose infamous presidency marked a decade of genocide against Mayan Indians in Guatemala (300,000), and in Nicaragua (50,000), El Salvador (75,000), Honduras (several thousands). It was Reagan who publicly defended General Rios Montt, the butcher of Guatemala, from criticism for human rights abuses ("He's getting a raw deal") and who praised the butchers of Afghanistan's secular society as "The moral equivalent of our founding fathers". The White House, Pentagon, State Department, CIA—each in its turn has its own "side show" of horrors: Colin Powell's blatant lies in the United Nations on weapons of mass destruction, the Pentagon promoting torture, the CIA practicing assassinations and now, with European complicity and full public exposure, a global policy of renditions.

The continuity of torture and mass murder, between the past Reagan regime and the present Bush regime was not merely due to the return to office of many of the same political criminals (Wolfowitz, Abrams, Cheney and Rumsfeld) but to the politics of imperial conquest, destruction and extermination. However, the House of Horrors does not merely replay the past scenarios for the same ideological and political interests. Today's horror show has many of the same cast but with different directors and producers. In Central America and Southern Africa, fanatical anti-Communists were in command, often in defense of American corporate interests, and much of the action was covert or sub-contracted. Today it is the extremist Zionist militarists in the Pentagon who direct the US Horror Show in Iraq. Unlike Reagan's Cold Warriors, today we have professors entrenched in law and other faculties of America's most prestigious universities who provide the justification for unrestrained state terrorism. More than ever in recent US history there is a long list of distinguished professors who line up to defend the House of Horrors, the Prisons of Torture, the Seminars on Dehumanizing Arabs. These professors have had no compunction about portraying millions of victims as terrorists—this serves all the better to justify their brutalization. All of them are unconditional supporters of Israel, its paranoid politics, its routinized torture, its nuclear threats to humanity, its savage assaults on Palestinians.

ZionCons still appear constantly in all the mass media, spewing their ideological venom: Perle, Abrams, Wolfowitz, Stern, Dershowitz, Cohen, Kagan, Kristol, Rubin, Adelman, Lewis, Pollock and many more. Their primary loyalty is in joining US imperialism and Israeli colonialism into one marvelous House of Horrors, under the big tent of a "Mid-East Democratic Reform Initiative".

Zionist influence on Washington's criminal policies in the Middle East in favor of Israel is transparent. We should remember however that while aggressive state policies pursued under the current "House of Horrors" have brought the United States to an unprecedented level of exposure and condemnation worldwide, potentially endangering its own best interests and well-being as never before, its search for empire has a history which *preceded* the Zionist ascendancy and will certainly continue after its influence has declined.

While we should forcefully expose the profound influence of the ZionCons in shaping America's Middle East war policy today, the long term, large scale problem is empire building—imperialism, itself—which provokes popular resistance, to which the empire responds with torture and genocide. To end torture and defeat colonial powers overseas, we must resolutely confront their supporters and ideologues at home, whatever their ethnic or religious affiliations. We must not let their ideological fanaticism and aggression silence us from engaging a growing majority among Americans opposed to US war(s) in the Middle East and Zionist terrorism.

ENDNOTES

1   Ze'ev Schiff, "On the origins of targeted assassinations", *Haaretz*, June 6, 2006.
2   Ibid.
3   Ibid.
4   Ibid.
5   Emad Mekay, "Iraq Conflict Fuels Rise in Global Refugees to 12 Million: Survey", Agence France Presse, June 15, 2006. According to the US Committee for Immigrants and Refugees (USCRI) "There are almost three million Palestinian refugees in 2005" while USCRI puts the global figure for refugees for 2005 at 12 million.
6   Sandy English, "Hundreds of Iraqi academics and professionals assassinated by death squads", World Socialist Web Site, March 6, 2006.
7   Ahmed Janabi, "Everyone is a target in Iraq now", Al-Jazeerah online, October 14, 2005.
8   See <http://www.uruknet.info/?p=22885>. To keep abreast of this topic, see the BRussells Tribunal website at <http://www.brusselstribunal.org>.
9   "John Pilger Detects the Salvador Option, *The New Statesman*, May 8th, 2006, <http://www.newstatesman.com/200605080016>
10   See English, supra, endnote 5.
11   "Iraq: Soldiers describe mistreatment by commanders" <http://hrw.org/english/docs/2003/04/04/iraq5486.htm>
12   See Michael Schwartz "How the Bush Administration Deconstructed Iraq" TomDispatch.com.

13   Ellen Knickmeyer, "US has End in Sight on Iraq Rebuilding", *Washington Post*, January 2, 2006.

14   See Bernard Lewis, *From Babel to Dragomans: Interpreting the Middle East*, Oxford University Press, 2004.

15   *Financial Times*, June 9, 2004, p.5.

CHAPTER 7

ISRAEL'S FINAL SOLUTION

THE ASSAULT ON GAZA

"It is the duty of Israeli leaders to explain to public opinion, clearly and courageously, a certain number of facts that are forgotten with time. The first of these is that there is no Zionism, colonization or Jewish state without the eviction of the Arabs and the expropriation of their lands."
Ariel Sharon, former Likud Party Prime Minister
Agence France Press, November 15, 1998

"We must expel Arabs and take their place."
David Ben Gurian, former Labor Party Prime Minister, 1937

"There's no such thing as a Palestinian people. It is not as if we came and threw them out and took their country. They didn't exist."
Golda Meir, former Labor Party Prime Minister

"Israel will create in the course of the next 10 or 20 years conditions which would attract natural and voluntary migration of the refugees from the Gaza Strip and the West Bank to Jordan."
Yitzak Rabin, former Labor Party Prime Minister

"You don't simple bundle people onto trucks and drive them away. I prefer to advocate a positive policy, to create, in effect, a condition that in a positive way will induce people to leave."
Ariel Sharon, August 24, 1988

"The partition of Palestine is illegal. It will never be recognized. Eretz Israel will be restored to the people of Israel. All of it. And forever."
Menachem Begin, former Likud Party Prime Minister

"I believed and to this day still believe, in our people's eternal and historic right to this entire land."
Ehud Olmert, Israeli Prime Minister, to the US House of Representatives, June 2006

"But this is not merely faulty reasoning; arresting people to use as bargaining chips is the act of a gang, not of a state."
Haaretz Editorial, June 30, 2006

"I want nobody to sleep at night in Gaza."
Ehud Olmert, July 2, 2006

Introduction

Beginning on the night of June 28, 2006, Israel launched a massive land and air assault on the Gaza Strip. As scores of helicopter gunships and fighter jets fired missiles and rockets into populated centers, destroying the basic infrastructure of over 1.4 million Palestinians, over 5,000 soldiers poured into the territory following hundreds of tanks and armored carriers. The Jewish State's pretext for total war was to free a single captured Israeli soldier held as a prisoner of war (erroneously described as a "kidnapped" soldier) held by a Palestinian resistance group.

Even the pro-Israeli *Financial Times* saw through Prime Minister Olmert's flimsy excuse, remarking that: "...the disproportion between the means and ends suggest this (the release of the Israeli prisoner) may be a pretext".[1] The *FT* goes on to argue that the purpose of Israel's assault was to destroy the democratically elected government, claim that it had no one to negotiate with, and then..."*unilaterally [set] new borders for an expanded Israeli state, by annexing large swaths of the occupied territory on which the Palestinians had hoped to build their independent state".[2]*

On July 6, Israeli forces led by armored carriers invaded Northern Gaza and declared that they were annexing territory as a *"buffer zone"*[3], confirming the predictions of the editorial writers of the *FT*, and moving a step further toward the 'Final Solution'. By the end of the day, Israeli Armed Forces had re-conquered a major swathe of Gaza in a North-South pincer operation, killing 22 Palestinian civilian and resistance fighters and wounding scores. While European and US politicians urged "restraint" the Israeli blitz drove deeper into Gaza, ignoring all the diplomatic niceties and Geneva Conventions, confident that the Lobby will ensure that no US (and therefore no European) constraints will be imposed. While 300 left and progressive British Jews signed an advertisement in the *Times of London*, no such statement has emanated from their US counterparts—perhaps they are waiting until Israel's re-conquest is a fait accompli...?

Israel's strategic goal as each and every one of its Prime Ministers—Labor, Likud or Kadima—have explicitly stated is the total control of all of Palestine by the Jewish state, the forcible seizure of Palestinian land and the expulsion of millions of Palestinians from the "Land of Greater Israel". This totalitarian vision of a Final Solution has advanced methodically over the years, accelerating over the past year through the systematic destruction of the elementary conditions for Palestinian survival.

From the Present to the Past

The 6/28 assault was directed at destroying the Palestinian leadership, as even the BBC pointed out.[4] Over sixty Palestinian leaders were arrested or driven from office; this included the arrest of eight cabinet ministers and twenty other members of Parliament. In justification for the arrest of the democratically elected Hamas cabinet ministers and deputies, Israeli Defense Minister and Labor Party leader, Amir Peretz, ranted, *"The masquerade ball is over... the suits and ties will not serve as cover to the involvement and support of kidnappings and terror".*[5] Peretz— the political executioner of the invasion—has been the darling of the US and European 'Center-Left' and the favorite of self-styled 'progressive' Jewish intellectuals and rabbis.

> **Over sixty Palestinian leaders were arrested or driven from office; this included the arrest of eight cabinet ministers and twenty other members of Parliament.**

The Israeli destruction of the Gaza electrical power station and water supply, its bombing of bridges connecting North and South Gaza, followed a systematic effort to starve the 1.4 million Palestinians living in Gaza. Under the total embargo imposed by the Jewish State to strangle the Palestinian economy in order to *"create the conditions for voluntary departure"*, as former Prime Minister Rabin so exquisitely described ethnic cleansing... *"over 48 of the 60 factories in an industrial park have (been) shut or are relocating to Egypt or other Arab countries".*[6]

The blockade of entry points and the systematic murder of civilians, including entire families, leading up the invasion formed a clear pattern of provocation, to justify the invasion. In the weeks leading up to 6/28, Israel mobilized its armed forces on the borders of Gaza in preparation for a massive attack, giving the lie to the claims by the Jewish state that it was 'responding' to the capture of its soldier. Throughout 2006, Israel waged psychological and military warfare throughout the Gaza territory. Between January and May 30, 2006, according to the Palestinian Center for Human Rights (PCHR), the Israeli military launched 18 assassinations, euphemistically referred to as 'extrajudicial executions' or 'targeted assassinations of militants'; between March 29 and May 30, there were 77 Israeli air strikes on population centers, government offices, infrastructure and productive facilities with nearly 4,000 artillery shells fired into Gaza by Israel.

As the Israeli armed forces positioned themselves for their 6/28 blitzkrieg, the Jewish state escalated its provocations, increasing its killing of Palestinian civilians. Between May 26 and June 21, a total of 44 Palestinians were killed, thirty of whom were civilians, including eleven children and two pregnant women.[7]

The Israeli tactic was to commit such grotesque crimes against defenseless civilians as to force the democratically elected Hamas government to renounce its eighteen-month voluntary ceasefire and retaliate in defense of its people. Hamas refused, and Israel, not to be denied its 'land grab', invented the pretext of the freeing of the Israeli soldier 'hostage', widely described as a "teenage" or "19-year-old" soldier, to increase empathy for the Franco-Israeli settler.

Concomitant with the terror campaign and preceding Israel's bloody June campaign, the Jewish State and its overseas political 'lobbies' in the US effectively halted all funding to the democratically elected government, including withholding hundreds of millions of dollars of tax revenue which was collected by the Jewish State on Palestinian imports and which belongs to the Palestinian Authority. Poverty levels quadrupled, and child and infant malnutrition multiplied. The salaries of 165,000 government employees, including medical workers, teachers and police, which directly support over 1 million Palestinians, went unpaid for months, raising the levels of extreme poverty to over 80% of the population in Gaza and 64% for all Palestinians. The poverty line for Palestinians set at $2.10 a day is an inadequate measure of living standards. Since the starvation blockade tactics of January-May were not sufficient to break Palestinian resistance, topple the Hamas government and facilitate the land grab, Israel escalated the civilian terror campaign in June, culminating in the invasion and physical destruction of what remained of the economy and the semblance of governance. The totalitarian methods of terror, starvation and enclosure were tightening the noose—implementing the Zionist Final Solution to the Palestinian Question, or as Yitzak Rabin—ostensibly the Israeli proponent of peace in Oslo—once stated, creating "the conditions which would attract natural and voluntary migration of the refugees from the Gaza Strip and the West Bank."

The Final Destruction of Six Myths about the Jewish State and the Lobby

Israel's storm trooper tactics—so devastatingly demonstrated in the invasion of 6/28 and its totalitarian vision of massive ethnic cleansing—leave few doubts about its ultimate goals and political methods. As John Dugard, UN Special Rapporteur on Human Rights in the Palestinian Territories, pointed out:

> Israel is violating in Gaza the most fundamental norms of humanitarian law and human rights law—its conduct is indefensible. Over 1,500 rounds of artillery have been showered on Gaza…Sonic booms terrorize the people. Transport has been seriously disrupted by the destruction of roads and bridges. Sanitation is threatened.[8]

In response, with all the cant, hypocrisy and arrogance for which Israeli politicians are infamously renowned, Israel's Permanent Representative to the United Nations in Geneva, Itzhak Levanon, blustered that the emergency meeting was a "planned and premeditated attack on Israel...We find ourselves in an absurd situation in which the Human Rights Council, convened into urgent session, ignores the rights of one state and holds a special meeting to defend the rights of the other side."[9]

Apparently the distinguished diplomat was referring to the Council's ignoring the "rights" of Israeli fighter and helicopter pilots to bomb Palestinians civilians into fleeing in terror across the Egyptian border.

1. Israel and Democracy

In December 2005, in the most democratic election ever organized in the Arab East, the Hamas Party was elected to power by the majority of Palestinian voters. Even President Bush, before he was chastened by the Jewish Lobby, publicly conceded the democratic character of the Palestinian election process. The Israeli State rejected the outcome and orchestrated a massive well-financed international campaign through its US and European Jewish lobbies to isolate and undermine the newly elected government. Instead of recognizing its democratic mandate, Israel applied the terrorist label to the new Palestinian government; it ignored Hamas' unilateral ceasefire, and escalated its murderous military attacks. Above all it succeeded in establishing an economic blockade, exercising its hegemony over the US and through the latter, over the European Union. Israeli animus to Palestinian democracy and its citizens' role in freely electing its representatives clearly marks Israel as an enemy to an open pluralistic Arab society. Obviously the same applies to the major Jewish organizations in the US—AIPAC, ADL, the Conference of Presidents of the Major Jewish Organizations, which parroted Israel's attack on Palestinian democracy, as they have done on every other policy, no matter how unconscionable, such as the murder of Palestinian children and families. The Israeli animosity to Arab democracy is widely transmitted into the US body politic by their Zionist followers in the lobbies, government, mass media and business.

2. Israel and Peace

The week prior to the Israeli invasion, Hamas and the PLO agreed to negotiate with Israel, giving tacit recognition to the State of Israel. Most of the mass media published reports of the accord and the European Union welcomed the agreement, stating it was

The week prior to the Israeli invasion, Hamas and the PLO agreed to negotiate with Israel, giving tacit recognition to the State of Israel.

the beginning of a process. The *Financial Times* reported:

> The crisis (Israeli invasion of Gaza) has overshadowed *a vital agreement* reached by Hamas and Mahmoud Abbas, Palestinian Authority President, on Tuesday that includes an implicit *Hamas acceptance of a two state solution* to the Middle East conflict. A copy released by Hamas...refers to the Palestinian goal of a state on all the land occupied in 1967... (Emphasis added)[10]

Israel responded by rejecting negotiations and launching the new war to destroy the Palestinian State. In fact the Israeli State never at any point even recognized the elected Hamas government as a negotiating adversary let alone a partner.

Since the 1980s, whenever the PLO have carried out a ceasefire, proposed a two state solution and explicitly recognized the State of Israel, it initiated an action which promptly threw the possibility out the window.

As Noam Chomsky has documented,[11] at every point since the 1980's that the PLO have carried out a ceasefire, proposed a two state solution and explicitly recognized the State of Israel, the Jewish state initiated an action which promptly threw the possibility out the window: it launched the invasion of Lebanon, assassinated prominent leaders or launched military assaults, killing activists and civilians, in order to force the Palestinians to withdraw their offer.

The Israeli regime absolutely refuses to accept a negotiated prisoner release and exchange proposed by Hamas, the Palestinian Authority, US client Hosni Mubarek and most of the European Union. Israel holds at least 9,000 Palestinian political prisoners including 335 children and several hundred women, most of whom have not been charged, and of whom almost all have been tortured. The great majority are civilians who were seized in their homes or in the street. In a word, most Palestinian prisoners are civilian kidnap victims of the Israeli Defense Forces, not captured combatants as is the case of the lone Israeli soldier. The Palestinians have repeatedly called on Israel at least to free the five hundred kidnapped Palestinian children and women hostages in exchange for their captured soldier. Israel responded by intensifying its military assaults and widening the net to include all Palestinians. At a cabinet meeting on July 2, Olmert stated, "I have given instructions to intensify the strength of action by the army and security services to hunt down these terrorists, those who sent them...and those who harbor them."[12] In other words, the resistance organizations (dubbed 'terrorists' although they are within their international legal rights under the Geneva Conventions to combat Israeli military incursions) include all major Palestinian organizations—those who *"send them"* includes all the elected political authorities; and those *"who harbor them"* includes hundreds of thousands of families, friends, neighbors, community and civic groups, doctors and nurses—in a word, Palestinian civil society. As the sentiment now has it in Israel, reflected in a poll published by the (Israeli) daily *Maariv*, the majority of Israelis desire the assassination of Hamas leaders".[13] So this is a totalitarian order to criminalize and target almost the entire political and civil society of Palestine.

3 *Israel and the Possibility of a Two-State Solution*

Israel's re-occupation of Gaza and imposition of martial law is accompanied by the criminalization of the entire electoral political class: cabinet ministers, parliamentarians and party activists. Israel's Deputy Prime Minister Shimon Perez told CNN: "They (Palestinian government officials) will be put on trial and they will be accused of participating and supporting terrorist acts against the civilian government [*sic*]."[14] How to make sense of such a statement? Which is the civilian government—the one whose duly elected members are now under Israeli arrest? Or was this a slip of the tongue, intentional or blundered, which marks the beginning of Israeli reference to Gaza as within Israel?

To make its point, in the best traditions of Chilean dictator Augusto Pinochet, the Israelis bombed the executive offices of the Palestinian Prime Minister, setting the building on fire. As if to demolish even the memory or thought of a Palestinian government, the Israeli military juggernaut is destroying the entire Palestinian infrastructural basis for political life: buildings, leaders, parties, and elections.

Systematically and with bureaucratic efficiency the Jewish State has proceeded with daily demolitions of every conceivable structure necessary for civilized life. On July 3, 2006 it bombed the university in Gaza City. On July 4 it bombed the Ministry of the Interior. On July 5 Israelis invaded Northern Gaza and the criminal story continues. For those who believed that this invasion was merely an incursion in search of a prisoner of war, Yuval Diskin, head of Israel's secret police, Shin Bet, stated that the "...operation in Gaza could last months."[15] With monumental cant and hypocrisy, Major General Amos Yadlin, Israeli Army Chief of Intelligence, having arrested or driven underground the entire Palestinian leadership, declared that "...mediation efforts were stymied because no one knows whom to talk to about Shalit (the Israeli POW)." Needless to say, no offer to negotiate was put on the table, for fear that a negotiator might actually appear...

4 *Israel and Terror*

While Israel was attempting to destroy the very basis of Palestinian organized collective existence as a people, it was also launching 24 hour artillery assaults, continual sonic booms by low flying jets, forcing the dehydration of the entire population in scorching heat by destroying drinking water supplies, forcing them to live in darkness, deprived of food and confined to their homes or shelters. An entire people, without an army of their own, under military siege, is holed up in an ever-shrinking territory! This is State Terror in its most expressive and malignant form: "Collective Punishment" is not directed at securing the release of the Israeli POW; it is directed at making life for the Palestinian people so unbearable, so lacking in the most basic conditions for survival, that they will either be forced to flee or rise up in a heroic last stand, to which Israel will apply all its murderous military might. This, the distinguished academics, journalists, ideologues and Conference of Presidents of the Major Jewish Organizations will describe as : *"a vigorous Israeli response to Palestinian terrorism"*.

5. *The Jewish Lobby: The Central Issue*

While the Israeli assault on Gaza grinds on, so does the propaganda and activism in its favor by all the major Jewish/Zionist organizations in the US and Europe. In a review of the *Daily Alert* (the daily organ prepared for the Conference of Presidents of Major Jewish Organizations in the US) since the beginning of the invasion of Gaza, one finds automatic and uncritical support for every single Israeli assault on Gaza: electrical power plants because they have "dual use"; water supplies and sewage treatment plants are "military targets" because they are used by the captors; terrorizing children and civilians is to "let them know what Siderot (an Israeli border community and home of the Defense Minister) has been going through"; intensified and prolonged Israeli repression of the Palestinian population occurs because "Hamas and Fatah are terrorist organizations and they must be treated as terrorists and crushed by all means necessary".[16]

There is a Zionist international division of labor: the military assassins operate in Israel, the verbal assassins operate out of the plush suites of the head offices of the Conference of Presidents of the Major Jewish Organizations.

Nothing captures the power of the Jewish Lobby as much as the Euro-American response to Israel's full-scale assault on Gaza. Bush supports Israeli action even when it grossly violates Washington's own 'rules' for the IDF offense: it destroyed a US-financed power plant, it blew up bridges, roads and water lines contrary to Bush's admonition to "avoid damaging infrastructure and harming civilians". Israel can stick its fingers in both of Bush's eyes and have his backing because it knows that the Jewish Lobby will mobilize a near unanimous Congressional endorsement, a favorable media focus on the Israeli 'hostage' and a virtual blackout on massive Palestinian suffering. Thanks to the Jewish Lobby, Israel's totalitarian terror directed toward a 'Final Solution' only elicits laughable proposals from the United Nations to negotiate a peaceful resolution, when the only legitimate elected negotiators are in jail or hiding and threatened with assassination.

On July 5 the European Union (EU) castigated Israel's *"dispropor-tionate measures"* but not Israel's invasion and violation of the United Nations Charter on the rights of nations to self-determination. This meek, shameful betrayal of the EU's own principles is exacerbated by its equating Israel's invasion with the Palestinian capture of an active military combatant.[17] The difference between Lobby-dominated US backing of Israel's invasion and that of the EU boils down to the *"appropriate amount of force"* which Israel should apply in invading Gaza.

What accounts for US support for Israeli ethnic cleansing, despite its impudently and blatantly repudiating the US "moderate" guidelines on destroying Palestinian democracy? No one in their right mind can claim that the Israeli assault on Gaza advances US policies, interests or US imperial power. The entire campaign from the beginning to end to destroy the democratically elected Hamas government was made and packaged in Israel and executed with the willing complicity of the executives among the Conference of Presidents of the Major Jewish Organizations in America—including but not confined to AIPAC. The daily assaults and assassinations in Gaza and the West Bank were carried out under the direction of Israeli generals, Shin Bet and Mossad, and approved by the Israeli Defense Minister and Prime Minister without their consulting or even feigning to publicly advise Washington in advance. The political campaign to isolate and destroy Hamas was overwhelmingly organized by the Jewish Lobby; it succeeded in securing a near unanimous endorsement in the US Congress and complete backing in Washington. It successfully got the Bush Administration to pressure the European Union to boycott the Hamas government.

There is no evidence that implicates Big Oil in the Israeli drive to 'cleanse' Palestine of Arabs. There is no evidence that Israel was acting on behalf of US strategists. There is a wealth of reports, documents, statements and actions taken by the Israeli regime and its US transmission belts indicating that they imposed US complicity, engineered the entire operation in accord with their own totalitarian methods at the service of their own designed strategy to secure the 'Final Solution': Jewish rule over the entire Palestinian territory.

The Jewish Lobby has dutifully followed every twist and turn in the Israeli propaganda line on its devious road toward a purely Jewish-populated former Palestine.

For example, Israel claimed it couldn't negotiate with the Palestinians because they refused to recognize Israel despite the fact that even Arafat publicly and categorically proclaimed he favored a Two State solution in the 1980's. The Lobby ignored Arafat's pledge, then labeled his proposal as unreliable, then turned around and endorsed his role as a legitimate interlocutor at the Oslo meeting after Israel passed the line that he was a statesman and not a terrorist. ... With Sharon finally scuttling the tarnished agreement, the Lobby switched to re-labeling Arafat a terrorist and blamed the PLO for failing to accept the creation of separate Palestinian Bantustans.

The Jewish State claimed that it couldn't deal with an illegitimate undemocratic regime. The Lobby parroted the line, calling Israel the "only democracy in the Middle East", even as it occupied and exercised colonial rule over 3.5 million Palestinians. Subsequent to the free elections which were won by Hamas, the Israeli State rejected the democratic outcome; the Lobby "forgot" about its democratic rhetoric and again parroted the line of its Israeli masters—democratically elected authorities who are not approved by Tel Aviv are not acceptable.

When Israel launched a series of measures to destroy the Palestinian economy and blockade trade and financial life, the Lobby automatically endorsed it, promoted US complicity, and supported the collective punishment of the Palestinian people for having been so irresponsible as to support a nationalist government inclined to eliminate corruption.

When Israel built the segregation wall and the World Court condemned it, the Lobby defended it, repeating the Israeli State line: It's a 'Security Fence'.

The evidence of the Lobby acting as a transmission belt for Israeli state policy under all conditions is overwhelming. In the face of all rational considerations, the Lobby automatically gives unquestioned support to Israel's violations of peace, democracy, human rights, international court rulings, United Nations resolutions. This is especially true even when the Israeli State blatantly ignores US policy. There is no question that the Lobby's primary political loyalties lie with the State of Israel.

The Jewish Lobby's wholehearted backing of Israel's assault on Gaza illustrates once again that there is no crime, no matter how terrible and perverse, that Israel commits, which will not be supported by the respectable professors, investment bankers, journalists, surgeons, policy advisers, real estate moguls, lawyers, school teachers and other ordinary folk who make up the activist base of the Major Organizations.

6 *Israel and Prisoner Exchanges: The Record*

The Israeli government and all its principle spokespeople have repeatedly rejected negotiations directed toward a prisoner exchange, calling the demand *"outrageous"*, *"extortion"* and likely to *"encourage terrorism"*. The Jewish State's line was predictably echoed and amplified by its representatives in the Conference of Presidents of Major Jewish Organizations (CPMJO) repeatedly throughout the Israeli invasion in their propaganda sheet, *Daily Alert*. The editorial pages of the *Washington Post*, the *New York Times* and the *Los Angeles Times* were full of opinion pieces supporting the Israeli line opposing prisoner exchanges written by members or supporters of the (pro-Israel) Jewish Lobby.

The historical record provides a totally different account of Israel's policy on prisoner exchange and extortion. Israel has on numerous occasions negotiated with so-called 'Palestinian terrorists' the exchange of prisoners, and consummated the deals. As Esther Wachsman, the mother of an Israeli soldier who died in an operation to release him, emphatically stated (and as everyone in Israel knows), "All this talk about not speaking to the terrorists is nonsense, in the end they released Palestinian prisoners with blood on their hands for three dead soldiers and they released Sheikh Ahmed Yassin for two Mossad agents."[18]

Equally the indignation of Israeli officials and the officials of the Jewish Lobby against *"extortion"* is laughable, were it not so tragic. Israel systematically holds family members, relatives and entire neighborhoods of suspected Palestinian activists hostage. Some are even imprisoned and tortured in order to extort information or force the suspects to turn themselves in.

The practice of accusing the victims of the crimes that the executioners themselves are about to commit, as Albert Camus once noted, is the hallmark of totalitarian regimes.

Beyond the Jewish State and Lobby's hypocrisy, cant and outright lies accompanying the refusal to negotiate a prisoner exchange is an equally important question: Why has the Israeli regime, contrary to its past practices, refused to negotiate? The explanation for Israeli intransigence is that it does not want its soldier released, at least not until it has devastated and re-occupied Gaza. The refusal to negotiate this time is a coldly calculated and cynical move to prolong the invasion and increase their stranglehold on the Gaza economy in order to accelerate the "voluntary" departure of the Palestinians and Palestinian businesses. The lowly corporal is being sacrificed to the Greater Good of Greater Israel; for all the sentimental photos of the lad published in the Lobby-influenced mass media, there is no accompanying concern at the cynical refusal of the Jewish State to negotiate his release.

The refusal to negotiate is a coldly calculated move to increase the stranglehold on the Gaza economy in order to accelerate the "voluntary" departure of the Palestinians and Palestinian businesses.

The danger is that Israeli fundamentalism is implicating not only the

US mass media and state, it's infusing US civil society, which already is suffering from police state regulation by our own rulers in the White House. Beyond the terrible plight and injustices of the Palestinians in Gaza, and US complicity, lies the larger question of a new air war against Iran. If Israel, through its Jewish lobby and backers in the government, can induce a US invasion of Iraq, if it can secure US and EU complicity in destroying a democratically elected government in Palestine in the course of ethnic cleansing and invading and destroying Lebanon, could the same power configuration lead to a full-scale attack on Iran? The precedents have been established. The political machinery is in place. Is it a question of timing or pretext? Can some as yet unforeseen or unpredictable event or political force intervene to forestall the Zionist juggernaut? The first step is to explain the problem: to name the pro-Israel power bloc at work, to expose the issue of dual loyalties, to face down the vicious slander campaigns emanating from the agents of the Israeli state, and to begin a nationwide educational and political campaign to end Israeli crimes against humanity and its Lobby's shameful apologetics for the 'Final Solution'.

Mass Media Propaganda at the Service of Ethnic Cleansing

As is predictable from past responses to Israel's savaging of Palestinian communities and civilians, the response of the mass media to the Israeli onslaught was almost entirely in line with the outlook of the Jewish Lobby. I have chosen to analyze one of the more reputable sources—the British Broadcasting Corporation (BBC), rather than the more overt Lobby mouthpieces like the *Washington Post, Los Angeles Times* and *New York Times,* or the blatant television and radio stations, to illustrate the problem. On July 1, 2006, Alan Johnston, the BBC News reporter in Gaza, provided an 'overview' of the war situation.[19] The key to the pro-Israel account is set in the background to the Israeli invasion: "The best of governments would struggle here. And Hamas came to the task with an attitude toward Israel that guaranteed that it would be engulfed by problems."

Hamas' "attitude"—at least what was expressed in its behavior,— was: (1) upholding a one-year cease fire with Israel, despite continued Israeli assassinations; (2) participation in the first free and open electoral process; (3) an offer to negotiate co-existence on the basis of equality and mutual respect with the Israeli regime, which Israel categorically rejected; and (4) the pursuit of peaceful means and appeals to the United Nations against the brutal Israeli boycott. In other words, the BBC turned the background to the invasion on its head: it was Israel's hostile and belligerent attitude (and behavior) that "guaranteed that it [Hamas] would be engulfed by problems".

The second "background" statement to frame the BBC's defense of Israel's invasion reads: "In the past Hamas suicide bombers have hammered at Israel's cities, taking hundreds of lives. Hamas called the bombs in the cafes and the buses resistance to occupation. But the West called it terrorism. It plunged the new government into economic and diplomatic isolation. And it will remain an international pariah until Hamas renounces violence and recognizes Israel's right to exist."

The BBC selectively reviewed Hamas activities of the past, ignoring much worse examples of Israeli state terrorism, including the murderous invasion of Lebanon, killing 25,000 people, 1,400 alone in Sabra and Shatila Refugee Camps; the Israeli killing of four times as many Palestinian civilians during the two Intifadas; the systematic murder of opponents, called "targeted assassinations"—all of which have been condemned by the UN and most of the Western governments (US excluded). If past behavior of terrorism provides a criteria to evaluate regimes, it is Israel, along with the US, which is cited most frequently by the majority of Western opinion polls as the greatest threat to peace. The very founding of Israel was based on terror and violent destruction of hotels, cafes, hospitals, schools, and other colonial and Arab properties. The preoccupation of the BBC with Israeli cafes and buses overlooks the Israeli destruction of Palestinian schools, hospitals and homes. By any measure of United Nations voting behavior, it is Israel that is the international pariah by at least a 10 to 1 margin. Hamas' election participation was endorsed by all Western regimes, including Washington, who initially welcomed the democratic outcome. The blockade of Palestine, led by Israel, the Lobby and the US, was not a result of past Hamas behavior, but of present electoral outcomes and Israel's vengeance on the Palestinian electorate, as top Israeli officials have publicly asserted. Moreover, as was pointed out earlier, one week before the Israeli invasion, Hamas, in signing off on an agreement with the PLO, had tacitly agreed to a two state solution. The BBC's prejudicial framework is designed to blame Hamas, the victim of the crimes which Israel, the Lobby and the US are perpetuating against them.

According to the BBC, the Israeli Lobby/US embargo is thus not imposed against a democratically elected government but against terrorists. Israeli assaults on Palestine in the lead-up to the invasion are justified by past Hamas actions, ignoring the provocative murder of 20 Palestinian civilians during bloody June 2006. The BBC's 'framework' for analyzing the Israeli invasion is a transparent frame-up of a re-colonized nation.

The Israeli re-colonization of Gaza, the bombing and the military mobilization prior to the capture of the Israeli soldier is totally ignored in the BBC overview. Instead we are presented with all the sappy melodrama of a third-rate soap opera in the service of a savage onslaught against 1.4 million Palestinian captives.

Hamas militants were among those who raided an army

post on Gaza's border on Sunday. In the dawn light they burst out of a tunnel and surprised a slumbering tank crew. The attacker killed two soldiers and led away 19-year-old Gilad Shalit. And when you see the pictures of his pale, bespeckled face on television, it is easy to believe that he is as he is described ' shy, bright, with a gift for math'. He is every Israeli's 'kid next door.' And now they are watching him live their nightmare. He is somewhere in the depths of Gaza in the hands of their most formidable enemy."[20]

The BBC projects the image of Arab child killers literally coming out of an underground—real live devils—and slaughtering sleepy and freckly-face (a ploy to associate Israeli soldiers with European, not Semitic—*Arab*—peoples) "kids", who we are not told had fired thousands of shells into Gaza when they were awake while scanning the horizon for any moving target. There are 9,000 Palestinian prisoners, many are civilians, some are pale or worse because of legalized torture, a good number are much younger than Gilad, some wear glasses, many are shy and bright with 'a gift for math'. Their families have lived the Israeli 'nightmare' of incarceration, anywhere from one to twenty years…not a few days, like the tank crew corporal. There are three hundred real Palestinian 'kids next door', younger than eighteen, who are rotting in Israeli jails—and there are thousands of others who have been blinded and crippled by Israeli live ammunition for protesting the occupation. For Israelis, the 'Israeli nightmare' takes place with $20,000 USD per capita income, with electrical appliances lighting up the house, swimming pools to lounge around, and beaches to distract themselves from the 'nightmare' of a single Israeli soldier, who, we are told by the BBC, "is in great danger" from the kid-killing "Palestinian militants". Written without irony or shame, the BBC omits to mention the living nightmare of 1.4 million Gaza inhabitants without water, sewage, electricity, and subject to daily barrages of artillery and missiles…

It is not difficult to see that the BBC has incorporated into its narrative the racist Zionist idea that one Israeli life is worth more than 1.4 million Palestinians, or that the psychological anguish of Israeli television viewers is more important than the hundreds of thousands of Palestinian families threatened with physical extermination.

Let it be said that the BBC's apology for Israeli terror is no worse than the propaganda that passes for news in the rest of the illustrious mainstream publications in the US.

What is striking about the media's reportage of Israeli aggression is the extent to which it justifies and legitimates the most heinous crimes.

What is striking about the media's reportage of Israeli aggression is the extent to which it justifies and legitimates the most heinous crimes, with the crudest imagery and sanctimonious language. Neither the Pope, nor Kofi Annan nor any other prominent governmental official—except the Swiss foreign minister—has raised a cry of indignation at this crime against humanity. Thus speaks the power of the Israeli lobbies here and abroad. When Mussolini invaded Ethiopia, the League of Nations wrung their hands and did nothing. When Hitler invaded Czechoslovakia, some Westerners cried appeasement but did nothing. When Israel rapes Gaza, Washington and the EU urge them on.

Since Israel is the aggressor and the Jewish Lobby is deeply engaged and the mass media is flashing the face of the lone Israeli military captive, the US peace movement is virtually dead to the Palestinians' nightmare. This, despite the fact that as activists, most are aware of the fallibility of the major media, and regularly rely on the internet for reportage closer to the truth.

Even the infamous disclaimers of the power of the Jewish lobby (Chomsky, Palast, Klare, Albert and an army of progressive intellectuals and journalists) would be hard pressed to find a 'Big Oil' interest buried in the sands and rubble of Gaza. Nor can US government support of Israeli aggression in Gaza be linked to any 'geo-political interests in the Middle East' as argued by Professor Steven Zunes. The Lobby has spoken and Washington has listened: Israel is to be supported, their lies are truths, their invasion is defensive, their 'anguish' is real, their life is a 'nightmare'; the 'others' are terrorists.

The Palestinians' tiny crowded strip of land is backed up against the sea. But the Palestinian people have held it for untold generations. It will require their utter physical annihilation by the Israeli storm troopers to remove their presence.

Epilogue

As the Israeli war machine grinds on inexorably toward the 'Final Solution' under the torrid summer sun, the killing fields of Gaza become saturated with Palestinian blood. As the Palestinian casualties mount by the dozen each day, the deaths exceeding a hundred and the wounded by three hundred by the middle of July, new evidence of Israel's criminal use of illegal gruesome chemical and experimental weapons comes to light. On July 9, the Palestinian Health Ministry released a report from surgeons in Gaza hospitals which revealed that "all 249 casualties inflicted by the Israeli war machine during the operation in Gaza…resulted from shrapnel of newly developed shells and explosives which cause amputation of limbs and burning of all the injured parts." In Shifa Hospital, Dr. al-Saqqa (who heads the hospital's emergency service) stated, *"Even bodies of the injured have been almost completely burnt. They have been deformed in a very ugly way that we have never seen before. When we try to x-ray dead bodies, we find no trace of shrapnel that hit the person killed. We are sure that Israel is using a new chemical or radioactive weapon in the new operation (assault on Gaza). More than 25% of the injured are children under 16.'*[21] The day after the World Cup Football Final, Israeli storm troopers murdered four teenagers playing football in a field.

Given the impunity granted them by the United Nations, the European Union and the United States, Israel intensified its attacks in Gaza to the point of blowing up fully occupied three-story apartment buildings, killing two women and two children on July 10.[22] The Israeli government repeated the usual war propaganda, claiming *"they were aiming for the terrorists"*. As usual, the major US-Jewish organizations echoed the Israeli line that *"there was no humanitarian crisis in Gaza"*.[23] Even as Israel denied any crisis, it proceeded to tighten the entry of foreign citizens (mostly US) of Palestinian ethnicity into the Occupied Territories for the first time since 1967.[23] This includes physicians, engineers, journalists and academics of Palestinian ancestry holding US or European citizenship ,separating them from their family members, patients and colleagues trapped in Gaza. It is clear that Israel is doing everything possible to block the full exposure of the extent of its terror campaign to isolate the Palestinians from the rest of the world and to break up families in order to create the *"conditions"*, as both Sharon and Rabin had once so poetically put it, for the massive Palestinian *"voluntary departure"*. Not to be outdone by their earlier brutality, on July 11, Israel dropped a 1 ton bomb on an apartment building in a crowded Gaza neighborhood, killing 23 Palestinians, fourteen described as civilians including nine from one family—mother, father and seven children all below the age of seventeen.

Predictably the 'Final Solution' or 'Palestinian Holocaust' deniers in the US media and especially the pro-Israel Jewish press continue to defend the invasion, the killings and the destruction without the least shame but rather with the self-righteous vehemence of unchallenged bullies. As the Israeli murderous campaign proceeds inside Gaza with impunity, it extends its power against a spineless European Union. On July 7, 2006 Israel imprisoned Hassan Khreshi, Vice-President of the Political Committee on Security and Human Rights of the Euro-Mediterranean Parliamentary Assembly (EMPA) of which Israel is a member. Clearly the EU's newly discovered impotence to openly criticize Israel's slaughter in Gaza has encouraged its rulers to even more bloody aggression—which does not stop at the borders of Gaza. On July 12, Israel invaded Lebanon after a border incident involving Hezbollah (a Lebanese Islamic-nationalist political-military organization). This resulted in the capture of two Israeli soldiers and the death of seven Israeli soldiers and two Lebanese civilians. As grassroots resistance in the Arab world increases, the Israeli war machine moves beyond its borders, now to Lebanon and likely to Syria and other neighboring countries where opposition to the 'Final Solution' is likely to develop.

Although in the US the Conference of Presidents of the Major Jewish Organizations and the opinion page writers in the major and minor US media unconditionally support the Israeli government's position opposed to negotiation with the elected Hamas leadership and their brutal bombing of Palestinian civilians trapped without food, water or electricity in Gaza, over 54 percent of Israeli Jews believe that the government has used excessive force, particularly in arresting elected Hamas officials, and 50 percent supported negotiating with Hamas over the release of the Israeli prisoner of war while 42 percent oppose negotiations.[24] As the *Jerusalem Post* summed up its poll results, "*the public as a whole is more open than the leadership to the possibility of dialogue with Hamas, a finding the Peace Index surveys has* pointed to consistently in recent months" (my emphasis).[25] According to the 'political criteria' of most major US Jewish organizations, Israel must be full of 'anti-Semites' and 'self-haters' or other such pejorative labels which are usually applied to American advocates of recognition of Palestinian rights and negotiation with Hamas.

ENDNOTES

[1]   *Financial Times*, July 1, 2006.
[2]   Ibid, p. 8.
[3]   BBC News July 6, 2006,
[4]   BBC News July 1, 2006.
[5]   BBC News, July 1, 2006.
[6]   *New York Times*, July 3, 2006.
[7]   PCHR, June 2006 Weekly Report on Israeli Human Rights Violations in Palestinian Territory.
[8]   John Dugard, United Nations Envoy to an emergency meeting of the United Nations Human Rights Council, July 4, 2006.
[9]   BBC News, July 5, 2006.
[10]   *Financial Times*, June 29, 2006. p. 8.
[11]   Noam Chomsky, *Fateful Triangle: the United States, Israel and Palestine*, Pluto, London, 1999.
[12]   Al Jazeera, July 2, 2006.
[13]   *La Jornada*, July 8, 2006.
[14]   CNN, July 2, 2006.
[15]   Al Jazeera, July 2, 2006.
[16]   *Daily Alert*, July 3, 2006.
[17]   *La Jornada*, (Mexico City), July 6, 2006.
[18]   BBC News July 1, 2006.
[19]   BBC News July 1, 2006.
[20]   BBC July 1, 2006.
[21]   Al Jazeera July 11, 2006.
[22]   Al Jazeera, July 10, 2006.
[23]   *Daily Alert*, July 12, 2006.
[24]   *Haaretz*, July 10, 2006.
[25]   *Jerusalem Post*, July 11, 2006.

CHAPTER 8

"MAD DOG" RAVAGES LEBANON

"Israel must be like a mad dog, too dangerous to bother."
General Moshe Dayan, Former Israeli Defense Minister

"Army Chief Dan Halutz has given the order to the air force to destroy 10 multi-story buildings in the Dahaya district (of Beirut) in response to every rocket fired at Haifa."
Israeli Army Radio, July 24, 2006

"I think it's important that we not fall into the trap of moral equivalency here. What Hizbollah has done is kidnap Israeli soldiers and rain rockets and mortar shells on Israeli civilians. What Israel has done in response is act in self-defense."
US Ambassador to the United Nations John Bolton

"Israeli leaders could be charged with war crimes."
Louise Arbour, UN High Commissioner for Human Rights, July 2006

*"The Third World War...has already started.
What we're seeing today in the Middle East is a chapter of it."*
Daniel Gillerman, Israeli Ambassador to the United Nations, July 2006

"Israel is the biggest threat to peace in the eyes of most Europeans."
Poll conducted by the European Union in early 2006

Kristalnacht, the 1939 Nazi assault on Jewish homes, stores and persons in 'reprisal' for a Jew killing a German Embassy officer, was a garden party compared to the Jewish State's ongoing destruction of Lebanon. The Nazi 'reprisal' led to the killing of several Jews and property damage in the millions of dollars. Israel's murder and destruction toll as at August 1st, 2006 already included over 828 Lebanese civilians dead, 3200 wounded, 750,000 (some say 900,000) refugees, hundreds of destroyed apartment buildings, thousands of homes, schools, factories, aqueducts, water and sewage treatment facilities, churches and mosques, radio and television stations, all the major bridges and highways, the airports and ports—in fact anything and anybody standing, hiding, or fleeing for safety.

Israel's deliberate 'total blockade' in addition to its carpet-bombing has created a humanitarian catastrophe for 2.5 million Lebanese, including the 750,000 refugees. According to the *Financial Times*, "The humanitarian situation has been made worse by an Israeli sea and air blockade and the targeting of roads and bridges that hinder the distribution of aid, both to the refugees and to the people who have stayed behind."[1] Refugees tell of days of Israeli shelling, shortages of water and food, power outages and cut phone lines. Even more sinister, many refugees "recount how they were first told by Israel to leave, only to be hit by Israeli shelling on the road to safety".[2] Even humanitarian aid and assistance was targeted. As the British *Guardian* reported on July 25, 2006:

> The ambulance headlights were on, the blue light overhead was flashing and another light illuminated the Red Cross flag when the first Israeli missile hit, shearing off the right leg of the man on the stretcher. As he lay screaming beneath fire and smoke, patients and ambulance workers scrambled for safety, crawling over grass in the dark. Then another missile hit the second ambulance.

No matter. All the major Jewish organizations in the US, Europe and Canada pledged fealty to the Israeli state and endorse its crimes against humanity as do all the mass media; they influence or control the US Congress, Executive branch and trade union confederations in the US. The 'Big Lie' of Israeli 'reprisals' has been repeated so often in the media and in official circles that it is taken as an accepted fact. If we return to the 'ancient history' of July 12, 2006, we discover that Hezbollah attacked an Israeli Army post on the border with Lebanon—a military target with no civilian significance. Immediately after this localized military incident, Prime Minister Olmert ordered massive bombing of Beirut and civilian targets throughout Lebanon. After Israel's carpet-bombing of civilians and civilian infrastructure throughout Lebanon, Hezbollah responded on July 14, 2006 by 'declaring war' on Israel, namely bombing Israeli cities. On July 14, 2006 the Jewish Lobby propaganda and power machine went into action criticizing Bush over his concern for the Lebanese client regime, which the White House had so laboriously put in place.[3]

Abraham Foxman, National Director of the Anti-Defamation League, sharply attacked Bush for asking Tel Aviv to show restraint and not undermine Lebanese Prime Minister Siniora. The Conference of the Presidents of Major American Jewish Organizations put its 52 groups into action. Bush quickly backtracked and forgot about his Lebanese client. Israel and the '52 Groups' pushed the US to supply more 5-ton bombs for its bombers to drop on a defenseless country without a functioning air force. The leading ideologues of the Jewish Lobby pushed for the US to bomb Iran and Syria, the 'hand behind Hezbollah'—hoping to start Israeli Ambassador Gillerman's World War Three.

The unanimity of the major Jewish organizations' support for Israeli ethnocide extends to the 'peace time' Israeli peace organizations and progressives like Amos Oz, who calls on Israel's peace organizations to close ranks behind the butchers of Beirut in the name of the 'defense' of Israel.

As Washington rushes a new supply of 5-ton bombs and 'precision missiles', there can be no doubt that the Israeli leaders' destruction of the civilian homes, apartments and infrastructure is a precisely calculated target.[4] As precision-guided missiles are playing a key part in Israel's military strategy, it is clear that the repeated bombing of hospitals, mosques, refugee caravans and ambulances on the highways, and the Muslim and Christian sectors of Beirut and other cities are an integral part of that strategy.

Professor Juan Cole argues persuasively that the war on Lebanon was planned for at least a year, citing the presentations by senior Israeli army officers to Washington think tanks, diplomats and journalists outlining the coming invasion.[5]

A year prior to the war on Lebanon, senior Israeli army officers made presentations to Washington think tanks, diplomats and journalists outlining the coming invasion.

The Israeli pretext of rescuing two captured soldiers is laughable given the instant massive offensive and the sustained destruction of all of Lebanon, including large areas of central and northern Lebanon where there are few if any Hezbollah.

It ill behooves us to ignore the recent historical context for the Israeli bombing and wanton murder of Lebanese. For several years the Jewish Lobby has pressured the White House and Congress to disarm and destroy Hezbollah; to accomplish that goal it was necessary to change the correlation of forces in Lebanon by forcing the Syrians out—which was successfully accomplished through the assassination of a prominent Lebanese politician (Hariri) then pinning the murder on Syrian intelligence—though it was demonstrably counter to Syrian interests, no proof was ever presented, and perjured testimony, later retracted, was the sole evidence. Subsequent to Syria's departure, a Lebanese assassin in the pay of the Israeli secret service, Mossad, was captured by the anti-Syrian Lebanese police, and admitted to committing numerous bombing assassinations on Lebanese citizens targeted by the Israelis.

With Syria out of Lebanon, Washington secured a one-sided UN resolution calling for the disarming of Hezbollah, without any military or territorial concession from Israel (such as the return of Israeli-occupied Lebanese Shebaa Farms) or the return of Lebanese or Hezbollah prisoners who had been languishing in Israeli prisons for up to ten years. That UN resolution, probably the only one Israel abides by for obvious reasons, subsequently provided part of the cover for Israel's invasion as it bombed Lebanon into a miserable state more like Afghanistan than the vibrant Mediterranean republic it had been just days before. Israel's strategy was transparent: it sought to isolate Hezbollah in the world, securing UN support via Washington, secured in turn by pressure from the Lobby on the Bush Administration, with a view to promoting an internal conflict in Lebanon between Hezbollah and the Lebanese government, in which the US/UN would then intervene in favor of its favored Beirut clients—likely the Christian Maronites, who presumably were to have been goaded into action against Hezbollah by the Israeli assault against its own sector.

Failing on both counts, Israel decided, in consultation with Washington, to launch a frontal murderous assault on Lebanon on the pretext of the captured soldiers and Israel's need to eliminate the "terrorist" organization, Hezbollah. The Israeli military attack presented several favorable future possibilities apart from the destruction of the anti-imperialist Hezbollah. One was the opportunity to isolate and create a pretext to attack Syria and Iran if they exerted any efforts on behalf of the Lebanese. Secondly Washington saw the Israeli invasion as a means to distract horrified world opinion away from the US genocidal occupation of Iraq. Thirdly the Bush Administration sought to secure the Jewish Lobby's continued powerful media influence in support of the US occupation of Iraq when a majority of US citizens were increasingly hostile. Finally, in acceding to supply Israel with weapons of mass destruction, like 5-ton bombs, the Republicans and Democrats sought to secure campaign funding from their millionaire and billionaire Jewish political supporters. Not to be left behind in the race for the hearts and minds of Israel supporters, Democratic National Chairman Howard Dean—once the beneficiary of an internet campaign by progressives supporting his drive for the presidency based on his condemnation of the war in Iraq—attracted wide media attention for his fulmination that the Iraqi Prime Minister was an "anti-Semite" for refusing to denounce Hezbollah.

For Israel, the military attack was directed toward destroying *all of Lebanon*, converting it into an economic wasteland while ethnically cleansing the Lebanese civilians from southern Lebanon, facilitating its declaring the country a 'free-fire' zone—to be bombed at will, killing any remaining persons on the grounds that they were Hezbollah sympathizers, activists, social workers, medics, and fighters. The strategy was to 'empty the pond (southern Lebanon and south Beirut—perhaps 40 percent of the country's population) to catch the fish (Hezbollah)'. (Hezbollah is a mass political and social movement with a mass base of 1.1 million Lebanese which, inter alia, provided social services to local populations in what might have been viewed as in the best traditions of progressive socio-political movements, had not racist bias and antipathy toward religion—or only specifically toward Islam, since if similar activity had been undertaken by Christian activists in Latin America, would it not have been embraced?—prevented western progressives from arriving at such an assessment.) In the process, Israel sought to create a client regime in Lebanon and to cut off the moral and material support that Hezbollah gives to the democratically elected Hamas government in Palestine.

In the course of events, Israeli and US assumptions failed. Israel's massive terror bombing undermined the pro-US Beirut regime and turned the great majority of Lebanese in favor of Hezbollah—as surely might have been anticipated, since recent infliction of collective punishment on the population of Iraq with a view to turning them against even such a tyrant as Saddam Hussein had miserably failed. In the total absence of the Lebanese government, it was Hezbollah that rushed victims to hospitals, provided food, evacuation convoys, and a modicum of relief to all Lebanese—regardless of affiliation. Washington's precautions to the Israelis to respect (Lebanese) civilians and civilian infrastructure were brazenly ignored by the Jewish state from the start, which knew full well that the Jewish Lobby in the US would ensure Washington's complicity in mass murder and the undermining of its own client regime.

There was never any question, when facing a choice between defending a conservative, recently installed Lebanese regime or supporting Israel's total war, that the White House would support the Lobby and Tel Aviv—hands down.

If the US miscalculated on Israel's 'precision intervention', the Jewish State over-estimated its capacity to bomb Hezbollah into submission. The Israeli regime then proceeded to launch a land war, which is extremely costly in the mountainous zones of South Lebanon. For the first time there were large-scale and mounting Israeli military casualties—not only innocent, unarmed Lebanese families targeted by Israeli planes and helicopters were dying.

In attacking and capturing two Israeli soldiers, Hezbollah had sought to come to the humanitarian aid of the besieged Palestinians of Gaza, who were suffering the hammer blows of Israel's invasion and daily assassinations. Neither Syria nor Iran had any influence on Hezbollah's decision to take Israeli pressure off the Palestinians. According to several Iran experts, "Iran has taken a pragmatic approach in its foreign policy and does not want to get into a serious confrontation with Israel".[6] Another expert argued "Iran was not looking for a crisis in Lebanon at a critical moment in the nuclear diplomacy".[7] An expert on Hezbollah pointed out "it was inconceivable that Iran had ordered Hezbollah to take Israeli soldiers prisoner. Hezbollah leaders are not the types to take orders from elsewhere".[8] This of course doesn't exclude the corollary motivations that Hezbollah sought to secure a prisoner exchange for some Lebanese political prisoners who had been held by Israel, some for over a decade, as well as to free Lebanese territory still under Israeli occupation.

By attacking Lebanon and focusing on Hezbollah, Israel sought to further isolate the Palestinian government and to continue its policy of bombing the Palestinian people into a 'voluntary' exodus. During the first two weeks of the Lebanese bombing, Israel continued its assassination and bombing campaign in Gaza and the West Bank, killing and maiming scores of civilians, children and resistance fighters. Perversely, by raising the death toll (to nearly 500), destruction (an estimated $2 billion dollars) and forced exodus of at least 750,000 civilians in Lebanon as at July 27, 2006, Israel has effectively distracted the philo-Israeli mass media from the daily murder and injury of dozens of Palestinians. Mass media coverage of Israeli genocide in Lebanon is at its worst: the television media—CBS, NBC, ABC, CNN, and National Public Radio and the respectable press—not only repeat the Israeli propaganda about "precision-guided missiles...destroying Hezbollah bunkers," but focus on the handful of Israeli deaths and injuries—sometimes resorting to news items of days earlier in order to try to project an image of Israeli suffering to correspond to that of the current daily images of Lebanese civilian deaths and injuries in the thousands, and of the million who are homeless, without electricity or water even while still subject to 5-ton bombs dropped by merciless unopposed Israeli pilots purportedly looking for 'bunkers' but locating multi-storied apartment blocks instead. "At least one third of Lebanese casualties are children," according to the UN's Jan Egeland after a field inspection. Less than one-tenth are Hezbollah fighters. Faced with massive civilian bombings, US Secretary of State Rice referred to the devastation as "the birth pangs" of a new order, just as her predecessors in the Third Reich justified the bombing of London during World War Two.

On July 24, 2006 the *Daily Alert*, the news sheet of the Conference of Presidents of Major American Jewish Organizations published and re-published articles written by apologists for Israel's bloody invasion. Not a single criticism of the flight of at least 750,000 refugees, not a word of the destruction of apartments, not even a passing mention of the murder of over 100 children. Quotes from President Bush opposing a ceasefire, from ultra rightist 'Israel Firster' Ambassador Bolton (US Ambassador to the UN) defending Israel's terror bombing, arguing that the relatively few rockets falling in Israel were of greater concern than the destruction of the entire infrastructure of Lebanon, the pollution of its entire coastline, and the killing and maiming of thousands of civilians, a third of whom were children...Op-Ed articles in the *Washington Post, Los Angeles Times, Wall Street Journal*, and *New Republic* supported Israel's bloodbath. Editorials in the *Washington Post, Wall Street Journal* and *Miami Herald* closely follow the Lobby's lines.

The entire massive Jewish and pro-Israel propaganda machine has covered the US media with messages of unconditional support for Israeli murder, denials of Lebanese suffering, and justification of the wanton destruction, presented as an act of heroic defense... by the 'mad dogs' (ref. Moshe Dayan) of Israel. The voices of Americans horrified by Israeli atrocities or who just feel sympathy for its victims go unheeded, or worse, are attacked and ridiculed. (The veteran octogenarian White House correspondent, Helen Thomas, of Lebanese ethnic origin, was taunted as the 'voice of Hezbollah' by the President's Press Secretary, Tony Snow.) The US peace movement, prohibited by its Jewish progressives from voicing outrage at Israel, let alone the Lobby, is moribund. Once again, Israel gets away with murder; its overseas political transmission belts dominate the mass media. The US Congress kneels to the Lobby's dictates. The entire White House Staff act as messengers for the Israeli Foreign Office, while Israel in turn broadcasts that it has US "permission" for its behavior—sweeping aside all niceties with no concern whatsoever for the evident public embarrassment (and private—what?) that this might cause its benefactor.

The US submission and complicity in the Gaza ethnocide and now the destruction of Lebanon without internal debate in Congress, in the mass media, or even in the so-called 'peace movements', speaks loudly and clearly to the stranglehold of Israeli power within the United States and to the enormous and continuing damage to our basic democratic freedoms. To stand against totalitarian terror and US complicity should be a common reflexive act of decency. Today under the Lobby's all pervasive domain, it is an act of courage, even though it may reach only a few tens of thousands through the alternative media.

Israel's idea of a 'ceasefire' parroted by the Israel Lobby and regurgitated by the US Secretary of State Condoleeza Rice to Lebanese leaders is first to allow Israel to continue the carpet-bombing of Lebanon with the newly shipped 5-ton American bombs, thus rejecting the Lebanese Prime Minister's pleas for an immediate ceasefire.[9] Once Israel has totally devastated the country, Washington will propose an 'international force' (of Israel's choosing) along with the Lebanese Army to occupy Southern Lebanon (currently under Israeli occupation with the remnant of the battered unarmed UN peace keepers). The 'international force' is then supposed to proceed to the total disarming and forced removal of all Hezbollah fighters and their half-million supporters in the South. At that point Israel would consider a ceasefire.

Apparently Israel's mad-dog disease is contagious and has affected the few remaining grey cells in the White House. According to the *New York Times*, there are no commitments for the proposed 'international force': "The US has ruled out its soldiers participating, NATO says it is overstretched, Britain feels its troops are overcommitted and Germany says it is willing to participate only if Hezbollah agrees."[10] Secondly following on the Israeli scorched-earth policy, and Hezbollah's tough resistance, few if any Lebanese soldiers will take up arms to implement Israel's conditions, as even the conservative Lebanese leaders reject a foreign occupation. Thirdly and most important, Hezbollah is prepared for and capable of engaging in a prolonged popular guerrilla war of resistance such as Israel has never faced before, in terms of organization, morale, and military capability. According to *Jane's Defense Weekly* analyst Nicholas Blandford: "(The Hezbollah) are well armed, well-motivated combat veterans from the 1990's. It's the old Mao Tsetung guerrilla strategy of retreating when the enemy advances and advancing when the enemy retreats."[11]

According to another expert on Hezbollah: "They operate in small isolated cells. One cell does not know what the other cell is doing…This decentralized structure is part of the group's military potency".[12] Hezbollah's military force, as large as 7,500 fighters, has, like the Vietnamese earlier, been preparing underground tunnels across South Lebanon and has built an advanced, well-stocked armory. Unlike previous Arab armies, which were heavily infiltrated and which fought 'standing wars' under highly centralized commands, Hezbollah works in small, decentralized groups that move quickly and have taken effective measures against Israeli informers. Hezbollah is waiting for a full-scale ground invasion to fight a guerrilla war in the mountains and on their terrain. According to Hezbollah Secretary General Hassan Nasrallah: "When the Israelis enter, they must pay dearly in terms of their tanks, officers and soldiers."[13] Israel is clearly not going to win a 'seven-day war'. Even in the first ten days, Alon Ben-David, a *Jane's Defence Weekly* correspondent, wrote that the Israeli military has suffered "considerable casualties" in its push north into Lebanon.

Epilogue

Thanks to the power of the US-Jewish Lobby and the reach of its international affiliates, the US government secured the agreement of the world's powers meeting in Rome on July 26, 2006 to give Israel's 'mad dogs' free rein to continue their genocidal policies in Lebanon and Gaza, a vote hailed by the mouthpiece of the Conference of Presidents of the Major Jewish Organizations.[14] Given the Lobby *supremos*' efforts to stifle dissent from genocide, special importance should be given to the fact that the Rome vote took place less than 24 hours after Israel deliberately murdered (decapitated) 4 UN peace keepers through direct targeting of their camp—even after having received over a dozen frantic phone calls from the beleaguered international peace keepers before, during and after the Israeli missile and tank shelling attack,[15] advising that they were being shelled, and pleading for cessation. Even UN Secretary General Kofi Annan couldn't stomach the Israeli claims of error. His statement that the Israelis deliberately attacked the unarmed UN observers in their clearly marked outpost provoked fits of indignation in Israel and among Israel Firsters in the US. Needless to say, the US Jewish Lobby automatically backed Israel's slaughter of the UN peacekeepers and published the demand of Dan Avalon, Israeli Ambassador to the US, that Secretary General Annan 'apologize' for his 'baseless' charges.[16] In the meantime, the respectable press, led by the ultra-Zionist *Washington Post*, continued to provide exclusive editorial and news space for the apologists of Israeli genocide in Lebanon. David Rivkin, Jr. and Lee A. Casey argued that the mass terror bombing of Lebanon (and by the same logic, of Gaza) are "within (Israel's) right" and went on to provide convoluted pseudo-legal arguments that would have made Goebbels blush.[17] Needless to say, we are told that both authors served in the Reagan Justice Department, apparently cutting their teeth sanitizing the Central American killing fields.

Israel and the compliant press immediately presented the 'Rome meeting' as having given Israel "permission" to commit every outrageous crime forbidden in the UN Charter under the rubric of "Crimes against Humanity". However, the succeeding coverage given to the denials that this had been the case—not only from the Finnish Foreign Minister whose country holds the EU presidency, but even from a senior spokesperson from the US State Department, who called the assertion "outrageous"—has been muted in the extreme.

After widely publicizing Israel's assertion it had world permission for its actions, the media muted coverage of denials by the EU and even the US State Department, which termed that notion "outrageous".

As the world's attention turned to the genocide in Lebanon, the Israeli military machine continued to slaughter Palestinian children and civilians. Reuters reported that 19 Palestinians, over half civilians, including 3 children under 4, were killed and 60 people wounded.[18] The toll of Palestinian dead and wounded in the Jewish state's month-long assault rose to over a thousand—a matter barely covered in the press, as if the longtime victimized Palestinians had somehow been implicated in their fate, whereas the Lebanese, still newly targeted, for the time being, at least, enjoy the aura of innocence, and hence merit greater coverage...

The official Israeli peaceniks have joined the war party, as have most of their followers, though not the astute and steadfast Uri Avnery. A poll published by Israel's Maariv daily newspaper states that 82 percent back the continued offensive and 95 percent say Israel's action is justified.[19] Since Israel is generally considered a democracy limited to its Jewish citizens, we can safely state that the overwhelming majority of Israeli Jews are *knowing and willing accomplices* to Israeli crimes against humanity. (Did Goldhagen ever find a consensus of 95 percent of Germans in favor of Nazi ethnic cleansing?) Likewise, in the United States and Europe, the great majority of Zionist organizations and their activists are extremely mobilized toward securing US support for Israeli genocide. The hidden horror and the voices of dissent of many US citizens are stifled by the overbearing dominance of the Jewish Lobby's monopoly of the mass media. It is as if the Lobby-promoted invasion of Iraq was a dry run for US backing for Israeli invasions in the Middle

East, aimed at provoking major wars with Iran and Syria.

Postscript

True to form, two days after Israel agreed to the UN-brokered cease fire backed by the US and France, Israel launched a commando attack deep into northern Lebanon, attempting to assassinate a Hezbollah leader

Once again the Israelis were driven back, suffering one dead and two wounded, while killing three resistance fighters

The Jewish Lobby, predictably, immediately endorsed this gross violation of the ceasefire agreement, which appears on the verge of an early collapse, given Israel's explicit threats to continue to attack the resistance communities throughout Lebanon.

ENDNOTES

[1] *Financial Times*, July 25, 2006 p. 3.
[2] Ibid.
[3] *Forward*, July 14, 2006.
[4] BBC News July 23, 2006.
[5] See <http://www.juancole.com>, July 23, 2006.
[6] *Financial Times*, July 18, 2006 p 3.
[7] Ibid.
[8] Ibid.
[9] *Financial Times*, July 25, 2006.
[10] *New York Times*, July 24, 2006.
[11] Cited in Christian Henderson, "Hezbollah proves its mettle," Al Jazeera, July 25, 2006.
[12] Saad-Ghoreyeb cited in Al Jazeera, July 25, 2006.
[13] Al Jazeera, July 25, 2006.
[14] *Daily Alert*, July 27, 2006.
[15] BBC News, July 25, 2006.
[16] *Daily Alert*, July 26, 2006.
[17] *Washington Post*, July 25, 2006.
[18] Reuters, July 26, 2006.
[19] BBC News, July 27, 2006.

PART II

ISRAEL AND MIDDLE EAST WARFARE

CHAPTER 9

ISRAEL'S WAR WITH IRAN

THE COMING MIDEAST CONFLAGRATION

Introduction

Israel's political and military leadership have repeatedly and openly declared their preparation to militarily attack Iran in the immediate future. Their influential supporters in the US have made Israel's war policy the number one priority in their efforts to secure Presidential and Congressional backing. The arguments put forth by the Israeli government and echoed by their followers in the US regarding Iran's nuclear threat are without substance or fact and have aroused opposition and misgivings throughout the world, among European governments, international agencies, among most US military leaders and the public, the world oil industry, and even among sectors of the Bush Administration.

An Israeli air and commando attack on Iran will have catastrophic military consequences for US forces, cause severe loss of human life in Iraq, and most likely ignite political and military violence against pro-US Arab-Muslim regimes, such as Saudi Arabia and Egypt, perhaps leading to their overthrow. Without a doubt Israeli war preparations are the greatest immediate threat to world peace and political stability.

Israel's War Preparations

Never has an imminent war been so loudly and publicly advertised as Israel's intended military aggression against Iran. When the Israeli Military Chief of Staff, Daniel Halutz, was asked how far Israel was ready to go to stop Iran's nuclear energy program, he said "Two thousand kilometers"—the distance of an air assault.[1] More specifically Israeli military sources revealed that Sharon had ordered Israel's armed forces to prepare for air strikes on uranium enrichment sites in Iran.[2] According to the London *Times*, the order to prepare for attack went through the Israeli defense ministry to the Chief of Staff. During the first week in December"...sources inside the special forces command confirmed that 'G' readiness—the highest state—for an operation was announced".[3]

On December 9, 2005, Israeli Minister of Defense, Shaul Mofaz, affirmed that in view of Teheran's nuclear plans, Tel Aviv should "not count on diplomatic negotiations but prepare other solutions."[4] In early December, Ahron Zoevi Farkash, the Israeli military intelligence chief, told the Israeli parliament (Knesset) that "if by the end of March, the international community is unable to refer the Iranian issue to the United Nations Security Council, then we can say that the international effort has run its course".[5]

In plain Hebrew, if international diplomatic negotiations fail to comply with Israel's (now extending) timetable, Israel will unilaterally militarily attack Iran. Benjamin Netanyahu, leader of the Likud Party and then-candidate for Prime Minister, stated that if Sharon did not act against Iran, "then when I form the new Israeli government (after the March 2006 elections) we'll do what we did in the past against Saddam's reactor."[6] In June 1981 Israel bombed the Osirak nuclear reactor in Iraq. Even the pro-Labor newspaper, *Haaretz*, while disagreeing with the time and place of Netanyahu's pronouncements,

If international diplomatic negotiations fail to comply with Israel's timetable, Israel will unilaterally militarily attack Iran.

agreed with its substance. *Haaretz* criticized "(those who) publicly recommend an Israeli military option..." because it "presents Israel as pushing (via powerful pro-Israel organizations in the US) the United States into a major war." However, *Haaretz* added... "Israel must go about making its preparations quietly and securely—not at election rallies."[7] *Haaretz*'s position, like that of the Labor Party, was that Israel should not advocate war against Iran before multi-lateral negotiations were over and the International Atomic Energy Agency made a decision.

In other words, the Israeli "debate" among the elite had not been over whether to go to war but over the *place* to discuss war plans and the timing to launch war. Implicitly *Haaretz* recognized the role played by pro-Israeli organizations in "pushing the US into the Iraq war", finding it advisable to perhaps insert a word of caution, resulting from increased US opposition to the activities of the Israel First campaigners in Congress (see below).

Israeli public opinion apparently does not share the political elite's plans for a military strike against Iran's nuclear program. A survey in the Israeli newspaper *Yedioth Ahronoth*, reported by *Reuters* (Dec. 16, 2005) showed that 58 percent of the Israelis polled believed the dispute over Iran's nuclear program should be handled diplomatically while only 36 percent said its reactors should be destroyed in a military strike.

Israel's War Deadline

All top Israeli officials pronounced the end of March 2006 as the deadline for launching a military assault on Iran. The thinking behind this date was to heighten the pressure on the US to force the sanctions issue in the Security Council. The tactic was to blackmail Washington with the "war or else" threat into pressuring Europe (namely Great Britain, France, Germany and Russia) into approving sanctions against Iran.

Israel knows that its acts of war will endanger thousands of American soldiers in Iraq, and it knows that Washington (and Europe) cannot afford a third war at this time. The end of March date also coincided with the IAEA report to the UN on Iran's nuclear energy program. Israeli policymakers believed that their threats might influence the report, or at least force the kind of ambiguities that could then be exploited by its overseas supporters to promote Security Council sanctions or justify Israeli military action.

Fixing a March date also *intensified* the political activities of the pro-Israel organizations in the United States. The major pro-Israel lobbies lined up a majority in the US Congress and Senate to push for the UN Security Council to implement economic sanctions against Iran or, failing that, endorse Israeli "defensive" action. Thousands of pro-Israel national, local and community groups and individuals have been mobilized to promote the Israeli agenda via the mass media and visits to US Congressional representatives.

The war agenda also plays on exploiting the tactical disputes among the civilian militarists within the White House, between Cheney, Bolton and Abrams on one side and Rice and Rumsfeld on the other. The Cheney line has always supported an Israeli military attack, while Rice promotes the tactic of "forced failure" of the European diplomatic route before taking decisive action. Rumsfeld, under tremendous pressure from practically all of the top professional military officials, fears that an Israeli war will further accelerate US military losses. The pro-Israel lobby would like to replace the ultra-militarist Rumsfeld with the ultra-militarist Senator Joseph Lieberman, an unconditional Israel First Zealot. The war, of course, has not yet materialized but the threat did increase the pressure from Washington on the Security Council to impose harsh economic sanctions on Iran.

US-Israeli Disagreements on an Iran War

As Israel and the Jewish lobbies intensified their efforts to provoke a US economic and military confrontation with Iran, disputes within the Washington Establishment surfaced. The conflicts and mutual attacks extended throughout the state institutions, and into the public discourse. Supporters and opponents of Israel's war policy represent powerful segments of state institutions and civil society. On the side of the Israeli war policy are practically all the major and most influential Jewish organizations, the pro-Israeli lobbies, their political action committees, a sector of the White House, a majority of subsidized Congressional representatives and state, local, and party leaders. On the other side are sectors of the Pentagon, State Department, a minority of Congressional members, a majority of public opinion, a minority of American Jews (Union of Reform Judaism) and the majority of active and retired military commanders who have served or are serving in Iraq.

Most of the discussion and debate in the US on Israel's war agenda has been dominated by the pro-Israeli organizations that transmit the Israeli state positions. The Jewish weekly newspaper, *Forward*, has reported a number of Israeli attacks on the Bush Administration for not acting more aggressively on behalf of Israel's policy. According to *Forward*, "Jerusalem is increasingly concerned that the Bush Administration is not doing enough to block Teheran from acquiring nuclear weapons…".[8] Further stark differences occurred during the semi-annual strategic dialogue between Israeli and US security officials, in which the Israelis opposed a US push for regime change in Syria, fearing the emergence of a possibly more radical Islamic regime. The Israeli officials also criticized the US for forcing Israel to agree to open the Rafah border crossing, upsetting their stranglehold on the economy in Gaza.

Predictably the biggest Jewish organization in the US, the Conference of Presidents of Major American Jewish Organizations (CPMAJO) immediately echoed the Israeli state line, as it has since its founding. Malcolm Hoenlan, President of the CPMAJO, lambasted Washington for a "failure of leadership on Iran" and "contracting the issue to Europe".[9] He went on to attack the Bush Administration for not following Israel's demands by delaying referring Iran to the UN Security Council for sanction. The leader of the CPMAJO then turned on French, German, and British negotiators, accusing them of "appeasement and weakness", and of not having a "game plan for decisive action"—presumably for not following Israel's 'sanction or bomb them' decisive action.

The role of AIPAC, the CPMAJO and other pro-Israeli organizations as transmission belts for Israel's bellicose war plans was evident in their November 28, 2005 condemnation of the Bush Administration agreement to give Russia a chance to negotiate a plan under which Iran would be allowed to enrich uranium under international supervision to ensure that its enriched uranium would not be used for military purposes. AIPAC's rejection of negotiations and demands for an immediate confrontation were based on the specious argument that it would "facilitate Iran's quest for nuclear weapons"— an argument which flies in the face of all known intelligence data (including Israel's) which says Iran is at least 3 to 10 years away from even approaching nuclear weaponry. AIPAC's unconditional and uncritical transmission of Israeli demands and criticism is usually clothed in the rhetoric of US interests or security in order to manipulate US policy. Accordingly, AIPAC chastised the Bush regime for endangering US security. By relying on negotiations, AIPAC accused, the Bush Administration would be "giving Iran yet another chance to manipulate [*sic*] the international community" and "pose a severe danger to the United States".[10]

Leading US spokesmen for Israel opposed President Bush's instructing his Ambassador to Iraq, Zalmay Khalilzad, to open a dialogue with Iran's Ambassador to Iraq. In addition, Israel's official 'restrained' reaction to Russia's sale to Teheran of more than a billion dollars worth of defensive anti-aircraft missiles, which might protect Iran from an Israeli air strike, was predictably echoed by the major Jewish organizations in the US. No doubt an important reason for Israel's setting an early deadline for its military assault on Iran was to act before Iran established a new satellite surveillance system and installed its new missile defense system.

Pushing the US into a confrontation with Iran via economic sanctions and military attack has been a top priority for Israel and its supporters in the US for more than a decade.[11] AIPAC believes the Islamic Republic poses a grave threat to Israel's supremacy in the Middle East. In line with its policy of forcing a US confrontation with Iran, AIPAC, the Israeli PACs (political action committees) and the CPMAJO have successfully lined up a majority of Congress people to challenge what they describe as the "appeasement" of Iran. According to the *Jewish Times*, "If it comes down to a political battle, signs are that AIPAC could muster strong support in Congress to press the White House to demand sanctions on Iran."[12]

Representative Ileana Ros-Lehtinen (R-Florida), who has the dubious distinction of being a collaborator with Cuban exile terrorist groups and unconditional backer of Israel's war policy, is chairwoman of the highly influential US House of Representatives Middle East subcommittee. From that platform she has echoed the CPMAJO line about "European appeasement and arming the terrorist regime in Teheran".[13] Ros-Lehtinen is "the main sponsor of two bills that have been front and center for AIPAC in recent months: the Iran Freedom Support Act, which was approved by the House last month [April 2006], and the Palestinian Anti-Terrorism Act, [which] is expected to be passed in the near future."[14] The Iran Freedom Support Act, H.R. 282, proposes "To hold the current regime in Iran accountable for its threatening behavior and to support a transition to democracy in Iran".

A similar bill was introduced by Senator Rick Santorum into the Senate in February 2005 which "codifies existing sanctions, controls and regulations in place against Iran; expands the list of entities that can be sanctioned under the Iran-Libya Sanction Act; and authorizes $10 million in assistance to pro-democracy groups opposed to the current Iranian regime."[15] Interestingly, the *Philadelphia Daily News* reported on May 22, 2006 that Senator Rick Santorum tops Public Citizen's list of Congressional receivers of lobbyist funds during the 1998-2004 election cycle. "Maybe voters, reporters," the *Philadelphia Daily News* concluded, "…should start asking more questions about just what Santorum might have done in return for all that dough."[16]

The pro-Israel Lobby's power, which includes AIPAC, the Conference of Presidents of Major Jewish Organizations, the PACs and hundreds of local formal and informal organizations, is magnified by their influence and hegemony over Congress, the mass media, financial institutions, pension funds and fundamentalist Christian organizations. Within the executive branch, their influence in these institutions amplifies their power far beyond their number and direct control and representation in strategic public and private institutions (which itself is formidable). AIPAC's "Progress and Policy Report for 2005"—published on its website—lists, among its accomplishments getting Congress to approve 100 pro-Israel legislative initiatives, $3 billion in direct aid and more than $10 billion in guaranteed loans, transfer of the most advanced military technology to Israel's multi-billion dollar arms export corporations, and the lining up of a 410 to 1 vote in the House of Representatives committing the US to Israel's security—*as it is defined by Israel.*

The pro-Israel Lobby's power, which includes AIPAC, the CPMAJO, the PACs and hundreds of local formal and informal organizations, is magnified by their influence over Congress, the mass media, financial institutions, pension funds and fundamentalist Christian organizations.

The conflict between the Israeli elite and the Bush Administration, to the extent that such appears to exist, has to be located in a broader context. Despite pro-Israeli attacks on US policy for its 'weakness' on Iran, Washington has moved as aggressively as circumstances permit. Facing European opposition to an immediate confrontation (as AIPAC and Israeli politicians demand) Washington supported European negotiations but imposed extremely limiting conditions, which were contrary to the terms of the Non-Proliferation Treaty, which allows uranium enrichment for peaceful purposes. The European "compromise" of forcing Iran to turn over the enrichment process to a foreign country (Russia) was not only a violation of its sovereignty, but also a policy that no other country using nuclear energy practices.

Given this transparently unacceptable "mandate", it is clear that Washington's 'support for negotiations' was a propaganda devise to provoke an Iranian rejection, and a means of securing Europe's support for a Security Council referral for international sanctions. Washington had absolutely no precedent to object to Russia's sale of defensive surface-to-air missiles to Iran, since it is standard in the arms export business. As for the Ambassadorial meetings in Iraq, the US has had great success in securing Iranian co-operation on stabilizing its Iraqi Shiite client regime. Iran has recognized the regime, has signed trade agreements, supported the dubious elections, and provided the US with intelligence against the Sunni resistance. Given their common interests in the region, it was logical for Washington to seek to bend Iran into further cooperation via diplomatic discussions. It is no surprise that the Zionist Organizations of America (ZOA) invited the most bellicose of US Middle East warmongers, UN Ambassador to the United Nations, John Bolton, to be its keynote speaker at its annual awards dinner.[17] The ZOA has loyally followed all the zigzags of Israeli policy since the foundation of the State.

Despite the near unanimous support and widespread influence of the major Jewish organizations, 20 percent of American Jews do not support Israel in its conflict with the Palestinians. Even more significantly, 61 percent of Jews almost never talk about Israel or defend Israel in conversation with Goyim (non-Jews).[18] Only 29 percent of Jews are active promoters of Israel. Even in Israel, the support fluctuates. As reported on NOW with Bill Moyers,

> **Sixty-one percent of Jews almost never talk about Israel or defend Israel in conversation with non-Jews. Only 29 percent of Jews are active promoters of Israel.**

> In late February 2002, a poll in Israel's largest paper, *Yediot Aharonot*, found majority support for evacuating all settlements in Gaza (57%) and some or all in the West Bank (59%). As tensions rose during the last year, national polls found a growing number of Israelis in favor of "transfer"—the removal of Palestinians from the West Bank. According to a June 2003 survey by Martin Indyk published in the journal FOREIGN AFFAIRS, found "Israeli public-opinion polls consistently show strong majorities in favor of a full settlement freeze and of evacuation of outlying settlements as part of a peace process that provides Israel with security."[19]

As for the settlers themselves, a further poll taken by Peace Now indicated that nearly 80 percent of the settlers moved to the West Bank to improve their quality of life[20]—expensive homes, swimming pools, gardens—a quality made possible by the American taxpayer.

It is important to note that the Israel First crowd represents less than a third of the Jewish community and hence their claim to speak for 'all' US Jews is false and a misrepresentation. In fact, there is more opposition to Israel among Jews than there is in the US Congress. Having said that, however, most Jewish critics of Israel are not influential in the big Jewish organizations and the Israel lobby; they are excluded from the mass media and mostly intimidated from speaking out, especially on Israel's war preparations against Iran. The minority Jewish critics cannot match the five to eight million dollars spent in buying Congressional votes each year by the pro-Israel lobbies.

The Israeli Defense Forces Chief of Staff, Daniel Halutz, has categorically denied that Iran represents an immediate nuclear threat to Israel, let along the United States. According to *Haaretz*,[21] Halutz stated that it would take Iran time to be able to produce a nuclear bomb—which he estimated might happen between 2008 and 2015.

Prior to the Israeli elections, Israel's Labor Party officials did not believe that Iran represented an immediate nuclear threat and felt that the Sharon government and the Likud war propaganda was an electoral ploy. According to *Haaretz*, "Labor Party officials…accused Prime Minister Ariel Sharon, Defense Minister Shaul Mofaz and other defense officials of using the Iran issue in their election campaigns in an effort to divert public debate from social issues".[22] In a message directed at the Israeli Right but equally applicable to AIPAC and the Conference of Presidents of Major Jewish Organizations in the US, Labor member of the Knesset, Benjamin Ben-Eliezer rejected electoral warmongering: "I hope the upcoming elections won't motivate the prime minister and defense minister to stray from government policy and place Israel on the frontlines of confrontation with Iran. The nuclear issue is an international issue and there is no reason for Israel to play a major role in it".[23] Unfortunately the Israel lobby made it a US issue and put Washington on the frontlines…

Post-election, however, with the departure of Sharon from the scene and Olmert having assumed power with the new Kadima party, the war agenda is back on track. On May 10, 2006, the Israeli *Yedioth Internet* headlined the program succinctly:

OLMERT TO ASK US ACT AGAINST IRAN:
PM set to visit Washington in two weeks for summit with President Bush; Olmert to point to link between Tehran nuclear threat, Hamas terror, demand Americans move against Iran.

Fabrication of Iran's Nuclear Threat

Israeli intelligence has determined that Iran has neither the enriched uranium nor the capability to produce an atomic weapon now or in the immediate future, in contrast to the hysterical claims publicized by the US pro-Israel lobbies. Mohammed El Baradei, head of the United Nations International Atomic Energy Agency (IAEA), which has inspected Iran for several years, has pointed out that the IAEA has found no proof that Iran is trying to construct nuclear weapons. He criticized Israeli and US war plans indirectly by warning that a "military solution would be completely unproductive".[24]

At one point, in a clear move to defuse the issue of the future use of enriched uranium, Iran even "opened the door for US help in building a nuclear power plant".[25] Iranian Foreign Ministry spokesman, Hamid Reza Asefi, speaking at a press conference, stated "America can take part in the international bidding for the construction of Iran's nuclear power plant if they observe the basic standards and quality".[26] Iran also plans to build several other nuclear power plants with foreign help. The Iranian call for foreign assistance is hardly the strategy of a country trying to conduct a covert atomic bomb program, especially one directed at involving one of its principal accusers, a state which has established as official policy its own willingness to use nuclear weapons, even against non-nuclear states.[27]

In April, 2006 Iranian President Mahmoud Ahmadinejad announced that Iran had successfully enriched uranium. However, at its current level of development, there is still no factual basis for arguing that Iran represents a nuclear threat to Israel or to the US forces in the Middle East, though Iranian pursuit of nuclear weapons would indeed be logical, given the blatant threat it faces from other powers determined to "transform the Middle East".

Israel's war preparations and AIPAC's efforts to push the US in the same direction based on falsified data or imminent threat is reminiscent of the fabricated evidence which was channeled to the White House through the Pentagon's Office of Special Plans led by Abram Shulsky and directed by Douglas Feith and Paul Wolfowitz, both long-time supporters of the Likud Party. Israel's war preparations are not over any present or future Iranian nuclear threat. The issue is over *future enrichment of uranium*, which is legal under the Non-Proliferation Treaty as is its use in producing electrical power. Iran currently is only in a uranium enrichment phase. Scores of countries with nuclear reactors by necessity use enriched uranium. The Iranian decision to advance to processing enriched uranium is its sovereign right as it is for all countries that possess nuclear reactors in Europe, Asia and North America.

The Iranian decision to advance to processing enriched uranium is its sovereign right as it is for all countries.

Israel and AIPAC's resort to the vague formulation of Iran's potential nuclear capacity is so open-ended that it could apply to scores of countries with a minimum scientific infrastructure. Even as the scare mongering proceeds apace, Brazil announced it had inaugurated a uranium enrichment center, capable of producing the kind of nuclear fuel that Iran wants to make despite international pressure against it.[28] There was no outcry against Brazil.

The European Quartet evaded the issue of whether or not Iran has atomic weapons or is manufacturing them and focused instead on attacking Iran's capacity to produce nuclear energy—namely the production of enriched uranium. It raised a bogus issue by conflating enriched uranium production with a nuclear threat, and nuclear potential with the danger of an imminent nuclear attack on Western countries, troops and Israel. The Europeans, especially Great Britain, had two options in mind: to impose an Iranian acceptance of limits on its sovereignty, more specifically on its energy policy and capacity to control the deadly air pollution of its major cities with cleaner sources of energy; or to force Iran to reject the arbitrary addendum to the Non-Proliferation Agreement and then to propagandize the rejection as an indication of Iran's evil intention to create atomic bombs and target pro-Western countries. The Western media would echo the US and European governments position that Iran was responsible for the breakdown of negotiations. The Europeans would then convince their public that since "reason" failed, the only recourse was to follow the US to take the issue to the Security Council and approve international sanctions against Iran where the US then would attempt to pressure Russia and China to vote in favor of sanctions or to abstain. However, it has become clear that neither country will agree, given the importance of the multi-billion dollar oil, arms, nuclear and trade deals between Iran and these two countries.

Having tried and failed in the Security Council, the US and Israel are likely to move toward a military attack. An air attack on suspected Iranian nuclear facilities will entail the bombing of heavily populated as well as remote regions leading to large-scale loss of life. Even a "limited" attack—bombing the Iranian Esfahan plant, alone—could lead to a horrific level of damage:

> A simulation of RNEP [Robust Nuclear Earth Penetrator] used against the Esfahan nuclear facility in Iran, using the software developed for the Pentagon, showed that 3 million people would be killed by radiation within 2 weeks of the explosion, and 35 million people in Afghanistan, Pakistan and India would be exposed to increased levels of cancer-causing radiation.[29]

The principal result will be a massive escalation of war throughout the Middle East. Iran, a country of 70 million, with several times the military forces that Iraq possessed and with highly motivated and committed military and paramilitary forces, can be expected to cross into Iraq. Iraqi Shiites sympathetic to or allied with Iran would most likely break their ties with Washington and go into combat. US military bases, troops and clients would be under tremendous attack. US military casualties would multiply. All troop withdrawal plans would be disrupted. The 'Iraqization' strategy would disintegrate, as the US 'loyal' Shia armed forces would turn against their American officers.

Beyond Iraq, there would likely be major military-civilian uprisings in Egypt, Saudi Arabia, Lebanon, Jordan, Palestine, and Pakistan. The conflagration would spread beyond the Middle East, as the Israel-US attack on an Islamic country would ignite mass protests throughout Asia. Most likely new terrorist incidents would occur in Western Europe, North America, and Australia and against US multinationals wherever their operations might be located. A bitter prolonged war would ensue, pitting 70 million unified Iranian nationals, millions of Muslims in Asia and Africa against an isolated US accompanied by its increasingly reluctant European allies[30] facing mass popular protests at home.

While the US effort to achieve sanctions at the UN appears to have failed, this does not mean that its effort to impose sanctions on Iran has ceased. Steven R. Weisman, writing in the *New York Times* on May 22, 2006, noted:

> Prodded by the United States with threats of fines and lost business, four of the biggest European banks have started curbing their activities in Iran, even in the absence of a Security Council resolution imposing economic sanctions on Iran for its suspected nuclear weapons program.

However, while the US appears determined to pursue sanctions by other means than through the UN, sanctions on Iran will not work because oil is a scarce and essential commodity. China, India, and other fast-growing Asian countries will balk at a boycott. Turkey and other Muslim countries will not cooperate. Numerous Western oil companies will work through intermediaries. The sanctions policy is predestined to failure; its only result will be to raise the price of oil even higher. An Israeli or US military attack will cause severe political instability and increase the risk to oil producers, shippers and buyers, raising the price of oil to astronomical heights, likely over $100 a barrel, destabilizing the world economy and provoking a major world recession or worse.

As for Israel, having failed in its attempt to precipitate a US military attack on Iran at the end of March, in large part because of the losses in Iraq, Israel then decided to raise tensions through an invasion and mass civilian bombing of Gaza and Lebanon, especially aimed at destroying Hezbollah, Iran's ally, in the hope of provoking an Iranian military response.

Conclusion

The only possible beneficiary of a US or Israeli military attack on Iran or economic sanctions will be Israel: this will *seem* to eliminate a military adversary in the Middle East, and consolidate its military supremacy in the Middle East. But even this outcome is problematic because it fails to take account of the fact that Iran's challenge to Israel is primarily *political*, and does not lie in its non-existent nuclear potential. The first target of the millions of Muslims protesting Israeli aggression will be the Arab regimes closest to

Israel. An Israeli attack would be a pyrrhic victory, if a predictable political conflagration unseats the rulers of Jordan, Egypt, Syria and Saudi Arabia. The consequences would be even worse if the US attacks: major oil wells burning, US troops in Iraq surrounded, long-term relations with Arab regimes undermined, increased oil prices and troop casualties inflaming domestic public opinion. An attack on Iran will not be a cleanly executed 'surgical' strike—it will be a deep jagged wound leading to gangrene.

No doubt AIPAC might celebrate "another success" for Israel in its yearly self-congratulatory report of missions accomplished. The Conference of Presidents of Major Jewish Organizations in America will thank their obedient and loyal congressional followers for approving the destruction of an 'anti-Semitic and anti-American nuclear threat to all of humanity' or some similar rubbish.

The big losers of a US-Israeli military attack on Iran are the US soldiers in Iraq and other Middle Eastern countries who will be killed and maimed, the US public which will pay in blood and bloated deficits, the oil companies which will see their oil supplies disrupted, and their new multi-billion dollar joint oil exploitation contracts undermined, the Palestinians who will suffer the consequences of greater repression and massive displacement, the Lebanese people who will be forcibly entangled in a new border war, and the Europeans who will face terrorist retaliations.

Already, it seems fair to say, the US is suffering geo-political repercussions from its unreasonable targeting of Iran and, in the eyes of the Muslim world, Islamic populations. While as yet they attend only as observers, Iran and also Pakistan are seeking to join the new Shanghai Cooperation Organization (SCO),[31] which, though not yet officially a mutual defense organization similar to NATO, has nonetheless already envisaged conducting joint military operations. While China has said that no new decisions on membership are immediately pending, Russian President Vladimir Putin "suggested that the alliance form an 'energy club' but offered no details in public sessions."[32] Clearly, this is far from the end of the matter:

> ...the SCO's influence in the region is on the rise... a stronger SCO, particularly one with a military component and Iran as a full member, might serve as a check to U.S. interests and ambitions in the region. "An expanded SCO would control a large part of the world's oil and gas reserves and nuclear arsenal," David Wall, an expert on the region at the University of Cambridge's East Asia Institute, told the *Washington Times*. "It would essentially be an OPEC with bombs."[33]

Has US policy towards Iran been serving its own imperial interests, then—or actually and unnecessarily pushing Iran into the arms of its former and future rivals?

It is important to stress that except for the Israeli lobby in the US and its grass root Jewish American supporters and allies among the Conference of Presidents of Major Jewish organizations, there are no other organized lobbies pressuring for this war. Sadly, neither has there been significant domestic resistance to it. The ritualistic denunciations of "Big Oil" whenever there is a Middle East conflict involving the US is in this instance a totally bogus issue, lacking any substance. All the evidence is to the contrary—Big Oil is opposed to any conflicts that will upset their first major entry into Middle Eastern oil fields since they were nationalized in the 1970's.

The only identifiable organized political force that has successfully made deep inroads in the US Congress and in sectors of the Executive Branch are the pro-Israel lobbies and PAC's. The major proponents of a confrontationist policy in the Executive Branch are led by pro-Israel neo-conservative National Security Council member (and Presidentially pardoned felon) Elliott Abrams, in charge of Middle East policy, and Vice President Cheney. The principle

Except for the Israeli lobby in the US and its grass root Jewish American supporters and allies, there are no other organized lobbies pressuring for this war.

opposition is found in the major military services, among commanders, who clearly see the disastrous strategic consequences for the US military forces and sectors of the State Department and CIA, who are certainly aware of the disastrous consequences for the US of supporting Israel's quest for uncontested regional supremacy. Doubt has extended even to those whose support might once have been assumed: analysts at the rightwing Heritage Foundation, and leadership elements within the Iranian exile community. [34]

The problem is that there is no political leadership to oppose the pro-Israel war lobby within Congress or even in civil society. There are few if any influential organized lobbies challenging the pro-war Israel Lobby either from the perspective of working for coexistence in the Middle East or even defending US national interests when they diverge from those of Israel. Although numerous former diplomats, generals, intelligence officials, Reformed Jews, retired National Security advisers and State Department professionals have publicly denounced the Iran war agenda and even criticized the Israel First lobbies, their newspaper ads and media interviews have not been backed by any national political organization that can compete for influence in the White House and Congress. As we draw closer to a major confrontation with Iran and Israeli officials set short term deadlines for igniting a Middle East conflagration, it seems that we are doomed to learn from future catastrophic losses that Americans must organize to defeat political lobbies based on overseas allegiances.

ENDNOTES

[1] *Financial Times*, Dec 12, 2005.

[2] *Times*, Dec 11, 2005.

[3] *Times*, Dec. 11, 2005.

[4] *La Jornada*, Dec. 10, 2005.

[5] *Times*, Dec. 11, 2005.

[6] *Times*, Dec 11, 2005.

[7] *Haaretz*, Dec 6, 2005.

[8] *Forward*, Dec. 9, 2005.

[9] *Forward*, Dec. 9, 2005.

[10] *Forward*, Dec. 9, 2005.

[11] *Jewish Times/Jewish Telegraph Agency*, Dec. 6, 2005.

[12] *Jewish Times*, Dec. 6, 2005.

[13] *Jewish Times*, Dec. 6, 2005.

[14] Ted Siefer, "Pro-Israel Congresswoman addresses AIPAC", *The Jewish Advocate*, May 12, 2006.

[15] Ron Strom, "Bill supporting freedom for Iran Introduced", WorldNetDaily.com. Interestingly, Senator Rick Santorum heads the list.

[16] Will Bunch, "Lobbyist Money: He's No. 1!, He's No. 1!", *Philadelphia Daily News*, May 22nd, 2006.

[17] ZOA Press Release, Dec. 11, 2005.

[18] *Jerusalem Post*, Dec 1, 2005.

[19] NOW with Bill Moyers: "Road to the Road Map", "<http://www.pbs.org/now/politics/settlements2.html>

[20] Ibid.

[21] *Haaretz*, Dec. 14, 2005.

[22] *Haaretz*, Dec. 14, 2005.

[23] *Haaretz*, Dec. 14, 2005.

[24] *Financial Times*, Dec. 10/11, 2005.

[25] *USA Today*, Dec. 11, 2005.

[26] *USA Today*, Dec. 11, 2005.

[27] Clinton Presidential Decision Directive 60. See Francis A. Boyle, *The Criminality of Nuclear Deterrence*, Clarity Press, Inc., 2002, pp. 46-48.

[28] Brazil Builds Nuke Facility", *Miami Herald*, May 7, 2006.

[29] Union of Concerned Scientists, May 2005. See <http://www.ucsusa.org/global_security/nuclear_weapons/the-robust-nuclear-earth-penetrator-rnep.html>

[30] While UK Foreign Secretary Jack Straw, who viewed war with Iran as "inconceivable", has now been replaced following an angry call from Bush ("Did Bush Force Straw Out?: London Papers: Foreign Secretary Jack Straw's Iran Stance Prompted Angry Bush Call To Blair" CBS News, May 7, 2006), British airfields are still off-limits, a difficulty addressed in the latest US strike plans aimed at Iran. "Strategists are understood to have presented two options for pinpoint strikes using B2 bombers flying directly from bases in Missouri, Guam in the Pacific and Diego Garcia in the Indian Ocean. RAF Fairford in Gloucester also has facilities for B2s but this has been ruled out because of the UK's opposition to military action against Tehran." "US Spells Out Plan to Bomb Iran", *The Herald*, May 16, 2006.

[31] Tim Johnson, "Iran, Pakistan Seek to Join Shanghai Cooperation Organization", Knight Ridder, June 15, 2006.

[32] Johnson, supra.

[33] Lionel Beehner, "The Rise of the Shanghai Cooperation Organization", International Institute for Strategic Studies website, <http://www.iiss.org/whats-new/iiss-in-the-press/june-2006/rise-of-the-shanghai-cooperation-organization> June 12, 2006.

[34] See Jim Lobe, "Iran Showdown Tests Power of Israel Lobby", IPS, April 11, 2006.

CHAPTER 10

THE CARICATURES IN MIDDLE EAST POLITICS

The centerpiece of the explosive confrontation between Islamic and Arab protestors, political leaders and governments, and the US and Western European regimes and publishers over caricatures published in Denmark is rooted in Israeli efforts to polarize the world in its favor and to promote isolation, economic sanctions and/or a military attack on Iran. There are several key questions, which almost all commentators and analysts have failed to address. These include:

• Why did the "cartoons" get published in Denmark?

• What is the political background of "Flemming Rose", the cultural editor of *Jyllands-Posten*, who solicited, selected and published the cartoons?

• What larger issues coincide with the *timing* of the cartoons publication and reproduction?

• Who "benefits" from the publication of the cartoons and the ensuing confrontation between the Arabs/Islam and the West?

• What is the contemporary political context of the Arab/Islamic protests?

• How is the Israeli secret service, Mossad, implicated in provoking the Western-Islamic/Arab conflict, and how do the consequences measure up to their expectations?

A starting point for analyzing the cartoon controversy, which has been a focus for attacking Muslims and Muslim countries as intolerant of Western 'freedom of expression' is the longstanding role of Denmark as a major operation point for Mossad activity in Europe. Re-phrased: How could a tiny Scandinavian country of 5.4 million citizens and residents (200,000 or less than 3% of whom are Muslim), renowned for fairy tales, ham and cheese, have become a target for the fury of millions of practicing Muslims from Afghanistan to Palestine, from Indonesia to Libya, pouring into the streets of cities all over the world with significant Muslim populations? Why, after the bombing of Baghdad, the tortures of Abu Ghraib, the massacres in Fallujah and the utter destitution of the entire Iraqi and Afghan people…would Muslims turn their anger at symbols of Denmark from its tinned cookies to its Embassies and overseas business offices?

The story, presented with straight faces by television newspeople, is of Mr. 'Flemming Rose', a crusading cultural editor of a widely read Danish daily newspaper who wanted to counter the growing 'political correctness' of Europeans about criticizing Muslims, which he compared to the 'self-censorship' he had witnessed in his native Soviet Union. The oddly-named Ukrainian-born editor of the culture page of the *Jyllands-Posten* commissioned Danish cartoonists to submit a series of cartoons depicting the Prophet Muhammad as they (the Danish cartoonists) might imagine him. However four of the twelve cartoons selected for publication were illustrated by 'Rose's' own staff, including the most controversial 'bomb in the turban' one. Braving Denmark's anti-blasphemy laws, Mr. Rose published the cartoons on September 30, 2005 and the rest is history…

A huge worldwide attack on what was portrayed as the West's "sacred right to free expression" erupted in the Muslim world with millions of shocked Europeans and North Americans rushing to defend their cherished freedoms in this 'clash of civilizations'. Syria and Iran were prominently blamed for the stirring up of furious believers in the streets of Damascus and Teheran, and in Beirut and the slums of Gaza. According to US Secretary Rice, "Iran and Syria have gone out of their way to inflame sentiments and to use this to their own purposes and the world ought to call them on it." The Pakistani and Libyan authorities[1] allied to the US fired on demonstrators, killing and wounding scores while numerous religious leaders were arrested. The Western governments urged their Arab and Muslim allies to prevent more attacks on Danish products and property, and blamed those unable to quell the fury with complicity and instigation. All of this was over a series of cartoons, or so we are told.

The cultural editor, 'Flemming Rose', who soon tired of being surrounded by a team of Danish police and security to protect him from assassination, and missing his daily jogs through his tranquil Copenhagen neighborhood, chose to seek safe haven in Miami, Florida (rather than his native Ukraine) among the Cuban exiles, Israeli *sayanim* and Mah Jong-playing retirees as the drama played on.

Denmark: Center of Mossad Activity

Why Denmark? Could this crudely manufactured controversy have been generated on the pages of any major London or New York paper? Who would wish to put Denmark at the center of this 'clash of civilization'—appearing as a script from some grade B Islamophobic thriller?

An interesting chapter in former Israeli Mossad agent Victor J. Ostrovsky's book, *By Way of Deception*,[2] outlines the close relationship between the workings of the Danish intelligence services and the Israeli Mossad over decades:

> The relationship between the Mossad and Danish intelligence is so intimate as to be indecent. But it is not the Mossad's virtue that is compromised by the arrangement; it's Denmark's. And that's because the Danish are under the mistaken impression that because they saved a lot of Jews in World War II, the Israelis are grateful and they can trust the Mossad.

The Mossad has the capacity to monitor the entire population of Arabs and especially Palestinians (presumably including those with Danish citizenship) in Denmark through their special relations with the Danes:

> …a Mossad man monitors all Arabic and Palestinian-related messages [among Denmark's Arab community] coming into their [the Danish Civil Security Service] headquarters…an extraordinary arrangement for a foreign intelligence service.

The Danish Intelligence officers' high regard for their Israeli Mossad office mates is apparently not, according to Ostrovsky, reciprocated:

> The Mossad have such contempt for their Danish counterparts that they refer to them as 'fertsalach', the Hebrew term for a small burst of gas, a fart…they tell the Mossad everything they do.[3]

In return for their servility, the Danes get valuable 'training' from the Israelis. "Once every three years, Danish intelligence officials go to Israel for a seminar conducted by the Mossad" which generates useful contacts for the Mossad "while perpetuating the notion that no organization deals with terrorism better than they (Mossad) do."

In the wake of the US debacle in Iraq and the world's resistance to a massive 'preemptive military attack' or economic and diplomatic embargo of

Iran, which could send oil prices to over $100 a barrel, Israel needed to turn the war of ideas on its head. It would make sense that a propaganda campaign, aimed to further whip up justifications to attack countries like Iran and Syria (at the time of the cartoons' publication, Israel's current enemy du jour), should emanate from one of the US' strongest European allies in the invasion and destruction of Iraq and Afghanistan, one whose national intelligence apparatus (so fondly known as 'fertsalach') would be eager to serve Israel's interest.

Flemming (or *Flaming*) Rose: Journalist with a Cause

Given Mossad's longstanding penetration of the Danish intelligence agencies, and its close working relations with the rightwing media, it is not surprising that a Ukrainian Jew, operating under the name of "Flemming Rose" with close working relations with the Israeli state (and in particular the far right Likud regime) should be the center of the controversy over the cartoons.

A Ukrainian Jew, operating under the name of "Flemming Rose", with close working relations with the Israeli state (and in particular the far right Likud regime), commissioned the cartoons.

"Rose's" ties to the Israeli state antedate his well-known promotional "interview" with Daniel Pipes (2004), the notorious Arab-hating Zionist ideologue. Prior to being placed as a cultural editor of a leading rightwing Danish daily, from 1990 to 1995 "Rose" was a Moscow-based reporter who translated into Danish a self-serving autobiography by Boris Yeltsin, godchild of the pro-Israeli, post-communist Russian oligarchs, most of whom held dual Russian-Israeli citizenship and collaborated with the Mossad in laundering illicit billions. Between 1996-1999 "Rose" the journalist worked the Washington circuit (traveling with Clinton to China) before returning to Moscow (1999-2004) as a reporter for *Jyllands-Posten*. In 2005 he became its cultural editor, despite little or no knowledge of the field, and over the heads of other Danish journalists on the staff. In his new position "Rose" found a powerful platform to incite and play on the growing hostility of conservative Danes to immigrants from the Middle East, particularly practicing Muslims. Using the format of an 'interview' he published Pipes' virulent anti-Islamic diatribe, probably to "test the waters" before proceeding to the next stage in the Mossad strategy to polarize a West-East confrontation.

Provoking Conflict Between Muslims and the West

While the Zionists succeeded in their goals in Iraq—establishing a beachhead in the northern Kurdish enclave ('Kurdistan'), and securing assets in the new "Iraqi" regime via Chalabi and others—Israeli strategic plans to extend US military operations to Iran and Syria were facing major challenges from within the US military and public and even sections of the mass media. Mossad assets in the *New York Times*, *Wall Street Journal* and elsewhere had to settle for puff pieces proclaiming Iran's (non-existent) nuclear weapons threat, right after the same plot with regard to Iraq was exposed as a total fabrication. Another line of propaganda was needed to silence war critics and heighten animosities towards the Islamists/Arabs in general and Iran in particular. This is where the "Flemming Rose"/Mossad operation came into the picture.

The Islamic-hate cartoons were published in Denmark in September 2005 as Israeli and US Zionists escalated their war propaganda against Iran. The initial response from the Islamic countries, however, was limited. The story wasn't picked up in the *International Herald Journal* until late December 2005. By early January 2006, Mossad "Katsas" (Hebrew for case officers) activated *sayanim* (volunteer Jewish collaborators outside of Israel) throughout Western and Eastern European media to simultaneously reproduce the cartoons on Feb. 1 and 2, 2006. One such *sayan* operation would have been the decision by *France-Soir* Senior Editor Arnaud Levy and Editor in Chief Serge Faubert to publish the cartoons. The paper's French-Egyptian Roman Catholic owner almost immediately fired the paper's Managing Editor, Jacques Lefranc, who, according to an interview with CNN, had initially opposed their publication, without touching Levy and Faubert.

After their first publication in September, 2005, drew little Muslim notice, the cartoons were then *simultaneously reproduced* throughout Western and Eastern European media on Feb. 1 and 2, 2006.

A strident campaign was launched in practically all the pro-Western mass media condemning the initial, relatively moderate Islamic protests, which had occurred between September to December 2005 and rapidly provoked the subsequent massive escalation, doubtlessly aided by covert Mossad operatives among Arab populations. Mossad's 'little farts', the Danish intelligence, fanned the fires by advising Denmark's rightwing Prime Minister Anders Fogh Rasmussen not to give way by refusing to apologize as the pro-Western Arab regimes requested and even refusing a request for a meeting with a group of Denmark-based diplomats from Arab and Muslim countries to discuss the 'situation'.

"Flemming Rose"/Mossad tried one more gambit to further heighten East-West tension. He publicly offered to publish any Iranian cartoons which would mock the Holocaust in 'his' paper. The senior editor of *Jyllands-Posten* apparently belatedly caught on to "Flemming Rose's" hidden agenda and vetoed the 'offer', asking Rose to take a leave of absence. Rose left for

Miami, not Tel Aviv—where his residency might raise suspicions about his claim to be merely an opponent of "self-censorship". In Miami, he no doubt will have the protection of the locally based *sayanim*, armed and trained for "self-defense" of threatened Zionists.

Sayanim—Defenders of Western Civilization

The *sayanim*, a name derived according to Victor Ostrovsky from the Hebrew word '*to help',* are a huge worldwide network of Jews in strategic or useful places (real estate, mass media, finance, car dealerships, etc.) who have agreed to help Israeli Mossad activities within their own countries. This has been ascribed to the supra-national loyalty *sayanim* offer to Israel, above and not always in the interest of, their home country. According to Gordon Thomas and Martin Dillon in their detailed biography, *Robert Maxwell, Israel's Superspy*,[4] the notorious media mogul, Robert Maxwell, was a super-*sayan*, providing cover, offices, political connections, money-laundering services *and* planting stories in the service of Israel at Mossad's behest.

The activities of these 'helpers' range from the spectacular to the more mundane and, according to Victor Ostrovsky, in his 1990 biography *By Way of Deception*, the *sayanim* represent a pool of thousands of active and inactive individuals who can provide services discretely out of loyalty to 'the cause of Israel' as defined by any current Mossad operation. The cynicism of this arrangement is clear: it makes little difference to the Mossad if an operation such as 'Flemming Rose' jeopardizes the national and economic interests of the *sayan's* own country and, if exposed, might harm the status of Jews in the Diaspora. The standard response from the Mossad would be: "So what's the worst that could happen to those Jews? They'd all come to Israel? Great." This recklessness clearly has ramifications for Jews who have refused to be recruited as Mossad helpers in affected countries.

Mossad War Propaganda and the "Cartoon Controversy"

Israeli leaders expressed their opposition to the Bush Administration's diplomatic efforts to engage the European powers in the Iran negotiations, which delayed action against Iran. Automatically and without question all the major Zionist and Jewish organizations in the US (AIPAC, Conference of Presidents of Major Jewish Organizations, ADL and others) unleashed a sustained national campaign to mobilize Congress and their "friends" in the executive branch to take immediate military action or to impose economic sanctions on Iran. However the Bush Administration, while in agreement, lacked public support in the US and among its European allies and their national electorates for such a policy.

The Mossad policy was to create a pretext to *polarize* public opinion between the Middle East (and beyond) and the West in order to escalate tensions and demonize Islamic adversaries to its Middle East hegemonic pretensions. The "Rose" cartoons served the Mossad perfectly. The issue could be presented as a free speech issue, a conflict of "values" not "interests", between the "democratic West" and the fundamentalist "totalitarian" (as characterized by Pipes-Rose) Islamists.

Nothing could be further from the truth. Rose had solicited and selected the Islamic caricatures while his paper had rejected similar cartoons of Jesus Christ in an earlier context. The image of Rose as a "cultural iconoclast"—while working for a **The Mossad policy was to create a pretext to *polarize* public opinion between the Middle East (and beyond) and the West.** rightwing daily whose daily fare was publishing anti-(Mid-East)immigrant "news stories" and favorable interviews with Zionist extremists—is prima facie not credible, although that image has been purveyed by all the major media outlets. Further, while "Rose" may have *initiated* the international tensions, the efforts of his liberal and neo-con colleagues and his comrades in and out of the Mossad publicizing the appearance of the caricatures were required even to be able to reach and thereby provoke the ire of the Arab and Islamic world. This explains the delay between the original publication of the cartoons, and the massive Muslim response that erupted months later.

The cartoons, the subsequent insults and calumnies attacking the Islamic protestors and their secular allies throughout Africa, the Middle East, Asia and Europe, eventually provoked major peaceful and then violent protests by millions of people. Visual images of violent protests and demonstrations were featured by the Western mass media, successfully creating the intended fear and apprehension against Muslim countries and minorities in Europe. Islamophobia gained momentum. Zionist propagandists in Europe and the US linked the "defense of free speech" issue to Israeli "security" policies. While the West was engaged in calumniating the Islamic protestors, Israel blockaded Gaza and the US and Europe cut off all funding to the Palestinians, threatening the population with mass starvation for exercising its democratic right to elect its own leaders! "Rose's" free speech charade revived the discredited ZionCon doctrine of the "Clash of Civilizations". Playing on European Islamophobia and the increasing sensitivity of practising Muslims and Arab nationalists to Western abuses, it is likely that Israeli psych-war experts pinpointed the "free speech" issue as the ideal detonator for the conflict.

The democratic electoral victory of Hamas—dubbed by Israel as a terrorist movement—accelerated Israeli efforts to convince Western governments to insist that regimes in Muslim countries repress the 'irrational Islamic masses' or face Western censure or elimination of aid. (The failure to crack down violently on demonstrators was presented by the Western media as official approval or instigation) The major US Zionist organizations were able to influence Secretary of State Rice into blaming Iran and Syria for fomenting the worldwide demonstrations from Gaza to the Philippines. The Israeli strategy was to use European outrage to weaken opposition to a military attack or economic sanctions on Iran and Syria—or preceding that, on Gaza and Lebanon.

Beyond Religious Blasphemy

While most establishment analysts have narrowly focused on the cartoon as the source and target of the massive global demonstrations, in fact it is at best the immediate detonator of a whole series of ongoing events of much greater *political* significance. From the "shock and awe" carpet bombing of Iraq, to the mass torture and routine everyday humiliation in occupied countries, from the utter destruction of Fallujah (now a symbol of American annihilation as Guernica has been for the Nazis) to Israeli devastation of Jenin and Palestine, from the everyday assassinations of Palestinians by the Israeli occupiers, to the smearing of the Qur'an with filth at Guantanamo, Israel, the US and Europe have attempted to demonstrate that no Muslims are safe anywhere—not in their schools, homes, offices, fields, factories or mosques—and that *nothing they hold dear is sacred*.

The reason that millions were demonstrating against a caricature of Muhammad published in an insignificant Scandinavian rightwing newspaper is that this was the last straw—the detonator—of a series of deliberate violations of fundamental social and political rights of Muslim, Arab and colonized peoples. While the Western media have focused exclusively on the religious content of the demonstrators, almost every country where massive sustained demonstrations have taken place has been subject to recent Western intervention, large-scale pillage of raw materials and/or experienced the destruction of their secular rights: countries invaded; homes, schools, hospitals, systems of health and clean water demolished; agriculture and natural resources looted; museums, libraries, and archeological sites pillaged and mosques desecrated. The West has rendered present conditions for material existence an inferno for all the peoples (both secular and observant) living in Arab or Islamic countries. Now their most profound historic, spiritual reference point, the Prophet Muhammad—the most cherished religious figure—has been repeatedly trampled with impunity by arrogant imperialists and their media servants, aided and abetted by the Israeli state and its overseas *sayanim* operatives. It is a gross misrepresentation to suggest that practicing Muslims could desecrate Jesus Christ with impunity when Jesus is among the revered prophets of Islam; that too is forbidden by the Qur'an, and would be abhorrent to the thought of Muslims.

As the Israeli strategists well knew in advance, the vilification of

Islam was not taking place in a political vacuum. The material conditions for an Islamic-Arab uprising were ripe: Hamas had swept the Palestinian elections, the US military were aware that they were losing the war in Iraq, Iran was refusing to capitulate, Bush was losing public support for ongoing and future Middle Eastern wars, AIPAC, Israel's main political instrument for influencing US policy, was under criminal investigation...Israel's strategy of having the US fight its wars was boomeranging. There was a need to revive the politico-military tensions which they had exploited after September 11, 2001 to Israel's advantage: hence the "Flemming Rose" provocation, hence the coordinated, widespread promotion of the act, hence the free speech agitation among Western *sayanim*, liberals, conservatives and neocon ideologues, hence the predictable explosion of protest, hence the 'recreation' of Mideast tension...and the advances of Israel's agenda.

Clearly the burgeoning confrontation portends more than simply a religious or free speech issue, more than the crude provocations of an errant cultural editor coddled by the 'little farts' of a penetrated Danish intelligence agency. What is at stake is the deliberate racist stereotyping of Arab, Islamic, and Third World peoples in order to sustain and deepen their oppression, exploitation and subordination, and Western willingness to accept this process, despite all protections against incitement of hatred, whether enshrined in international or domestic law.

What is at stake is the deliberate racist stereotyping of Arab, Islamic, and Third World peoples in order to sustain and deepen their oppression, exploitation and subordination, and Western willingness to accept this process.

The most pervasive, prolific, and influential sources of racist Arab stereotypes are Israel and its overseas (particularly US and European) academics, terror 'experts', and psychologists at the most prestigious universities and think tanks, who have provided the "psychological profile" to torture, humiliate, provoke, and repress the millions struggling for self-determination against colonial and imperial dominance.

Once again Israel and especially its overseas operatives have placed the expansion and militarist interests of Israel above the interests of the peoples of the US and Europe. The criterion "Is it good for the Jews?" as defined by the Israeli state, has led to the blind alley of massive confrontations and deepening animosity between Arab/Muslim peoples and Western regimes. What appeared so clever to the 'Roses' of the world and their *Katsas* and docile *sayanim*, in provoking confrontation, may once again boomerang: The uprisings may go beyond protesting symbols of vilification to attacking the substance of power, including the Arab and Muslim pro-consuls and collaborators of Euro-American political and economic power. While the Mossad is very astute in infiltrating and provoking oppressed groups, it has been singularly inept in controlling and containing the resultant uprisings as the recent victory of Hamas demonstrates and the success of the Iraqi resistance illustrates. The next controversial cartoon may show Moses leading his people into the desert.

Epilogue

While the Mossad-provoked controversy between the West and the Islamic peoples—framed as 'free speech versus blasphemy' rather than 'free speech versus incitement to hatred'—continues to deepen, Israel has proceeded to impose a Nazi-like economic siege over 4 million Palestinians *intended* to starve them into surrendering their democratic freedoms. Intended is the concise term, Gideon Levy, columnist for the Israeli daily newspaper *Haaretz*[5] records Dov Weissglas, advisor to the Israeli Prime Minister, jokingly telling top officials: *"Its (the economic blockage—which may include electricity and water, as well as food) like an appointment with a dietician. The Palestinians will get a lot thinner but won't die."* The Israeli officials "rolled with laughter". As Levy points out "more than half of all Palestinians are already living in poverty…last year 37% had difficulties obtaining food… 54% of the residents of Gaza cut back the amount of food they consume…child mortality rose by 15%…unemployment reached 28%." Planned pre-meditated mass starvation of a ghettoized population, jokingly discarded by its executioners as a 'visit to the dietician', is an exact replica of the internal policy discussion of the Nazi high command over the population in the Warsaw Ghetto. Israel's capacity to impose and implement a genocidal policy has been greatly facilitated by the symbolic sideshow that the Mossad-'Rose' orchestrated in Western Europe. "Cultural" conflict at the service of genocide—is hardly a clever ruse or merely a violation of Islamic sensibilities, it is a crime against humanity.

ENDNOTES

[1]   However, the Libyan parliament suspended the Minister of the Interior following the deaths of 11 protesters.

[2]   Victor Ostransky, *By Way of Deception,* New York, St. Martin's Press, 1990, pp. 231-232.

[3]   Ibid.

[4]   Gordon Thomas and Martin Dillon, *Robert Maxwell, Israel's Superspy*, Carroll and Graf Publishers, 2002

[5]   *Haaretz,* Feb. 19, 2006.

PART III

EXPERTS ON TERROR OR TERRORIST EXPERTS?

CHAPTER 11

EXPERTS ON TERROR

LOOKING IN THE MIRROR

After reading hundreds of books and articles and listening to scores of speeches and interviews by experts on terrorism and terrorists from the US, Canada, Israel, Europe, Latin America, Asia and South Africa, I have come to the conclusion that there are recurring patterns. They use a common language to describe their subjects and their environment, they are extremely ideological under a thin veneer of scientific jargon, they possess a keen sense of selective observation, they always pretend to possess a psychological understanding though few if any have dealt close up with their subjects in any clinical sense except perhaps under conditions of incarceration and interrogation.

Their style is righteous, highly moralistic, vitriolic, given to hyperventilation, and yet facile with euphemisms to describe the violence of their partisan states. Their analysis is almost always filled with highly charged personalistic/individualistic invective, and views their subjects as devoid of any political motivations.

This psychobabble provides a "legitimate-sounding" channel for expressing deep-seated hostility, a method for assuming a posture of civilized superiority in the face of their dehumanized subjects. The dehumanization process is central to the whole terrorist-political-academic enterprise—for the purpose is to present "the terrorist" as one with no redeeming features, with no 'place' in the world, no 'time' for affection—in other words, worthy of physical extermination. The Terrorist Experts are the "set-up" people. They **The purpose is to present "the terrorist" as one with no redeeming features, with no 'place' in the world, no 'time' for affection—in other words, worthy of physical extermination.** motivate the colonial and imperial conquerors and reinforce their idea that the terrorists are not worthy of ruling or being ruled in regions of wealth or even of living in any territory contiguous to "civilized" or "chosen" people.

The Terrorist Experts project the violence of the rulers, their conquistadorial ambitions, their greed to seize land and resources, and their savage destructive impulses onto their victims while the responses of the victims, the survivors, are clothed in the rhetoric of pathological behavior. The really clinical pathologies are to be found, however, in the minds of the verbal assassins—who cannot decipher the causal relation between the repeated rapes and tortures committed by their patron-states and the desperate cries and attempts at self-defense of the excluded, displaced, and exploited, or arrive at any appropriate moral conclusion.

Almost all the terror experts have a chronic psychological blindness to the systematic and comprehensive violence inflicted by the West and Israel on particular groups. Today it is the "Arabs"; at others times it is all insurgents who respond to imperial violence with violence.

Almost all the terror experts have a chronic psychological blindness to the systematic and comprehensive violence inflicted by the West and Israel on particular groups.

The all-pervasive practice of torture is a means of breaking and converting militants, and then infiltrating resistance movements. This interrogation method receives ideological justification and moral support from the Terror Experts. In their writings, insurgents or 'terrorists' are described as beyond the human pale— as sub-human, in a "trance". Their leaders are described as cynical profiteers and manipulators who have no human values or goals. Their communities are "lawless pockets". Once committed to the cause (the merits of which remain unacknowledged, undiscussed), they know no law, no justice—only death, murder, and martyrdom. They live in failed states. They have no history or culture (or at least one inferior to 'Western', 'Judeo-Christian' civilization). In a word, the world will be better without them.

To the torturer, this means his or her work is in the best interest of civilization. The Terror Experts are offended when the practitioners of torture are exposed, their handicraft of brutality photographed and published throughout the world's media. The Terror Experts are grieved, not for the acts of moral degradation, but because it confirms what the "terrorists" have been saying—that they revolt out of the outrage and humiliation they suffer at the hands of their US/Israeli/European torturers, soldiers, mercenaries and bosses. Terror Experts protest at the *public exposure*: the dirty secrets absent from their analysis have become public knowledge and raise the specter of causality. After all, they had attributed feelings of "anger" and "humiliation" to the purported personality disorders, childhood or family or cultural/religious dysfunctions of the "terrorists". The statements of the Terror Experts become less convincing in the face of publicized facts of physical humiliation by the armies and states of the purported "civilizers".

The Terror Expert Genre

A lead article published in the *Weekend Financial Times* by Professor Jessica Stern titled "How Terrorists Think"[1] is emblematic of the Terror

Expert genre. Stern is identified as a lecturer at Harvard's John F. Kennedy School of Government and the author of a recent book, *Terror in the Name of God: Why Religious Militants Kill*.[2] Published in the most prestigious business newspaper, employed by a leading elite private university, with a book edited by a major publisher, Stern has all the right credentials to be regarded as a Terror Expert rather than a propagandist.

The Terror Experts operate and see themselves on two levels: as 'scholarly researchers' and as political prosecutors and 'security' advisors. As 'experts' their work is of dubious quality despite the self-declared wealth of sources they claim to have consulted. Many of the alleged "terrorists" were interviewed in jail where they most likely had been tortured and drugged. Their conversations would have been monitored. They hardly enjoyed the minimum conditions required to give a fair interview. Even so, the Terror Expert can be expected to edit out any excerpts that provide a political context for their actions, as their psychology-based methodology requires that they seek a sub-text, which ipso facto renders the actual text irrelevant. They are likely to pay more attention to their own jaundiced "impressions" of how the 'terrorist' looks, speaks or listens, usually fixing on their own pre-conceived "meanings" of particular facial expressions or body movements.

The Terror Experts excel in selecting the worst-case sample as "representative" of the leadership of the terrorists—the boastful, the moneygrubber, the affluent. They omit the norm of persecuted resistance fighters who are modest, sacrificing, in solidarity with their people, upon whom they have many times to depend for food, medical care, and refuge.

They omit the fact that there are highly educated "fundamentalist" Muslims who in every way pursue modern, science-based professions, use Western critiques of colonialism and imperialism, who find it compatible to seek self-determination, majority rule and practice their religion.

There are also fundamentalist Muslims who are pietistic—seeking solace in spiritual practices, living in a narrow circle of work, mosque and family—who have experienced the violent disruption of their pietistic life and respond, not only because the imperialists have transgressed the sacred, but because they have destroyed the family network and intergenerational codes of existence. Such pietistic Muslims avoid political engagement until their intimate human and spiritual circle is violated.

In the midst of the chaos, violence, dislocation, pillage, and occupation of a country, a whole people are adversely affected. As they reach out to respond, to protest, to survive, they seek movements and institutions that have some resources, a modicum of power. In the past there were powerful nationalist, socialist, and communist parties, dynamic trade unions and peasant movements. In a few countries these are still active and a force to be reckoned with. In many regions, however, they have been decimated by US client regimes, local secular or "religious" dictators, and by the disintegration of the Communist parties. Under harsh conditions requiring clandestine activity and mass support, many secular activists have joined politically-oriented religious movements, which embrace anti-colonial, anti-imperialist, and social warfare programs. The catalyst for secular "conversion" to Muslim-inspired movements is politics, not religion. Leon Trotsky once advised his followers during the Nazi occupation of Europe that it might be necessary to join the Catholic Church if that was the only space available for political action. Given the mass base of the Muslim movement, given its engagement in the anti-colonial struggle, it is no surprise that many secularists (who may be leftists, nationalists and democrats) have joined these movements—and may later turn to other political movements.

To subsume the rich mosaic of resistance fighters to one ideological formula because of formal affiliations—as these Terror Experts do—is an egregious error. They are eager to prescribe a *general repressive solution* to the "terror" problem, truckling to the political interests of their paymasters in the big foundations or state apparatus. They repress inconvenient complexities, diverse motivations, conjunctural convergences between secular and spiritual. Terror Experts evoke the emotive phrase 'Islamic Fundamentalist Terrorists' to end debates and considered analysis that might require the public to reconsider their support for imperial wars and Israeli conquests, and their opposition to Iraqi nationalists and Palestinian resistance fighters.

Interrogation: Questions for the Terror Experts

Terror Experts (TE) claim that objective conditions, or what they refer to disparagingly as "exploitation", "oppression" or "imperialism" (predictably always with quotes), are only a veneer covering some deeper "personal need". The TE then proceed to "unmask" the "true" motives—with a stream of psychobabble. In fact the resort to crudely conceived and applied psychological categories is the principle method that the TE use to suppress the "objective " world, which impinges on their interpretation of the action of the resistance fighter.

The external world in which violent resistance movements emerge is, by any measure, very hostile. The US and Israel, for example, are recognized the world over as very aggressive, non-normative actors, considering themselves unaccountable to any and all international laws. The TE can avoid this fundamental 'fact' impinging on the resistance fighters' behavior by focusing on their supposed "inner world" and "immediate" face to face relations. This allows the TE to avoid the unpleasant aspects of their own state loyalties—the primitive, tribal, clan, ethnic, religious, colonial, imperial loyalties which underlie *their* veneer of respectability, their phony defense of civilization and humanity.

The TE were horrified by the *photos* of US torture in Iraq—not the *acts.* The revelations unmasked the savagery of their accomplices, the practitioners of their prescriptions, the whole underworld of crime and punishment that is logically derived from the totalitarian pseudo-science of the Terror Experts. It brings the TE of Harvard, Princeton, Yale, and Johns Hopkins closer to the savage scenes of homo- and heterosexual rape, mass sequential genital violence. The TE, of course, strike a pose of indignation towards the brutal guards, interrogators, the military commanders. They are silent as their current paymasters are pilloried—Rumsfeld, Bush—knowing full well that the next President will also employ their services. In any case who is going to look deep and far from the scenes of torture and identify the torture accomplices among the TE?

The TE simply pronounce their diagnosis of the armed resistance fighters: incurable psychopaths, extremely dangerous when at large. The politicians dictate the commands: capture, confine, torture, or kill. The Special Forces break through doors in the middle of the night, cut throats, or take prisoners. The prison commandants establish the rules of "interrogation". The guards torture. This is s very coherent international division of labor, in which the TE play an important part in elaborating the rationale. They ply a morally and scientifically justified war-unto-death of the "untermensch" the "inferior" peoples, the "fundamentalist Arab Muslims", the "suicide bombers", the "Terrorists". A common language is spoken between the TE and their state patrons, and then promoted in and by the mass media.

Here are some questions for the TE: first, why do the imputed terrorists' "personal needs" find expression through politics (and not in a thousand and one personal, familial, cultural, socio-economic or civic channels)? Why do the terrorists' "personal needs" find expression against a certain enemy (the dominant power) rather than a host of other more direct objectives, which might be less dangerous and easier to access? Why do the terrorists' "personal needs" express themselves in *favor* of a particular group (family, neighborhood, nation, or class) and not another (foreign powers, exclusive elites, etc?) Why do the terrorists' "personal needs" find expression at a particular time (during invasions, occupations, etc.) and place (locus of imperial power, military and political institutions, mercenary police stations)?

Why do the imputed terrorists' "personal needs" find expression through politics, against a particular enemy, in *favor* of a particular group (family, neighborhood, nation, or class) and at a particular time and place?

Obviously the "personal" has multiple forms, objects, places, and times for expression. To explain specific political *actions* one must examine the political, ideological, and class relations, the state and international configuration of power.

The second set of questions is a refinement of the first: Why don't "personal needs" express themselves in other nonviolent forms of political action such as running in elections, for example, instead of becoming a guerrilla or suicide bomber, etc.? More specifically, what political obstacles or literal or figurative walls prevented other than violent forms of political action? We can hypothesize that the greater the *closure* imposed on the political system (colonial and neo-colonial rule, long-term military occupation, racist exclusive ideology and practice, systematic widespread torture of "suspects"), the greater the degree of *uprooting* or *ethnic purging*, the more likely the choice posed by the ruling power is simply: subject yourself or revolt. Under such circumstances there is a greater likelihood of violent resistance, individual or collective.

Suicide bombings are a form of individual sacrifice, of individual resistance taken in the name of a collective. In Western society, individual sacrifice to defend the nation in war merits the highest military medals— the distinguished medal of honor, with distinctive military and religious ceremonies. In the Middle East, similar honorific activities accompany the **Suicide bombings are a form of individual sacrifice, of individual resistance taken in the name of a collective.** suicide bombers: they are cited as 'martyrs' to the cause of national liberation. Why do the TE ascribe pathological behavior to the Middle Eastern resistance fighters and not to their own military heroes who died for the bloody empire? Why is one culture which honors its sacrificial martyrs called civilized and another a fanatical, violent, barbarian culture?

This question is especially relevant because throughout history in all nations facing superior arms, organization and technology from an imperial conqueror, resistance has included sacrificing one's life in the course of inflicting the highest number of casualties on the enemy. Just think of Leonides at the pass of Thermopylae, with a few hundred soldiers facing the advancing Persian imperial army: was he engaged in a form of "suicide" defense of Athens? Why is it 'glorious' to be the equivalent of a suicide bomber in ancient Greece and not in modern Palestine?

History teaches us that there have been and always will be self-sacrificing individuals or collectives (nations/people etc.) still prepared to defend nation and home when faced with superior arms—irrespective of the likely cost. Countries (especially imperial states) with superior arms rarely practice, either individually or collectively, the use of the human body as a missile or weapon. Japanese kamikaze fighters were not used in the conquest of China or the Philippines—this only came into practice when Japan was faced with the superior air and sea power of the US.

TE attempt to denigrate the politics of popular resistance by attributing the struggle to the manipulation of ignorant or uninformed followers by leaders with unworthy motives. This overlooks all mass movements, which have by their nature a whole range of leaders, activists and sympathizers, and who face grave personal danger in order to follow them. Terror Experts imagine leaders who are in search of "money", "status", "power", "jobs," etc. Once again the "unmasking" technique fails to explain obvious facts. Overwhelming evidence throughout the world, past and present, demonstrates that those who struggle against a dominant colonial, imperial power suffer severe material losses of life, family, jobs, income, houses, and property. In the case of the Palestinians, the Israeli Jews punish the whole extended family, steal personal belongings and heirlooms, and destroy generations of old orchards and cultivated fields. With resistance movements, it is very rare that "leaders" enrich themselves in the midst of a life and death struggle. Those leaders who do enrich themselves usually do so after the struggle has ended, especially if they turn to embrace the neo-colonial paymasters of the TE. In fact it is the Terror Experts' closest collaborators and their informants who enrich themselves by spying and turning in the patriots whom the experts call 'terrorists'.

Repeatedly the TE engage in role reversal, turning the victims into executioners and the executioners into victims. This has been a common ploy used by totalitarian imperialist ideologues to justify the use of force—from the Nazis to the present day US, European, and Israeli colonialists. To justify their preposterous claims, the TE comb the world to find some groups or individual leaders who will fulfill their stereotype and titillate their readers in New York, Tel Aviv, Washington or London. The Terror Expert meets a leader (Muslim, of course) who just happens to lead a "group known for beheading foreigners and for its close alliance with Osama bin Laden". The TE has touched all the right buttons to evoke the conditioned response—only they are the wrong buttons. Millions engaged in violent resistance do not "behead" foreigners—only a very small handful do and then under questionable circumstances.

The selective vitriolic libeling of a subject prepares the Western reader to accept the emotionally charged imputation of pathologic behavior. Harvard academic Jessica Stern provides us with a typical example—almost a parody—of these polemical ejaculations. She describes the purpose of her study as "to identify some common themes that might help to explain how violent Islamic nihilism continues to spread beyond the lawless pockets and failed states where terrorists tend to thrive and into the cities of the west".[3] Nihilism presumes no goals, no values, and no alternatives. Most observers would disagree based on a simple reading of most of the Islamic revolutionary or radical web sites: they have goals—to replace Western dominance with national Islamic rulers. Their values include both traditional religious and modern variants, and their alternatives to submission are guerrilla, mass or individual resistance.

The neighborhoods, cities, and communities where the putative "nihilists" originate were far more stable, norm-guided and law-abiding *before* the forceful intrusion of imperial and colonial power, which tears asunder the networks that bind collectivities. "Lawless pockets", to the degree in which they exist, are products of the unwillingness or incapacity of the conquering powers and their proxies to establish a just and stable social order. Moreover, one can observe in many cases that "lawlessness" is selective: occupied peoples disobey colonial 'laws', 'edicts' or 'fiats' while abiding by the laws or rules declared by their own legitimate authorities. Moreover, it is generally the case that newly liberated areas run by guerrillas are more lawful than under previous military or colonial occupation with their drugs, brothels and bars.

The notion of "failed states" has achieved a certain notoriety among Western pundits, academics and especially the TE. Its exponents use it to describe the collapse of nations that have been devastated by surrogate pro-Western militarists, and/or pillaged by Western banks under the tutelage and protection of the IMF and the World Bank. No doubt there have been gangster rulers in the former Soviet Union, Eastern Europe, and the Third World—but they have more often than not been trained by Western foundations or universities and send their ill-gotten fortunes to Western, Israeli, or "off shore" banks. The Terror Experts, in labeling their former progeny as failed rulers, disown their own offspring. What imperial ideologues mean by "failed states" is the failure of clients to establish a stable neo-liberal regime, necessitating "successful" Euro-US imperial intervention to create "prosperous democracies"—like in post-invasion Kosova, Afghanistan, Iraq, and Haiti where white slavery, drug trafficking, warlords, and death squads rule with the aid of US helicopter gunships hovering over and firing into unruly neighborhoods.

Stern and other verbal assassins strip the victims of their humanity ("nihilists"), denigrate their place of birth ('lawless pockets"), deny the historical authenticity of their nations ("failed states"), all the better to oversee their extermination, their ghettoization in economically ravaged and unsustainable regions, and their torture. Through the eyes of the Terror Experts, Euro-US and Israeli bombing of these population centers is seen as doing "humanity" a great favor: preventing the 'spread' of terrorists into the cities of the West.

The shrill anti-Arab/Muslim rhetoric of the TE encourages 'moderate' Western politicians to impose more rigid and humiliating administrative and legal measures against Arab, Middle Eastern and South Asian travelers, immigrants, visitors, religious leaders, academicians and business people. Targeted by and subject to systematic denigration by the Western mass media, state functionaries, immigration police, hostile embassy personnel, academic terror experts, the secret police, and special assassination teams, oppressed people are forced to transform themselves to meet a chronic "na-

tional emergency". Ruler-ruled relations are a series of perpetual imposi-
tions, unwelcome visits by colonial operatives granted license by the imperial
Terror Experts, purportedly to restore order. Faced with a systematic effort
to lower their self-esteem, the oppressed people "find" themselves in their
own organizations, public and clandestine, religious and secular. This reaffir-
mation finds expression in a reassertion of a religious or secular identity,
embodied in a mosque, church, political movement or resistance organization.

Colonial/imperial power disrupts the *daily routine* of the general population: 'going to work' entails passing through roadblocks, work places are
destroyed, fruit trees are uprooted. "Taking care of the family" becomes a
daily life and death struggle of securing food at black market prices, facing
unpredictable hostile fire in the marketplace. 'Enjoying leisure' becomes a
memory of the pre-colonial/pre-imperial past. Now there is 'forced leisure'—
jobless, policed, futureless—in the street, where individual discontent is
socialized by local opinion leaders who provide a focus for action. Taking
sides, addressing the oppression, the hardening of attitudes is a fundamental effort to recover the 'daily routine'.

The complex interweaving of powerful spiritual loyalties, family re-
sponsibilities, and workplace displacement leads to a commitment to direct
action and a political movement. This is a rational and complex process.
The Terror Experts' colonial preconceptions blind them to this reality. For
example, Stern sees the committed resistance fighter as being in a "kind of
trance"—irrational, dogmatic, and simplistic.

The Terror Experts repeat ad nauseum that the "terrorists" join their
organizations in their search for strength—a common response of all those
who engage in politics and social action. The TE turn a commonplace phenomenon which has a lineage of over 3,000 years or more into a particular
feature of "terrorists". The resistance fighters do have a sense of altruism
and an idea of the public good—which the Terror Experts refuse to take
seriously. To do so would require a profound re-examination of their own
loyalties, and collaboration with imperial/colonial powers, and a deep critical
self-examination of their institutional location and motives. This would be a
difficult psychological and material experience for Terror Experts since their

The resistance fighters do have a sense of altruism and an idea of the public good—which the Terror Experts refuse to take seriously. To do so would require a profound re-examination of their own loyalties, and collaboration with imperial/colonial powers.

prestige, income, status, and influence might be threatened. Their critical
introspective analysis might lead them to question their paymasters, their
institutions, their colonial/imperial states. Which foundations would pay a

'renegade' Terror Expert to bear witness to their colleagues' prejudices, falsifications, and close ties to politicians who sanction torture and murder? Would their former colleagues describe the renegade as being in a "kind of trance", "victim of the Stockholm complex" (accepting the views of their captors)?

The colonial practitioners and their academic experts specialize in verifying each other's stereotypes of resistance fighters. They oversimplify their motives, decisions, and commitments. They rely on blanket categories that obscure deeper structural realities in favor of subjective labeling. Above all they banish any objectivity. Relations of power and dominance, state violence, violent intrusions into Arab, Muslim, and Latin American countries, towns, and villages are described by the TE as "defensive", or "retaliation". As the limbs and body parts of Palestinian babies, women and grandparents are exploded over the ruins of homes and neighborhoods, Harvey Morris, the Zionist Bureau Chief of the *Financial Times* in Israel writes of Israeli "retaliation". Banishing objectivity means the incapacity to empathize with the human condition of the colonized victims—for that reason the experts must present the victims as sub-human. Because the Terror Experts are condemning the most abused victims in the name of the most vicious powers, they convince themselves that their vitriolic diatribes are merely a service to truth and science. The TE have invented a new paradigm—scientific diatribes in the service of intellectual dishonesty.

The TE are masters of euphemism, especially in dealing with the muck and gore of empire building. Imperialists become "one worlders". Colonial occupation is called "nation building". Murderous sequential destructive offensive wars become "humanitarian interventions". While the TE are the driving force in the change of lexicon, what is remarkable is the extent to which ordinary academics pick it up. Above all the Terror Experts celebrate triumphal imperialism: the defeated

While the TE are the driving force in the change of lexicon, what is remarkable is the extent to which ordinary academics pick it up.

colonial peoples, we are told, are "resentful"—"those who feel they can't keep up". How is a Palestinian farmer going to "keep up" with a Jewish settler who seizes his land and water, and supported by local thugs and Israeli soldiers acting under government authority, blocks his access to the market? Anything short of resentful would be masochistic. Is it any wonder that the deracinated and dispossessed risk their lives to convert resentment into resistance? By all means. When the tanks roll into Iraqi neighborhoods after shelling homes and mosques, is it any wonder that furious neighbors swarm around an ambushed tank and dance on the shards of smoking metal and corpses? Is it a frightful spectacle of pitiless terrorists or jubilant neighbors, who have silenced the sound of shells bursting over their heads and into their neighbors' homes?

The Terror Experts existed before the Iraqi resistance and they will exist after it. Wherever the oppressed rise and effectively resist imperial rule there will be academic chairs, foundations grants and centers for international studies for the ambitious upwardly mobile TE. The Imperial State will demand their services, prestigious councils of foreign relations will offer memberships, and universities will reward them with distinguished professorships. They will become celebrities—the mass media talk shows will feature them. They will be far from the killing fields but their spirit will be there, on the front lines and in the torture chambers, guiding the hands that place the hoods over the unredeemable nihilists, Muslims, Marxists or national patriots.

ENDNOTES

[1] *Financial Times*, June 13, 2004/
[2] Jessica Stern, *Terror in the Name of God: Why Religious Militants Kill*, Harper Collins, 2003.
[3] Jessica Stern, "How Terrorists Think", *Financial Times*, June 12/13, 2004, w1-w2.

BIBLIOGRAPHY

1. Jessica Stern, "How Terrorists Think", *Financial Times Weekend*, June 12/13, 2004 W1-2.
2. Alan Dershowitz, *Why Terrorism Works*, R.R. Donnelley and Sons, 2002.
3. Scott Altran, "Genesis of Suicide Terrorism", *Science,* March 7, 2003, p.1534.
4. Rafael Patai, *The Arab Mind*, W.W. Norton and Co., 1973 with preface by Norvell B. De Atkine.
5. Harvey Morris, "The State They're In", *Financial Times Weekend*, July 3-4 p. W1-2. 2005.
6. D. Long, *The Anatomy of Terrorism*, Free Press, New York, 1990.
7. E. Stout (ed), *The Psychology of Terrorism*, Praeger, Westport CT, 2002.
8. Hector Qirko, "'Fictive Kin' and Suicide Terrorism", *Science*, April 2, 2004 p 49.
9. "The Sociology and Psychology of Terrorism", Federal Research Division, Library of Congress, Washington DC, Sept. 1999.

CHAPTER 12

SUICIDE BOMBERS

THE SACRED AND THE PROFANE

Introduction

One of the least discussed but most important aspects of the 'suicide bombers' (SB) attacks is the Anglo-American (AA) systematic and profound degradation of that which the Islamic religion holds most sacred: its code of ethics, its mode of spiritual practice, its religious rituals, its sacred texts, and its respect for the observant believer.

The neo-conservative, liberal and pro-Israel propagandists, both journalists and academics, focus on what they choose to call the "pathologies" of young Muslims, the "fanaticism" of their beliefs, their "gratuitous" violence, the "generational anger", the "frustration" of living in "failed states" and a long litany of irrational behaviors which purportedly exonerates the AA and Israeli violence and torture.

A progressive school of thought emphasizes the 'reciprocal nature of violence"—Anglo-American wars, invasions and occupations which engender Arab or Islamic terror as part of a spiral of violence. In some versions, the religious element is subordinated to the political concern for self-determination in explaining the behavior of SB.

While the progressive approach has the advantage of advancing beyond the vitriolic psychobabble of the neo-conservative and Zionist 'experts' on the "Arab Mind", it fails to account for the depth and scope of the suicide bomber or martyrdom phenomena, especially the sharpening intensity during the occupation.

Beyond the general mayhem induced by Anglo-American wars, invasions and occupations, there are two forms of violence derivative from the general conception of war, which stand out as the direct determinants of suicide bombing.

The AA have theorized and put in practice the idea of 'total war'—a war without legal, moral, geographic, temporal or spatial boundaries. As Bush, Rumsfeld,

The Anglo-American alliance has theorized and put in practice the idea of 'total war'—a war without legal, moral, geographic, temporal or spatial boundaries.

and the Pentagon Zionists (Perle, Wolfowitz, Feith, and Company) declared, this is a different war in which the 'enemy' is everywhere and attacking at all times. The final solution is to search out and destroy them, their sanctuaries, their accomplices, their neighborhoods, families, religious institutions, and any who might offer material or spiritual support, protection or encouragement. The theory and practice of 'total war' obliterates the distinction between combatants and civilians, between military installations and civilian facilities, between military infrastructure and civilian transport systems, between the sacred and the profane.

The AA have imposed new norms of warfare and new practices for engaging the enemy which have been increasingly taken up by sectors of their adversaries. If AA imperialism can act with unrestrained violence against all military and civilian targets, so, it can be argued, in recognition of the universality principle, can the resistance—including the suicide bombers—whether they are Islamists or secular, poor or middle class. What influences the reaction of the adversaries of AA imperialism are their own rules of engagement—the notion of 'total war'.

The Anglo-American new norms of total warfare have been increasingly taken up by sectors of their adversaries.

Total War: Content and Consequences

There are different forms of imperial conquest. In one variant the method is to work through local elites who become the tribute collectors and gendarmes of the colonial powers, gaining control of the agro-mineral wealth and financing their privileged position via local taxes.

In another variant, the imperial powers destroy the pre-existing society and governing system, frequently uprooting the population and in the process physically annihilating its members and culture in the course of seizing its wealth. The degradation of the sacred is a prelude to attempts to impose a new set of beliefs more conducive to submission and exploitation.

A third variant is a combination or a sequential process of destruction, degradation, and exploitation followed by efforts to "reconstruct" a colonized military, police, and political structure willing and able to repress and contain anti-colonial resistance.

The US invasions of Iraq and Afghanistan follow the third variant. In the initial phase, the imperial armies engaged in total occupation, unrestrained pillage of historical sites, utter degradation of the population, destruction of cultural institutions, and the systematic assassination of leading members of the local political, civil service, and professional classes. Following the growth of massive resistance by secular and religious forces, uprooted and divorced from their essential everyday living, under constant physical and spiritual assaults, the AA occupation regime moves toward the "reconstruction" of a colonial repressive apparatus and governing bodies—beyond the walls, barbed wire enclosures, and watch towers of the colonial army.

'Total war' doctrine continues to wreak havoc with minor concessions to enclaves of collaborators, most of whom are 'dual citizens', exiles whose loyalties are first and foremost to the empire, whose homes, pensions, and even families (not to mention bank accounts and English rose gardens) are located in the cities of the imperial countries.

Total War and the Resistance

The practitioners of 'total war' borrow heavily from the practice and doctrine of the Israeli colonial occupation of Palestine: practices of collective punishment, erasure of historical sites, destruction of homes, eradication of orchards and productive farms, bombing of small factories, building of ghetto enclosures (walls), massive forcible evictions, and especially torture and interrogation techniques designed especially to violate Islamic beliefs and the Arab identity. These techniques have been transmitted via Israeli advisers and training sessions to US interrogators and incorporated into their manuals. It is precisely the common methods of both Israeli and Anglo-US interrogation-torture techniques linked to the doctrine of 'total war', which has led to the common practice of SB against them.

Insofar as the interrogation-terror techniques strip their victims of all that is essential to their 'spiritual self', they also force upon the victims and their sympathizers a 'new morality', one that no longer abides by the older moral-religious precepts, not as it concerns fighting back—Islam is not a pacifistic religion (by the Qur'an, fighting is to be disliked but it is nonetheless enjoined so long as it is in the way of God, which is further specified as in the way of justice and self-defense, in the way of the widow, the orphan, and the oppressed)—but as it concerns the protection of the enemy's "innocents". In its place the 'new morality' is the mirror image of the practitioners of 'total war'. The SB act without concern for civilians, locations, time, and circumstance. Like their interrogators, they seek to inflict the maximum damage to the "Western mind"—exposing their weaknesses, increasing their anxieties and fears, while undermining their everyday routines. The key to the conversion of Islamists and the secular opposition to martyrdom attacks and the practice of the 'new morality' is not merely the political-military colonial occupation and war, but the resort to the specific practices of degradation inflicted on the colonial victim.

Degradation: The Logic of Total War

The Israelis have practiced torture by degradation for decades and have a powerful army of overseas supporters—professors, neo-con officials, liberals, bankers, professionals, artists, journalists, and media moguls—providing justifications in the form of 'ameliorating circumstances' and 'moral equivalences'.

The Anglo-American practitioners of total war, impressed by the power of Israel to sustain its colonial occupation of Palestine and its impunity, overlooked the negative effects: the SB phenomenon, and Israel's repugnancy to the non-European world (and even to many Europeans).

Degradation is specifically designed to 'break' the 'Arab' or 'Islamic' Mind—as the Israeli psychological war experts labeled it—and secure an army of informers, agents and docile, terrorized released prisoners who would serve as exemplars to other would-be resistance fighters. While a few prisoners were 'turned' through torture and blackmail and others were released as 'broken' men and women incapacitated by profound psychological disorders, millions reacted not by submission but with indignation, anger, and violence—which in some cases has taken the form of SB. The words of the victim-survivors of Israeli brutality and visual images provided a terribly graphic reality of the systematic degradation of all that Arabs—Islamist or secular—hold sacred.

The perception of the victims, their families, their people, their fellow believers, and their nation is that degradation of Iraqi prisoners is a technique authorized and approved by the highest levels of power and executed by the terror experts, from elite psychologists down to the lowest jailers. Nobody can claim, "they didn't know". Nobody, in a volunteer army, can claim they were just obeying orders. Citizens in electoral systems who not only failed to adequately protest the degradation, but actually went on to vote for the imperial executioners post facto cannot claim innocence. All are complicit in the eyes of the suicide-bomber..

Degradation is a technique authorized and approved by the highest levels of power and executed by the terror experts, from elite psychologists down to the lowest jailers.

The Technique of Degradation: The Larger Meaning

The book of virtuous living for the Islamist and even, to a lesser degree, the secularists among Muslim populations, is the Qur'an. It is the 'divine book', which provides a moral guide and existential meaning to life. The torturers defecated and urinated on the Qur'an. They stomped on the Qur'an with muddy army boots. They flushed pages, held most sacred by the victims, down the toilet. They violated the most sacred single source of moral life.

The torturers systematically denied their victims water to clean themselves before prayer. Instead they defiled them with filth, scantily clad female interrogators smeared fake 'menstrual' blood on bound prisoners, forced them to defecate on themselves and ridiculed their victims' intense religious distress. They violated every taboo, every norm, including the deepest held moral codes. They forced (and photographed) deviant sex, prolonged nudity, raped men and women with cattle prods and other torture devices. They wrapped prisoners in the Israeli flag.

Such humiliating techniques have lifetime psychological consequences preventing the victims from ever marrying and maintaining normal family relations. The torturers specifically told their victims that the films and photos of their degradation would be shown to their families and neighbors to intensify the anguish after their release. These torture techniques specifically focused on Muslims and Arabs, but in general should be regarded as defiling the sense of modesty of all normal men and women. The torturers used gross sexual humiliation designed to break all political bonds between the colonized people and the degraded victims. Women prisoners in Abu Ghraib reportedly sent out messages begging the resistance to kill them in their cells by mortar attacks. Mosques were destroyed or turned into slaughterhouses; wounded men huddled in the sacred halls were executed at point blank range.

The AA political leaders promoted Christian evangelical military chaplains who incited the executioners to 'fight Satan' as they encircled and destroyed the city of Fallujah. Jewish and Christian 'terror experts' (often in the behavioral sciences) provided the emotional vitriol in pseudo-scientific jargon by projecting the psychopathic behavior of the executioners onto the victims. We need to view the policymakers as war criminals ...as formulators of the modus operandi of the Suicide Bombers...

Political Consequences of Defiling the Sacred

The profound systematic effects of 'total war' and its derivative defilement of the sacred has far-reaching effects on Muslims and Arabs, including secularists, in terms of geography, political practice, intensity of reflection and feeling about the practitioners, their government and their 'civilization'. The impact of defacing the sacred is strongest on those collectivities that share the same ethnic, religious and cultural values as those who are violated. The degradation of the sacred texts and religious sanctuaries impinge on the spiritual and physical existence of the groups and individuals whose lives have been guided by the defiled texts. The message relayed to millions by the torturers and their leaders is that 'nothing is sacred'—everything and everybody is equally an acceptable instrument for conquest, domination, and control. The whole process of degradation from the indiscriminate bombing of civilian communities to the usurpation of public space, to the pillage of a cultural heritage, to the arbitrary arrest and assassination of passersby, culminates in utter depravity, the attempt to literally turn the spiritual symbols and texts and moral guides into trash.

The denial of what is sacred to the oppressed is inherent to the process of creating a hierarchical chain—

The oppressors' process of degradation culminates in utter depravity, the attempt to literally turn the spiritual symbols and texts and moral guides into trash.

the greater the degradation of the 'other', the greater the power and self-esteem of the torturers. The lower the stature of the torturers—(those who, outside the torture chambers, have no access to the real spoils of conquest, the war profiteering, the 'reconstruction' racket or the military officers who can 'cream' the contracts)—the greater the inducement to achieve 'superiority' (symbolic rewards) by debasing the shackled and manacled, the naked and the humiliated, to please their superiors with tidbits of irrelevant 'intelligence'. Much of this is documented in General Antonio Taguba's report.

The chain of command dictates the license to torture; the word of the imperial executive informs the practitioners of degradation. The celebrants of imperial 'Judeo-Christian' values flaunt their impunity in the security of their technological and military might. The 'special people', the chosen nations, aggravate the experience of degradation. Imagine Rumsfeld and other officials and senators reviewing General Taguba's report describing the young son of an Iraqi Army officer stripped, smeared with filth and abused before his captive father (Seymour Hersh describes the shrieks of young boys being raped)—and projecting their own perversities onto the victimized people.

Suicide Bombers: A Response to the Desecraters

Some of the more intelligent of the generally benighted claimants of 'expertise' in terrorism have discovered that the SB are not necessarily poor, not necessarily 'direct victims' of imperial invasions, and are not necessarily Islamic fundamentalists. Faced with this incongruence with their earlier depictions, most of them ramp up the complexity of their psychobabble, citing 'alienation', 'generational conflict', and other behavioral pathologies, strikingly more descriptive of the TE's own societies. These Anglo-American and pro-Israeli 'experts', who pathologically ignore the monstrous crimes committed against the essential values and beliefs of the oppressed, see themselves, with all solemnity, as actually fit to diagnose the ills of others. A handful of the 'experts' claim that the terrorists, the SB, are political people and that these acts are 'political'—a response to the Anglo-American war, invasion and conquest. Closer to the truth, but still inadequate, some add the response to the 'humiliation of a conquered people'.

What drives the SB is an effort to redeem the Sacred from the Desecraters. The desecration includes, but goes beyond, the material destruction inflicted by the Anglo-American invaders and Israeli colonists. Degradation and defilement of the sacred texts, the deep inner values and the disciplined customs produces a class of individuals who sense the bonds of humanity have been irrevocably broken.

The SB believes that spiritual wrath can counter the desecraters of the Sacred. For the future SB, resistance, marches, protests, strikes, civil disobedience, even resistance in the homeland does not restore the 'Sacred'. The conflict rages in their neighborhoods, their houses; markets and transport are destroyed. The SB believe that only by reversing the violence, bringing it 'home' to the invaders, will they redeem and reassert the ascendancy of what has been defiled—the Sacred—by responding in kind to the 'total war' advocates, apologists, and even to innocent victims—your innocent victims for our innocent victims...

Recognition of the licensed defilement of the sacred is now out of the box—whether it continues in one form or another, videoed or hidden in military archives, it is now embedded in the minds of tens of millions—it is their very cultural—psychological—moral existence. Everyday life has been put to the test.

Conclusion

From the 'Shock and Awe' bombing of cities to the killing, maiming and destruction of millions, to the torture and profanation of the sacred, the *orders* have come from distant, faceless generals, presidents, secretaries of war, and have been *executed*, face to face, by average people, workers, employees, clerks...who 'elected' these leaders. The many faces of these ordinary people reflect, in the eyes of the SB, the faces and acts of those who have degraded the sacred and attempted to destroy what gives meaning to their everyday life.

To the SB, "the face of the enemy" is the face of "their people"—rich and poor, powerful and powerless, general and foot soldier. Hence the suicide bomber, whose normal bonds with the sacred and moral have been heightened by systematic degradation, until the SB feels no compunction in attacking ordinary people going about their everyday tasks in office buildings or subways, enduring personal immolation to reassert the sacred despite the overwhelming power of its desecrators, and at whatever cost. The victims whose homes, streets, innocents, and dear ones have been bombed and obliterated respond in kind against the homes, streets, innocents, and dear ones of the perpetrators.

Our analysis suggests a close relation between the Anglo-American practice of 'total war' and its derivative policies of systematic degradation and the emergence of 'suicide bombers'—one of the ultimate forms of rejection of tyranny. If this analysis is correct, the demise of suicide bombers is most likely to occur when the practice of 'total war' is ended. This can only come about through a defeat of the 'colonial revivalist' strand of imperialism in both its US, European and Israeli variants. The question is how long it will take for domestic and external political discontent to coalesce a political alternative capable of formulating a strategy of military withdrawal and abiding by international law.

Reconciliation between the Anglo-American and Islamic and Arab peoples can be achieved through a war crimes tribunal, similar to the Nuremburg Trials after the Second World War. The practitioners and proponents of crimes against humanity beginning with the President of the United States and the Prime Minister of Great Britain should be brought to trial and accorded exemplary punishment to establish a major milestone in civil society's global campaign to end impunity. Peace and reconciliation is only possible if justice is meted to the architects and practitioners of total war and human degradation.

PART IV

DEBATES

CHAPTER 13

NOAM CHOMSKY AND THE PRO-ISRAEL LOBBY

FIFTEEN ERRONEOUS THESES

"Reflexes that ordinarily spring automatically to the defense of open debate and free enquiry shut down—at least among much of America's political elite—once the subject turns to Israel, and above all the pro-Israel lobby's role in shaping US foreign policy… Moral blackmail—the fear that any criticism of Israeli policy and US support for it will lead to charges of anti-Semitism—is a powerful disincentive to publish dissenting views. It is also leading to the silencing of policy debate on American university campuses, partly as the result of targeted campaigns against the dissenters…Nothing, moreover, is more damaging to US interests than the inability to have a proper debate about the Israeli-Palestinian conflict…Bullying Americans into consensus on Israeli policy is bad for Israel and makes it impossible for America to articulate its own national interests…."

Financial Times, Editorial, Saturday, April 01, 2006.

Introduction

Noam Chomsky has been called the leading US intellectual by pundits and even some sectors of the mass media. He has a large audience throughout the world, especially in academic circles, in large part because of his vocal criticism of US foreign policy and many of the injustices resulting from those policies. Chomsky has been reviled by all of the major Jewish and pro-Israel organizations and media for his criticism of Israeli policy toward the Palestinians, even as he has defended the existence of the Zionist state of Israel. Despite his respected reputation for documenting, dissecting, and exposing the hypocrisy of the US and European regimes and acutely analyzing the intellectual deceptions of imperial apologists, these analytical virtues are totally absent when it comes to discussing the formulation of US foreign policy in the Middle East, particularly the role of his own ethnic group, or the Jewish pro-Israel Lobby and their Zionist supporters in the government. This political blindness is not unknown or uncommon. History is replete with intellectual critics of all imperialisms except their own, staunch opponents of the abuses of power by others, but not of one's own kin and kind. Chomsky's long history of denying the power and role of the pro-Israel lobby in decisively shaping US Middle East policy culminated in his recent conjoining with the US Zionist propaganda machine in attacking a study critical of the Israeli Lobby. I am referring to the essay published by the *London Review of Books* entitled "The Israel Lobby" by Professor John Mearsheimer of the University of Chicago and Professor Stephan Walt, the Academic Dean of the Kennedy School of Government at Harvard University. (A complete version of the study was published by the Kennedy School of Government in March 2006.)

Chomsky's speeches and writing on the Lobby emphasize a number of dubious propositions:

1) The pro-Israel Lobby is just like any other lobby; it has no special influence or place in US politics.

2) The power of the groups backing the Israel Lobby are *no more powerful* than other influential pressure groups.

3) The Lobby's agenda succeeds because it coincides with the interests of the dominant powers and interests of the US State.

4) The Lobby's weakness is demonstrated by the fact that Israel is 'merely a tool' of US empire-building to be used when needed and otherwise marginalized.

5) The major forces shaping US Middle East policy are "big oil" and the "military-industrial complex", neither of which is connected to the pro-Israel Lobby.

6) The interests of the US generally coincide with the interests of Israel.

7) The Iraq War, the threats to Syria and Iran, are primarily a product of "oil interests" and the "military-industrial complex" and not due to the role of the pro-Israel Lobby or its collaborators in the Pentagon and other government agencies.

8) The US behavior in the Middle East is similar to policies that it has pursued elsewhere in the world, and this policy precedes the Lobby.

While in general Chomsky has deliberately refrained from specifically discussing the pro-Israel Lobby in his speeches, interviews, and publications analyzing US policy toward the Middle East, when he does, he follows the above-mentioned repertory.

The problem of war and peace in the Middle East and the role of the Israel Lobby is too serious to be marginalized as an afterthought. Restrictions on our right to speak freely and critically regarding Israeli and the Lobby's policies severely reduces the possibilities for political action. Repression of free thought allows for the formulation and enactment of policies that are damaging to the interests of the American people, particularly where their best interests may diverge from those of their elites.

It is incumbent therefore to specify and examine the fifteen erroneous theses of the highly respected Professor Chomsky in order to move ahead and confront the Lobby's threats to peace abroad and civil liberties at home.

Chomsky's Fifteen Theses

1) Chomsky claims that the Lobby is just another lobby in Washington. Yet he fails to observe that the Lobby has secured the biggest Congressional majorities in favor of allocating three times the annual foreign aid designated to all of Africa, Asia and Latin America to Israel (over 100 billion dollars over the past 40 years). The Lobby has 150 full time functionaries working for the American-Israel Public Affairs Committee (AIPAC), accompanied by an army of lobbyists from all the major Jewish organizations (Anti-Defamation League, B'nai Brith, American Jewish Committee, etc.) and the nationwide, regional, and local Jewish Federations which hew closely to the line of the "majors", are active in policy and local opinion on Israel, and promote and finance legislative candidates on the basis of their adherence to the Lobby's party line. No other lobby combines the wealth, grass roots networks, media access, legislative muscle and single-minded purpose of the pro-Israel Lobby.

No other lobby combines the wealth, grass roots networks, media access, legislative muscle and single-minded purpose of the pro-Israel Lobby.

2) Chomsky fails to analyze the near unanimous Congressional majorities which yearly support all the pro-Israel military, economic, immigration privileges, and aid promoted by the Lobby. He fails to examine the list of over 100 successful legislative initiatives publicized yearly by AIPAC even in years of budgetary crisis, disintegrating domestic health services, and war-induced military losses.

3) Chomsky's cliché-ridden attribution of war aims to "Big Oil" is

totally unsubstantiated. In fact the US-Middle East wars prejudice the oil interests in several strategic senses. The wars generate generalized hostility to oil companies with long-term relations with Arab countries. The wars result in undermining the likelihood of new contracts opening in Arab countries for US oil investments. US oil companies have been much friendlier to peacefully resolving conflicts than Israel and especially its Lobbyists as any reading of the specialized oil industry journals and spokespeople emphasize. Chomsky chooses to totally ignore the pro-war activities and propaganda of the leading Jewish pro-Israel organizations and the absence of pro-war proposals in Big Oil's media, and their beleaguered attempt to continue linkages with Arab regimes opposed to Israel's belligerent hegemonic ambitions. Contrary to Chomsky, by going to war in the Middle East, the US sacrifices the vital interests of the oil companies in favor of Israel's quest for Middle East hegemony, responding to the call and at the behest of the pro-Israel lobby. In the lobbying

Chomsky chooses to totally ignore the pro-war activities and propaganda of the leading Jewish pro-Israel organizations and the absence of pro-war proposals in Big Oil's media.

contest there is absolutely no contest between the pro-Israel power bloc and the oil companies whether the issue is war or oil contracts. The former always predominate. But Chomsky never examines the comparative strength of the two lobbies regarding US policy toward the Middle East. In general this usually busy researcher devoted to uncovering obscure documentation is particularly lax when it come to uncovering readily available documents, which shred his assertions about Big Oil and the Israel Lobby.

4) Chomsky refuses to analyze the diplomatic disadvantages that accrue to the US in vetoing Security Council resolutions condemning Israel's systematic violations of human rights. Neither the military-industrial complex nor Big Oil has a stranglehold on US voting behavior in the UN. The pro-Israel lobbies are the only major force pressuring for the

Chomsky refuses to analyze the diplomatic disadvantages that accrue to the US in vetoing Security Council resolutions condemning Israel.

vetoes—against the US' closest allies, world public opinion and at the cost of whatever role the US could play as a 'mediator' between the Arabic-Islamic world and Israel. The public defense of Israeli crimes has nowhere been so evident—or disadvantageous to US global standing—as its refusal to condemn the Israeli strikes on the civilians of Lebanon.

5) Again, for one so rigorous as Chomsky, it is striking that he fails to discuss the role of the Lobby in electing Congress people, their funding of

pro-Israel candidates and the over fifty-million dollars they spend on the political parties, candidates and propaganda campaigns. The result is a 90% congressional vote on high priority items pushed by the Lobby and affiliated local and regional pro-Israel federations. The congressional vote on a measure with genocidal consequences—to cut off all aid to the Palestinians pushed by AIPAC and all the Jewish majors—was approved by a vote of 361 to 37 with 9 abstentions. The Jewish pro-genocide regime overrode the tiny liberal group of Jewish opponents allied with the Catholic Church and the World Council of Churches, referred to by the *Jerusalem Post* as "leftists". Worse, the Lobby almost shuts down the political system as a tool through which the American people democratically assert their preferences on major issues—witness the near-unanimous support of the Democratic Party for the Iraq war, and even a possible war against Iran, despite polls that now indicate that a majority of Americans desire otherwise.

Chomsky fails to discuss the role of the Lobby in electing Congresspeople and its impact on them.

6) Nor does he undertake to analyze the cases of candidates defeated by the Lobby, or the abject apologies extracted from Congress people who have dared to question the policies and tactics of the Lobby, and the intimidation effect of its 'exemplary punishments' on the rest of Congress. The "snowball" effect of punishment and payoffs is one reason for the unprecedented majorities in favor of all of AIPAC's initiatives. Chomsky's feeble attempts to equate AIPAC's pro-Israel initiatives with broader US policy interests is patently absurd to anyone who studies the alignment of policy groups associated with designing, pressuring, backing and co-sponsoring AIPAC's measures: the reach of the Jewish lobby far exceeds its electoral constituency—as the one million dollar slush fund to defeat incumbent Georgia Congresswoman, Cynthia McKinney demonstrated. That she was subsequently re-elected on the basis of low keying her criticism of Israel reveals the Lobby's impact even on consequential Democrats.

7) Chomsky ignores the unmatchable power of elite convocation that the Lobby has. The AIPAC annual meeting draws all the major leaders in Congress, key members of the Cabinet, over half of all members of Congress who pledge unconditional support for Israel and even identify Israel's interests as US interests. No other lobby can secure this degree of attendance of the political elite, this degree of abject servility, for so many years, among both major parties. What is particularly important to bear in mind is that the "Jewish electorate" is less than 5% of the total electorate, while practicing Jews number less than 2% of the population, of which not all are 'Israel Firsters'. None of the major lobbies like the NRA, AARP, the National

Association of Manufacturers, the National Chamber of Commerce, can convoke such a vast array of political leaders, let alone secure their unconditional support for favorable legislation and Executive orders. No less an authority than the former Prime Minister of Israel, Ariel Sharon, boasted of the power of the pro-Israel lobby over US Middle East policy. Chomsky merely asserts that the Pro-Israel lobby is just like any other lobby, without any serious effort to compare their relative influence, power of convocation and bi-partisan support, or effectiveness in securing high priority legislation.

Chomsky merely asserts that the Pro-Israel lobby is just like any other lobby, without any serious effort to compare their relative influence.

8) In his analysis of the run-up to the US-Iraq War, Chomsky's otherwise meticulous review of foreign policy documents, analysis of political linkages between policymakers and power centers is totally abandoned in favor of impressionistic commentaries completely devoid of any empirical basis. The principal governmental architects of the war, the intellectual promoters of the war, their publicly enunciated published strategies for the war were *all* deeply *attached* to the Israel Lobby and *worked* for the Israeli state. Wolfowitz, number 2 in the Pentagon, Douglas Feith, number 3 in the Pentagon, Richard Perle, head of the Defense Policy Board, Elliot Abrams in charge of Near East and North African Affairs for the National Security Council, and dozens of other key operatives in the government and ideologues in the mass media were lifelong fanatical activists in favor of Israel, some of whom had lost security clearances in previous administrations for handing over documents to the Israeli government. Chomsky ignores the key strategy documents written by Perle, Wurmser, Feith and other ZionCons in the late 1990s demanding bellicose action against Iraq, Iran, and Syria, which they subsequently implemented when they took power with Bush's election. How can a first rate intellectual critic of US foreign policy ignore, as Chomsky totally ignores, the disinformation office set up in the Pentagon by ultra Zionist Douglas Feith—the so-called 'Office of Special Plans'—run by fellow ZionCon Abram Shulsky to channel bogus "data" to the White House—bypassing and discrediting CIA and military intelligence which contradicted their disinformation? Non-Zionist specialist in the Pentagon's Middle East office Colonel Karen Kwiatkowski described in great detail the easy and constant flow of Mossad and Israeli military officers in and out of Feith's office, while critical US experts were virtually barred. None of these

How can a first rate intellectual critic of US foreign policy ignore the Office of Special Plans set up in the Pentagon by ultra Zionist Douglas Feith?

key policymakers promoting the war had any connection to the military-industrial complex or Big Oil, but all were deeply and actively tied to the State of Israel and backed by the Lobby. Astonishingly Chomsky, famous for his criticism of intellectuals enamored with imperial power and uncritical academics, pursues a similar path when it concerns pro-Israel intellectuals in power and their Zionist academic colleagues. The problem is not only the "lobby" pressuring from outside, but their counterparts within the State.

9) Chomsky frequently criticized the half-hearted criticism by liberals of US foreign policy, yet he nowhere raises a single peep about the absolute silence of Jewish progressives about the major role of the Lobby in promoting the invasion of Iraq. At no point does he engage in debate or criticism of the scores of *Israel First* academic supporters of war with Iraq, Iran or Syria. Instead his criticism of the war revolves around the role of Party leaders, the Bush Administration, etc... without any attempt to understand the organized basis and ideological mentors of the militarists.

10) Chomsky fails to analyze the impact of the concerted and uninterrupted campaign organized by all major US pro-Israel lobbies and personalities to silence criticism of Israel and the Lobby's support for the war. Chomsky's refusal to criticize the Lobby's abuse of anti-Semitism to destroy our civil liberties, hound academics out of the universities and other positions for criticizing Israel and the Lobby, is most evident in the recent smear campaign of Professors Walt and Mearsheimer. When the Lobby successfully pressured Harvard to disclaim Professor Walt and may have eventually forced his resignation from the Deanship at the Kennedy School at Harvard, despite Walt's own disclaimer, Chomsky joined the Lobby in condemning their extensive critical scholarship and meticulous analysis. At no point does Chomsky deal with the central facts of their analysis about the Lobby's contemporary power over US Middle East policy. The irony is Chomsky, himself an occasional victim of academic Zionist hatchet jobs, this time is on the givers' end.

Chomsky fails to analyze the impact of the concerted and uninterrupted campaign organized by all major US pro-Israel lobbies and personalities to silence criticism of Israel.

11) Chomsky fails to assess the power of the Lobby in comparison with other institutional forces. For example top US Generals have frequently complained that Israeli armed forces receive new high tech military hardware before it has become operational in the US. Thanks to the Lobby, their complaints are rarely heeded. US defense industries (some of whom have joint production contracts with Israeli military industries) have bitterly com-

plained of Israel's unfair competition, violation of trade agreements, and the illegal sale of high tech weaponry to China. Under threat from the Pentagon of losing all their lucrative ties, Israel canceled sales to China, while the Lobby looked on... During the run-up to the US invasion of Iraq, many active and retired military officials and CIA analysts opposed the war, and questioned the assumptions and projections of the pro-Israel ideologues in the Pentagon. They were overruled, their advice dismissed by the ZionCons and belittled by their ideological backers writing in the major print media. The ZionCons in the government successfully overcame their institutional critics in large part because their opinion and policies toward the war were uncritically accepted by the mass media and particularly by the *New York Times* whose primary war propagandist, Judith Miller, had close links with the Lobby. These are well-known historical linkages and debates of which a close reader of the mass media like Chomsky would have been aware. But Chomsky deliberately chose to omit and deny these, substituting more 'selective' criticism of the Iraq war based on the exclusion of vital facts.

12) What passes for Chomsky's 'refutation' of the power of the Lobby is a superficial historical review of US-Israel relations citing the occasional conflict of interests in which, even more occasionally, the pro-Israel lobby failed to get its way. Chomsky's historical arguments resemble a lawyer's brief more than a comprehensive review of the power of the Lobby. For example, while indeed, in 1956 the US objected to the joint French-British-Israeli attack on Egypt, does this mitigate the fact that over the next 50 years the US financed and supplied the Israeli war machine to the tune of $70 billion dollars, thanks largely to the pressure of the Lobby? In fact, in 1967 the Israeli air force bombed the US intelligence gathering ship, the *USS Liberty,* in international waters and strafed US Naval personnel, killing or wounding over 200 sailors and officers. The Johnson Administration in a historically unprecedented move refused to retaliate and silenced the survivors of the unprovoked attack with threats of 'court-martial'. No subsequent administration has ever raised the issue, let alone conducted an official Congressional investigation, even as they escalated aid to Israel and prepared to use nuclear weapons to defend Israel when it seem to be losing the Yom Kippur War in 1972. The US defense of Israel led to the very costly Arab oil boycott, which brought on a massive increase in the price of oil, and the animosity of former Arab allies, threatening global monetary stability. In other words, in this as in many other cases, the pro-Israel lobby was more influential than the US armed forces in shaping US response to an Israeli act of aggression against American servicemen operating in international waters. In recent years, the power of the Lobby has seriously inhibited the FBI's prosecution of the scores of Israeli spies who entered the US in 2001. The most that was done was their quiet deportation. The recent arrest of two AIPAC

officials for handing confidential government documents over to Israeli embassy officials has led the pro-Israel lobby to mobilize a massive media campaign in their defense, converting an act of espionage against the US into an 'exercise of free speech'. Editorials and op-ed articles in favor of dismissal of the charges have appeared in most of the leading newspapers in what must be the most unprecedented campaign in favor of agents of a foreign government in US history. The power of the propaganda reach of the Lobby far exceeds any countervailing power, even though the case against the AIPAC officials is very strong, and includes the testimony of the key Pentagon official convicted of handing them the documents.

13) Chomsky, a highly reputable critic of the bias of the mass media, attributes corporate ties to their anti-worker news reports. However when it comes to the overwhelming pro-Israel bias he has never analyzed the influence of the Israel Lobby, the link between the pro-Israel media elite and the pro-Israel bias. Merely a blind spot or a case of ideologically driven intellectual amnesia...?

14) Chomsky cites Israel's importance for US imperial strategy in weakening Arab nationalism, its role in providing military aid and military advisers to totalitarian terrorist regimes (Guatemala, Argentina, Colombia, Chile, Bolivia and so on) when the US Congress imposes restrictions to direct US involvement. There is little doubt that Israel serves US imperial purposes, especially in situations where bloody politics are involved. But this ignores the corollary that Israel benefited from doing so (and perhaps did so for this very reason)—it increased military revenues, gained backers favoring Israel's colonial policies, provided markets for Israeli arms dealers and in general established the appearance of a quid pro quo in what would otherwise demonstrably be a ludicrously one-sided relationship. However a more comprehensive analysis of US interests demonstrates that the costs of supporting Israel far exceed the occasional benefit, whether we consider advantages to US imperial goals or even more so from the vantage point of a democratic foreign policy. With regard to the costly and destructive wars against Iraq, following Israel's lead and its lobbies, the pro-Israel policy has severely undermined US military capacity to defend the empire elsewhere, has led to a loss of its prestige and perception of its power, and discredited US claims to be a champion of freedom and democracy. From the viewpoint of democratic foreign policy it has strengthened the militarist wing of the government and undermined democratic freedoms at home. Israel benefits

A more comprehensive analysis of US interests demonstrates that the costs of supporting Israel far exceed the occasional benefit.

of course because the war destroyed a major secular adversary and allowed it to tighten its stranglehold on the Occupied Territories.

Leftist apologists for what Israelis call the US "Jewish Lobby" like Noam Chomsky and Steve Zunes argue that US behavior in the Middle East is similar to policies that it has pursued elsewhere in the world, and this general policy is said to precede the lobby. This argument goes against most of US post-World War Two history. Voluminous evidence demonstrates that the US opposed colonialism and communism in Asia, Africa and Latin America, seeking to replace European and Japanese colonial regimes, to open markets and investment opportunities for US multinational corporations. Israel is the only colonial power opposing non-communist movements that the US has supported. For example during the Suez crises of 1956, when Britain, France and Israel invaded and occupied the Egyptian Suez and Sinai, the US opposed their effort to restore colonial rule. Subsequently by the late 1960's as the Jewish Lobby increased its power the US supported with arms, billions of dollars and diplomacy Israeli colonization, territorial grabs, and air assaults throughout the Middle East—a policy which it did not and does not support any place else in the world, particularly colonial state attacks aimed against some countries which have ties to US oil companies.

Unlike most of the rest of Asia, Latin America and Africa where the US has developed close ties with elected neo-liberal regimes, the US cannot replicate this policy in the Middle East because electoral processes result in negative outcomes, in part because of the US ties to the Israeli colonial state and its policy of territorial conquest. The major premise of US imperial foreign policy is to extract huge profits from Africa, Latin America and Asia—which is routinely accomplished, except in relation to Israel, which extracts from $3 to $10 billion dollars of tribute each and every year. This is so evident as to be ridiculous. In an interview with the *Wall Street Journal* (April 12, 2006), Israeli Prime Minister Olmert announced he would seek $10 billion (USD) to relocate 70,000 Jewish colonists in the West Bank. The Jewish Lobby immediately lined up scores of Congress people to support the outrageous Israeli proposal, at a time when hundreds of thousands of Hurricane Katrina victims are without any housing, employment or future. Never has the US engaged in an imperial war in which its major economic interests have either opposed that war or remained silent. If we examine the cases cited by Chomsky and his acolytes: Guatemala 1954, Iran 1954 and Chile 1973, the major economic groups supported US intervention: United Fruit in Guatemala, Standard Oil in Iran, Anaconda and

Never has the US engaged in an imperial war in which its major economic interests have either opposed that war or remained silent.

ITT in Chile. In the current Middle East and South Asian wars there is no comparable influence by major economic (oil) associations or even individual enterprises. Chomsky has not cited a single public statement or confidential memo or oil industry lobby, which is pushing the war agenda. In contrast there are over 2000 statements, press releases, conferences, interviews, op-eds articles, documents by all the major Jewish lobbies and their leaders which promoted the Iraq invasion and presently promote a pre-emptive attack on Iran. No other foreign policy area in the recent history of the United States has been subject to such a long-term, large-scale propaganda effort by a lobby acting on behalf of a foreign power, as is the case of the Jewish Lobby on behalf of Israel. The analogies with the old China lobby are laughable— both in terms of scope and influence in Congress. Likewise the anti-Castro lobby has failed to block $1 billion USD in US exports to Cuba backed by a formidable array of business interests. Moreover the anti-Cuban lobby does not pursue the state policies of a foreign government, and lacks the financing, media influence, and organization of the pro-Israel Jewish Lobby. Except in the Caribbean and Central America, the US has not invaded or gone to war to overthrow a regime in Latin America, unlike the case in the Middle East. The US utilizes domestic surrogates, military officials in alliance with local ruling classes, to depose nationalist or democratic regimes. In the case of Iraq, however, the US has engaged in a direct military invasion, and it plans future air and land wars against Iran and Syria. The different strategies reflect different policies designed by policymakers with conflicting priorities in US empire building: the neo-cons seek to destroy Israeli adversaries even if it means prejudicing US economic interests, while the neo-colonialists seek to conquer resources, not territories. US foreign policy frequently involves debates, discussion, alternatives— even within the framework of empire building. There is no such

The neo-cons seek to destroy Israeli adversaries even if it means prejudicing US economic interests, while the neo-colonialists seek to conquer resources, not territories.

debate on the Middle East, which involves policy related to Israel. The Lobby mobilizes between 90 to 98 per cent of Congress members. US behavior in the United Nations on human rights resolutions, sanctions, and peace proposals affecting Israeli colonial policy is profoundly influenced by the Lobby. On no other foreign policy issue has the US used its veto to protect a consistent violator of international law as it has with Israel. Except for the resounding UN opposition to the US economic blockade of Cuba, only the US policy condoning Israeli colonial expansion and violent intervention in Palestine has evoked such worldwide opposition. To conflate US imperial policies, policymakers and relations with Israel as similar to its configuration related to the rest of the world is historically false, empirically without foundation, and lacking in any analytical sophistication. No other regional foreign policy had so many key policymakers in the State Department and Pentagon organically linked and politically loyal to a foreign state as is the case in the contemporary Middle East. No other foreign policy area has been so uncontested in the mass media as is the Israeli colonial expansion and its sustained violation of human rights. US Middle East experts who are not unconditional supporters of Israel are labeled by the Lobby as "Arabists" or worse, "Anti-Semites", and have been totally marginalized in the State Department, the military and the CIA or driven from Congressional office. On no other regional policy area has this occurred. To argue that US Middle East policy is the same imperial policy applied elsewhere is to ignore the different alignments and power groups involved in determining policy and more importantly, the uses to which imperial power is applied and for what interests.

The unconditional commitment to the Israeli colonial state has eroded US relations with the richest and most populous states in the Arab and Islamic world. In market terms, the difference is between hundreds of billions of dollars in sales versus defending a receiver of massive US aid handouts. The economic losses far outweigh any small-scale questionable military benefits. The Arab states are net buyers of US military hardware. The Israeli arms industry is a stiff competitor.

US oil and gas companies are net losers in terms of investments, profits and markets because of the US ties to Israel which, because of its small market, has little to offer in each of the above categories. Big Oil was indeed interested in investing in Saddam's Iraq—it was excluded by US policy banning US corporations from entering that market. The

In market terms, the difference is between hundreds of billions of dollars in sales versus defending a receiver of massive US aid handouts. The economic losses far outweigh any small-scale questionable military benefits.

ban was part of the ZionCon strategy dating back to the Clinton Presidency, itself heavily influenced by the pro-Israel lobby and Middle East policymakers (Holbrooke, Albright, Ross, Indyck, Sandy Berger etc). That France, China, Russia, Japan and several other countries had an interest in Iraq oil and have signed several billion-dollar oil contracts with Iran is *not the cause* of US war policy but the consequence of it. Certainly big US oil companies could compete and have a better than even *chance* of competing successfully for exploration contracts under normal market conditions if the US war policy did not prohibit them. The role of the ZionCons in power in diminishing the US MNC presence in the Iranian oil fields demonstrates the supremacy of the Jewish Lobby over Big Oil.

The argument that the war policy was designed to keep global oil trading in US dollars when Saddam was thinking of moving into Euros or that the dollar-denominated oil trade is threatened by Iran's proposed oil bourse has no basis. Saddam's or Iran's moving to the Euro would have minimal or no impact on the currency market, accounting for less than 1% of currency transactions. The big holders of dollars, by a multiple of a hundred, are the Asians (China, Japan, Taiwan etc), the Middle Eastern oil countries led by Saudi Arabia, Kuwait, etc.—none of whom are known to be unloading dollars or following Iran's, or earlier, Saddam's monetary agenda. To do so would require a major wrench in their present relations with the US, one which would be fraught with consequences.

Finally the Lobby's effective campaign to secure US vetoes against international resolutions condemning Israel's ethnic cleansing of Palestinians and its assault on Lebanon puts the US publicly and very visibly on the side of widespread, legalized torture, legalized extrajudicial executions, and massive illegal population displacement, i.e. of war crimes, and crimes against humanity. The end result is the weakening of international law and increased volatility in an area of great strategic importance. Chomsky takes no account of the geo-strategic and energy costs, the losses in our domestic freedoms resulting directly from the Middle East wars for Israel and even less of the rise of a virulent form of Zionist neo-McCarthyism spreading throughout our academic, artistic, and other public and private institutions. If anything demonstrates the Zionists' growing power and authoritarian reach, the brutal and successful campaign against Professors Mearsheimer and Walt confirm it, in spades.

Conclusion

In normal times one would give little attention to academic polemics unless they have important political consequences. In this case, however, Noam Chomsky is an icon of what stands for the US anti-war movements and intellectual dissent. That he has chosen to absolve the pro-Israel Lobby and its affiliated groups and media auxiliaries is an important political event, especially when questions of war and peace hang in the balance, and when the majority of Americans oppose the war. Giving a 'free ride' to the principal authors, architects and lobbyists in favor of the war is a positive obstacle to achieving clarity about whom we are fighting and why. To ignore the pro-Israel Lobby is to allow it a free hand in pushing for the invasion of Iran and Syria. Worse, to distract from its responsibility by pointing to bogus enemies is to weaken our understanding not only of the war, but also of the enemies of freedom in this country. Most of all it allows a foreign government a privileged position in dictating our Middle East policy, while proposing police state methods and legislation to inhibit debate and dissent. Let me conclude by saying that the peace and justice movements, at home and abroad, are bigger than any individual or intellectual—no matter what their past credentials.

Yesterday the major Zionist organizations told us whom we may or may not criticize in the Middle East, today they tell us whom we may criticize in the United States, tomorrow they will tell us to bend our heads and submit to their lies and deceptions in order to engage in new wars of conquest at the service of a morally repugnant colonial regime.

CHAPTER 14

CONFRONTING ZIONISM AND RECLAIMING AMERICAN MIDDLE EAST POLICY

The problems of peace and war, humane treatment of all racial and ethnic groups, of allocating foreign aid to those in the Third World who need it most and not to an aggressive colonial state with the 28th highest per capita income[1] are foremost on our agenda. Confronting Zionism—the colonial state itself and its overseas loyalists—requires us to face up to the interrelated challenges of opposing US military and economic imperialism and its class and ethno-religious backers, regardless of their claims of being a special people with a unique history, cause or claims on humankind.

Many profound questions are pending and will be certainly raised after the Iraqi military debacle, which cost so many US lives and bled the budget of so many billions that should have been spent on tens of millions of US citizens and residents without health care and adequate living standards. While eventually there may be a call for a Congressional investigation to answer the questions "Why did the US launch the war?" "Why did the US lose the war?", and above all—"Who was responsible?", the likelihood of any such full scale inquiry pushing forward at this time will depend on the ability of the neo-cons in government to forestall it. The investigation of Douglas Feith by the Pentagon's Inspector General and the Senate Select Committee on Intelligence (SSCI) headed by Committee Chairman Pat Roberts was a non-event.[2] The limited inquiry called for by Congresswoman Barbara Lee has been placed on a slow boat to China.[3] While the FBI may have succeeded in forcing Wolfowitz' transfer to the World Bank, there has not yet been any public, official inquiry into or condemnation of his role.

Should such an inquiry take place at some time in the future, however, the series of questions which will provoke the most vehement and concerted opposition would focus on the role of the Pentagon Zionists, their advisers, collaborators and supporters in and out of the Bush regime. This line of inquiry will predictably be opposed by the neo-conservatives, liberals and philanthropic Jewish organizations and their non-Jewish allies in and out of the government, including those who did a magnificent job of exposing the non-Zionist militarists in the Bush Administration, but curiously enough forgot to even mention the Zionist cohorts and their ideological and organized backers in "civil society".[4]

Such an inquiry could serve as an educational experience in informing US citizens on the profoundly undemocratic nature of decision-making in questions of war and peace, the threats that civilian-militarists represent in relation to international law and the rights of national self-determination, and the real threat of highly organized internal elites who become transmission belts for colonial mini-states carving out regional empires.

There are two possible lines of inquiry with regard to the disastrous Zionist influence on US war policy in the Middle East. One line is from the "nationalist" empire builders who see the problem of Zionist power in terms of the negative effect that the Iraq war and the Israeli assault on Lebanon had on US empire building.[5] They are likely to testify that the Israel loyalists isolated the US from its European and conservative allies by pushing for a unilateral military conquest strategy, instead of engaging in joint diplomatic and economic strategies, and pressuring Israel to act like a "normal state" by negotiating a 'peace for land' two-state solution. These conservative empire builders will seek to publicize the role of the Zionists in the Pentagon and their slavish adherence to Israeli state interests, its devastating effects on the US's world politico-economic position by focusing on its loss of leverage over Arab and Muslim oil producers, and highlighting the mindless threats to Saudi Arabia.

In particular the professional military and intelligence officials will seek to demonstrate how the Zionists seized control over decision making, marginalized and manipulated them, and ignored internal intelligence reports in favor of "cooked reports" by their specially invented cohort and Israeli intelligence in order to maximize Israeli interests. The professional officials will especially emphasize the deliberate and wanton disregard of internal experts who warned against the war, the futility of looking for weapons of mass destruction, the irrationality of a series of Middle East invasions, and the likelihood of greater resistance during a colonial occupation. The NATO oriented military will point out how the Israeli-oriented policy makers deliberately provoked needless hostilities to empire-building among their European allies by orchestrating virulent "anti-Semitic" campaigns against France and Belgium because they were critical of Israel's territorial expansion and ethnic cleansing.

In a word, the conservatives (political, military and intelligence officials) will argue that the Zionists, by putting Israel in the center of their policymaking, undermined US empire building, draining troops, resources, money and public support to further Israel's quest for regional domination.[6]

Another line of inquiry, from the left or progressive side, should address the question of Zionist power over war and peace in the Middle East and elsewhere by focusing on the usurpation of democratic rights of US citizens in the making of foreign policy: the fact that a small elite of several thousand highly organized, affluent and well-funded lobbyists can control the voting behavior of Congressional members, intimidate or defeat political representatives who criticize Israel's colonial policies, and buy, silence and/or intimidate media outlets and public spokespeople who dare to raise questions about Iraqi-Israeli inter-connects. The progressive critique will be directed not only at the role of the Pentagon Zionists in twisting US war policy to favor Israel but their whole world view drawn from the Israeli view of its relation to the world: a paranoid and self-serving vision of eternal external enemies everywhere and unreliable allies, of perpetual repudiation of international law, covenants and Geneva Accords, of shrill polemics and deep penetration of ostensible allies' military and intelligence apparatuses.

Progressives will attack the Israeli view that labels adversarial states mortal enemies who only understand force and that considers negotiation a cynical device to be used only to neutralize critics, and to disarm adversaries in order to create new "facts on the ground" through force and violence. Progressives will have to courageously make the connection between the Pentagon Zionists, their affinity for Israeli ideology and their destruction of diplomacy, international law and co-operation.

But a true inquiry would have to extend much further than reviewing policy inputs and preferences with a view to democratizing American foreign policy. Whether any such official process would ever be possible in America seems questionable, given that it would have to address a level of crimes parallel to those of the Nazis in World War II—that the architects of the Iraqi war planned a series of aggressive wars of conquest based on the principle of domination by violence, torture, collective punishment, total war on civilian populations, their homes, hospitals, cultural heritage, churches and mosques, means of livelihood and educational institutions. These are the highest crimes against humanity.

Crimes against humanity are inevitable in "total wars" based on ideologies of exclusive ethno-religious loyalties, whether Jewish, Christian, Hindu or Muslim. The worst crimes are committed by those who claim to be a divinely chosen people, a people with "righteous" claims of supreme victimhood. Righteous victimology, linked to ethno-religious loyalties and directed by fanatical civilian militarists with advanced weaponry, is the greatest threat to world peace and humanity. Progressives must forcefully reject "righteous victimology" by exposing its contemporary imperialist agenda and the fact that many descendants of victims have now become brutal executioners. They must reject "special exemptions" preventing the naming of

Zionists power brokers and decision makers, especially by their Jewish colleagues on the Left. Selective criticism not only weakens the political substance and credibility of the critique, but is morally reprehensible as it denies an important truth—the politics of the Zionist architects of US imperial policy making.

Progressives must reject all imperial politics with or without Israeli design. The US must return to republican principles, but in promoting this goal, progressives have to point to the incompatibility between a democratic republic and empire building, between narrow, explicit or implicit, ethno-religious loyalties and internationalism, between expansionist capitalism and democratic socialism. In order to pursue the progressive line of inquiry and alternative political perspective, we should expect a prolonged, vitriolic and irrational assault.

The first line of ideological attack, particularly by the ZPC's, will be the "labeling" tactic—hard hitting critical analysis will be labeled "anti-Semitism" to inhibit readers and listeners from discussing the evidence and substance of the issues. The response to Mearsheimer and Walt, predicted in their own article, serves as yet another instance. The examination of linkages between the Israel-centered Pentagonistas and the Israeli state will be labeled "pages from the 'Protocols of Zion'" and other such spurious analogies.

The second line of attack will be to conflate Zionist power today with that of the not too distant past (1940's-1950's) when Zionism was only one of several views among US Jewry and when it was less organized and influential in politics, the media, and economy. The purpose of this dishonest amalgamation is to polemicize by citing past examples of relative Zionist weakness and to falsely attribute to the critics a worldview of a worldwide, long-term Jewish conspiracy.

The third line of attack, and the most morally reprehensible, is to conflate the victims of the Holocaust with the state terrorists of the Israeli state and their intellectual apologists and supporters among US Zionists. The use of "blood ties" to make this connection when there is no social-economic-political similarity only reveals the irrational, mystical, and reactionary nature of the current ideology of the Zionist right. The purpose of course is to secure public acquiescence to Israeli and US/Zionist crimes against humanity by presenting their actions in terms of "defensive" or "survival" tactics even as they unleash another holocaust-in-the-making upon Muslim populations, most recently again in Lebanon. No evidence is needed—just breathless, vicious invective by the holocaust-in-the-making deniers.

For the Zionist ideologues Israel is presented as the incarnation of universal values of democracy, liberty and justice, and those who criticize Israel are then labeled as supporters of "Arab" dictatorships, repression, injustice and terrorism. The stated universal values are worth upholding but abundant evidence exists that they are not practiced in Israel—where Arabs, both Muslim and Christian, are treated as second-class citizens; where death, destruction and ethnic genocide is daily fare for the Palestinians; and where Israel's nuclear arms threaten its Middle East neighbors.[7]

Finally one will hear from Zionists the "relativist" argument: "Israel's crimes are no worse than many countries in the world". However, few countries (except the US) are engaged in colonizing a neighbor, bombing adversaries with impunity (and killing massive numbers of innocent bystanders), storing nuclear warheads with an offensive doctrine, securing the largest proportion of US foreign aid including its most advanced technology, controlling US congressional voting on Mideast issues, shaping the Mideast political agenda for both Presidential candidates, routinely torturing thousands of political prisoners (and sending advisers throughout the world to teach how to do likewise), and practicing the totalitarian law of collective punishment for popular resistance.

There are many and profound reasons to single out Israel for condemnation, because while many countries practice some of the Israeli injustices, Israel and its overseas network in the US contain a whole configuration of power relations which threaten not only the oppressed people of Palestine but the rights of people throughout the world.

Facing this ideological attack will not be easy because media access is totally unequal. The opposition is well organized, strategically located and well financed. But as the crimes and failures of policy become more evident, particularly as the Iraqi debacle deepens and the Israeli destruction of Lebanon unfolds, and still the Neocons plow onward with an even more perilous agenda directed against Iran, many more Americans have become increasingly involved in seeking answers, providing the critics of the Israel-Zionist-Pentagon connection with a grand opportunity to expose and weaken the ties that bind.

Moreover, outside the US, we have mass public opinion in our favor. Latin America, Europe, Africa, Asia—the great majority see Israel as a threat, not a force for peace. Secular, democratic Jews anywhere else in the world have no problem criticizing US Zionists and their leading policymakers in the Pentagon. Nowhere do the Israeli-centered Zionists have such power as they have in the US. Even in Israel there is a minority of Jews, who openly despise the Pentagon-Zionists and their proposed serial wars; they especially despise Zionist ideologues like Richard Perle and Douglas Feith, who from afar were willing to sacrifice the last Jewish soldier for their megalomaniacal idea of "Greater Israel".

In this battle of ideas we have many allies around the world, our ideas and questions are relevant and will resonate in this time of deep anxiety among the American people. Let's move ahead and de-colonize our country, our minds and politics as a first step in reconstituting a democratic republic, free of entangling colonial and neo-imperial alliances!

ENDNOTES

[1]   See Global Income Per Capita 2005, compiled from World Bank Development Indicators, at <http://www.finfacts.com/biz10/globalworldincomepercapita.htm>

[2]   John Byme, "Prewar intelligence probe grinds towards end as parties accuse each other of delay" Tuesday April 11, 2006 appearing on the Rawstory website. http://www.rawstory.com/news/2006/Prewar_intelligence_probe _grinds_to_end_0411.html Byme noted that Democrats say that "Roberts stalled the inquiry until November" and that "the Committee has yet to interview any public officials about their statements on Iraq's capabilities leading up to the war."

[3]   In July, 2005, Congresswoman Barbara Lee (Dem., Calif.) introduced a Resolution of Inquiry in the House of Representatives (H. Res 375) which, if passed, would require the White House and the State Department to "transmit all information relating to communication with officials of the United Kingdom between January 1, 2002, and October 16, 2002, relating to the policy of the United States with respect to Iraq." The bill had 83 co-sponsors. On September 16, 2005, this bill was placed on the House Calendar, Calendar No. 87; however the order in which bills are considered and voted on is determined by the majority party leadership.

[4]   In the entire body of exposés by Seymour Hersh in *The New Yorker* during April-June, 2004, the role of the Zionist Pentagonistas is not discussed.

[5]   On June 16, 2004, 27 retired top diplomats and top military officials released a statement calling for Bush's electoral defeat and in May 2004 a more specific open letter to President Bush signed by 60 retired diplomats referred to the damage the US-Zionist relationship had done to US prestige and influence in the Muslim world and in Europe.

[6]   US Senator Ernest Fritz Hollings, "Bush's failed Mideast Policy is creating more terrorism", *Charleston Post and Courier,* May 6, 2004 and "The United States Has Lost Its Moral Authority", *The State*, June 23, 2004.

[7]   Yulie Khromchenco, "Poll: 64% of Israeli Jews support encouraging Arabs to leave", *Haaretz*, June 22, 2004. Citing a survey by the Haifa University National Security Study Center, a remarkable 25% of Jewish Israelis would support the banned racist Kach Party in an election.

INDEX